THE

GOSPEL IN LEVITICUS.

HOLY TYPES;

OR,

THE GOSPEL IN LEVITICUS.

A SERIES OF LECTURES

ON

THE HEBREW RITUAL.

BY

JOSEPH A. SEISS, D.D., LL.D.,

AUTHOR OF LECTURES ON THE GOSPELS AND EPISTLES OF THE CHURCH
YEAR, ON DANIEL, ON THE APOCALYPSE, ETC.

WIPF & STOCK · Eugene, Oregon

Wipf and Stock Publishers
199 W 8th Ave, Suite 3
Eugene, OR 97401

Holy Types
The Gospel in Leviticus on the Hebrew Ritual
By Seiss, Joseph Augustus
ISBN 13: 978-1-5326-3759-9
Publication date 7/19/2017
Previously published by St. Thomas Press, 1859

PREFACE TO NEW EDITION.

After the delivery, in 1859, of the discourses contained in the following pages, a request, numerously signed, was addressed to the author in these words:

Respected Sir:—Having heard with much pleasure your recent series of Sabbath Evening Discourses on the Book of Leviticus, and believing that we are expressing the wish of many members of our own congregation, as well as others, in requesting you to have the same published in book form, we would respectfully solicit your kind compliance with this request; hoping that, should you deem such publication advisable, it may redound to the glory of God in the edification of any who will give it the attention it merits.

In response to this, the first edition of one thousand copies was issued, under the title of *The Gospel in Leviticus*. Without the knowledge of the author, the same was soon thereafter republished by Thomas C. Jack, 30 Ludgate Hill, London. The first American edition was quickly exhausted, but failed to be followed by a second until a change of publishers was effected. Later, several successive editions were issued by Smith, English & Co., until that firm ceased to exist. For years since then the book has been practically out of print. But calls for it continue, and a new issue seems to be desirable, and so is here adventured.

The aim of the book is, to supply a popular exposition of the Levitical rites and ceremonies, to trace their typical import and relations, and to set forth the great features of the Gospel as therein adumbrated by types of God's own choosing. It thus covers a field comparatively unoccupied, but one of much interest and importance. It professes to find in these divine appointments and directions a symbolic foreshowing of the whole plan of grace and salvation through Jesus Christ.

Many are disposed to look with disfavor upon figurative or allegorical interpretations of Scripture, by reason of wild extravagances and perversions. But, if some have transgressed or gone too far, we dare not discard all figurative meanings of the sacred records, nor condemn the devout investigation of them, lest we censure the great Apostle of the Gentiles, and condemn the Lord Jesus himself, who found typical references in the manna in the wilderness, in the brazen serpent, and in the engulfment of Jonah in the stomach of the fish. There are extremes both ways, equally to be deprecated. And it is questionable, indeed, whether Christian theology can be thoroughly understood without the help of the Mosaic appointments, and the blending of the light of ancient symbolism with the facts of New Testament history.

It is believed, however, that nothing will be found in these pages that violates the proprieties of sober interpretation, or teaches what is not well established in the plain import of the divine Word in general. The testimonies, from various high and trustworthy sources, to the usefulness of former issues have been so numerous and gratifying as to beget expectation that this new edition will serve a good purpose, and also be received with favor. May it be of value to those to whom it comes. May it tend to enhance believing appreciation of the Scriptures and of Him "of whom Moses in the law did write." May the God of all grace and truth bless it to every one who reads it, and make it fruitful of good in the holy cause to which alone it is devoted. And to the Father, Son, and Holy Ghost be all glory for ever.

TABLE OF CONTENTS.

FIRST LECTURE.

INTRODUCTION.

Moses and his Third Book — What is the Gospel? — The many ways in which it is presented—Natural Symbols of Christ—The value of Types in conveying instruction — Nature and Revelation............... PAGES 13-28

SECOND LECTURE.

THE BURNT-OFFERING.

Origin of Sacrifices—Man a religious being—Revelation the assistant of Nature — Necessity for a Mediator — The Victim — Its Fate — What it availed—Its Freeness for all—The whole picture surveyed for the joy of the Saint and the alarm of the Sinner............................. 29-45

THIRD LECTURE.

THE MEAT-OFFERING.

Its relation to the Burnt-offering—Denotes the Sinner's offering of himself to the Lord—The best demanded—The oil of Unction—Frankincense —Leaven and Honey excluded—Salt demanded—Was Eucharistic in its nature — The Mercies of God........................... 46-62

FOURTH LECTURE.

THE PEACE-OFFERING.

Religion a thing of gladness — Our whole Salvation dependant on the Blood of Atonement—True Peace requires a full surrender of Self first —God must have the Best — The Christian's ground for Joy — Feasts on Sacred Food — The subjects of his rejoicing........................ 63–79

FIFTH LECTURE.

THE SIN AND TRESPASS-OFFERINGS.

The Christian in this life still subject to Sins of Infirmity—These lingering defects are real sins — Their guilt graded by the Rank of the Offender — The remedy for them — Sundry lessons..................... 80–97

SIXTH LECTURE

SUPPLEMENT TO THE LAW OF OFFERINGS.

Division of the Bible into Chapters and Verses—Miscellaneous Observations — Gospel Morality —The Personality of religious requirements — Faith — The Church.. 98–116

SEVENTH LECTURE.

AARON AND HIS CONSECRATION.

All religions founded upon Priesthood—Man must have a Mediator—All priesthoods sum up in Christ — The Ceremonies by which Aaron was consecrated — His Baptism — His Vestments — His Anointing — His marking with the Blood of Sacrifice — Our High-priest.............. 117–135

EIGHTH LECTURE.

THE CONSECRATION OF AARON'S SONS.

Two Orders of Priesthood—Inferior priests the sons of the High-priest— Particulars connected with their Consecration—The Consecration itself — Baptism — The Robe of Righteousness — The Lord's Supper — The Days of Waiting...... 136–155

CONTENTS. ix

NINTH LECTURE.

AARON IN THE DUTIES OF HIS OFFICE.

Salvation connected with the shedding of blood — The bloody rites of Greece and Rome — An argument for the inspiration of the Scriptures from their unity on the doctrine of Salvation by blood—Aaron's sacrifice for himself — Recollections of sin — Aaron's duties at the altar — Christ officiating at his own Immolation—Was made Sin for us—Aaron's entry into the Sanctuary the symbol of Christ's Ascension and investiture in heaven — His Coming again — Particulars connected with his second Advent... 156–176

TENTH LECTURE.

THE FALL OF NADAB AND ABIHU.

An Episode — The nature of their Sin — Intemperance — Will-worship — Holy fire—Early corruptions of the Gospel—The fate of usurpers and corrupters — Natural affection with respect to the Lost — Christ's intercessions not hindered by Apostasies — He is still the only High-priest and Savior... 177–196

ELEVENTH LECTURE.

THE CLEAN AND UNCLEAN.

Moses a Naturalist—Design of these distinctions in Meats—A system of wholesome Dietetics—Separation from the rest of mankind—Training in the perception of moral distinctions — A picture of Sin........... 197–214

TWELFTH LECTURE.

BIRTH-SIN AND ITS DEVELOPMENTS.

Cavils on the doctrine of native Depravity — The doctrine explained — Sin a disease — Symbolized by Leprosy — The analogy traced 215–233

THIRTEENTH LECTURE.

THE LEPROSY OF GARMENTS.

Corruption in our surroundings — Government — Domestic relations — Business — Education and literature — The Church — How such infections are to be treated — Christian Reform 234–251

FOURTEENTH LECTURE.

THE LEPER CLEANSED.

Cure to precede the cleansing — The two Birds — The Instrument of cleansing — The work of the Leper himself — Sacrifice necessary — Seven days of waiting required — The final Release........................... 252–269

FIFTEENTH LECTURE.

THE POOR — HOUSE LEPROSY — SECRET UNCLEANNESS.

The Poor.—Modifications for their benefit—More demanded of the Rich. *House Leprosy.*—The Earth infected—Its ultimate cleansing. *Secret Uncleanness.* — Involuntary corruption — A good moral and spiritual discipline 270–286

SIXTEENTH LECTURE

THE DAY OF ATONEMENT.

In the Seventh month — Once a year — For all at once — This day as regarded the High-Priest — as regards the Atonement itself — The two goats—This day as regarded the People—A day of Penitence and soul-sorrow............... 287–306

CONTENTS. xi

SEVENTEENTH LECTURE.
LAWS FOR HOLY LIVING.

The sense in which Salvation is altogether of Grace—The sense in which it is to be wrought out by Ourselves—What is a holy life—The means and elements of it—Keeping in view the blood-shedding of Jesus—Reformation of life—The cultivation of pure affections—Conformity to the Moral Law—A chapter of Penalties.................................. 307–325

EIGHTEENTH LECTURE.
PERSONAL REQUIREMENTS OF THE PRIESTS.

Suggestive of requisites to efficiency in the Gospel ministry—Why the priest had to be physically perfect—Why purely mated—Why his children should be pure—Why required to be holy—The moral character of the Lord Jesus—Why the priest was not to give way to grief at the death of relatives—Christ's greatest sympathies not carnal but spiritual 326–344

NINETEENTH LECTURE.
THE HOLY FESTIVALS.

Their social, political, and commercial benefits—Their value in a religious aspect—Congregational worship—The Passover—The Feast of Unleavened Bread—The first sheaf of Barley harvest—The Feast of Weeks or Pentecost, and the two loaves of Wheat harvest—The corners and the gleanings—The Feast of Trumpets, or Gospel call—The Feast of Tabernacles—The Sabbath........................... 345–365

TWENTIETH LECTURE
THE SANCTUARY AND ITS FURNITURE.

The three Apartments of the Tabernacle—Types of the three states of man in his progress from Condemnation to complete Redemption—The Golden Candlesticks—The Shew-bread—Salvation in the Church only—True members of the Church have but a veil between them and heaven—Shelomith's son... 366–383

TWENTY-FIRST LECTURE.

THE SABBATIC YEAR AND THE JUBILEE.

The stress laid on the number "seven" — The year-Sabbaths — How the people were to be supplied during the Sabbatic years — An argument for the Divine legation of Moses — How the truth of the Gospel is proven by these ancient laws — The Sabbatic periods in their typical signification — The "Jubilee" — Not properly the Gospel dispensation, but the final consummation to which the Gospel refers — A Sabbath to come — A period of Restitution — Of Release — Of Return home — Of Feasting upon the supplies of our years of toil — Conclusion....... 384–403

THE

GOSPEL IN LEVITICUS.

FIRST LECTURE.

INTRODUCTION.

LEV. CHAP. I.

Moses was one of those miraculous men, of whom there have been but a few. History tells not of another like him, unless it be the Savior, whom he so much resembled. Christ and he stand out upon the records of the past, as two great mountains, broad and high — the Alps of the ages — where earth and heaven touch; where the human connects with the divine. They head the two great dispensations of God thus far. All that the heavenly Father has delivered to us as yet, is comprised in the Law and the Gospel; and the one was "given by Moses," and the other "came by Jesus Christ." About one-third of the Old Testament was written by this remarkable man. It was through him that inspiration first broke forth in a steady and continued stream. He was, and remains, the great Lawgiver and Historian of the world.

LEVITICUS is the third in the order of his inspired writings. It is a book which treats of the offices, rites, services, and feasts of the Hebrew religion, as given in the charge of the priests — the sons of Levi. Hence its title, Λευιτικον — Leviticus — that is, what relates to Levi. The Talmudists denominated it "*The Law of the Priests*"—"*The Law of the Offerings.*" Either of these titles sufficiently describes it.

That Moses was really the writer of this book can hardly be doubted If what it contains be true, as all those best qualified to judge have never questioned, it is impossible to suppose that any but he could have written it. And Nehemiah, Luke, the writer of second Chronicles, and other inspired penmen, refer to it as a genuine production of him whose name it bears, as well as a veritable communication from God. And if it be a history at all, it must be received as inspired. It contains but little else than God's own utterances. It is more entirely made up of the very words of the Lord than any other book of the Bible. Jehovah himself speaks in every chapter, and in almost every verse, whilst Moses merely sits by, and hears, and writes, as the amanuensis of the speaking Lord.

It has been remarked, however, and not without reason, that this book "constitutes a part of the sacred canon, less read, and usually accounted less interesting and important, than almost any other." Many regard it as the mere record of an obsolete economy, inapplicable to our times, and containing little or nothing of practical value to us. How few have ever heard a chapter read, or a text taken, from this part of Scripture! How generally is it passed by, even by Christians, as of no account! From such an esti mate and treatment of it, I feel constrained to enter my dissent. So far from being a mere collection of curiosities for the antiquarian, it is a book of impressive, sublime, evangelical instruction. Here, as much as in any portion of Scripture, hath wisdom prepared her feast, and crieth: "Come, eat of my bread, and drink of the wine which I have mingled." What were all these ancient institutes but living pictures of the truth as it is in Jesus? Paul says of the Tabernacle and its services, that it "was a $\pi\alpha\rho\alpha\beta o\lambda\eta$ — *a parable, illustration, outline, figure* — for the time then present." In another place, he speaks of "the Law" as "having a $\sigma\kappa\iota\alpha\nu$ — *adumbration, shadow* — of good things to come." And elsewhere, referring to God's doings in connection with the administrations of Moses, he says: "These things were our $\tau\upsilon\pi o\iota$ — *types, patterns, examples.*" Nathaniel says, that "Moses in the law did write of Jesus of Nazareth." Christ himself says: "Had ye believed Moses, ye would have believed me, for he wrote of me." And the whole epistle to the Hebrews is one grand argument for Christianity, extracted from the rites and services of the Levitical economy. It must, therefore, be taken, as the teaching of the New Testament, that its outlines and characteristics are contained in these ancient institutes. The matter may be somewhat veiled in type and symbol, but there is as much Gospel in Leviticus as in Daniel, Ezekiel, or Isaiah. This very obsolete law of the priests and offerings, as I hope to make evident in the course of these discourses, contains an evangelism as pure and divine as that which dropped from apostolic lips, or stands written in apostolic records. Christ himself, and all h s mediatorial doings, from first to last, are nothing more than the fulfilment and complement of the laws herein written. "Think not," said he, "that I am come to destroy the law or the prophets: I am not come to destroy, but to fulfil." It is indeed astonishing, when we come to consider it, and a strong proof of the divine source of the Bible, how completely Christ is woven into its entire texture. Open the book anywhere, and we are sure to find something of Jesus. He is its Alpha and Omega; its beginning and its ending; its first and its last. "In the Law of Moses, and in the prophets, and in the Psalms," it is "written concerning him." Nor is it saying too much for this third book of Moses, to call it *The Gospel according to Leviticus*, just as the third book of the New Testament is called "The Gospel according to Luke." The one tells of Jesus and redemption through him, as well as the other; and if we do not find it full and overflowing with clear and beautiful evangelical instruction, it is because we know not how to read it.

WHAT IS THE GOSPEL? Not, what is the specific meaning of the word here or there; but, generalizing its various applications, and combining its several shades of signification into one view, What is the Gospel? Is it a particular set form of words? Certainly not. If it were, no man could preach it, except by the mere repetition of those words. Then, what is it? To answer briefly, I would say, *It is God's proclamation of a plan of mercy to sinners*. It is the divine revelation of grace to fallen man. It is the publication of forgiveness and eternal life through the mediation of Jesus Christ. Hence, whatever announces Christ as the Redeemer, and holds forth forgiveness and salvation through him, comprises and proclaims the Gospel. We call that the Gospel which narrates the Savior's history, simply and only because it is an account of the Redeemer. We apply the same term to the peculiar doctrines, ordinances and precepts which constitute the Christian system, for the reason that in these Christ is proposed and given to the believing and obedient in all his saving efficacy. The same word is used to denote the scriptural promises of forgiveness and mercy, in contrast with the exactions of the law; but all these various applications are easily resolvable into the one great, original idea of *God in Christ reconciling the world unto himself*.

Man is fallen and depraved. It is upon this assumption that the Gospel starts, and takes its peculiarities as the Gospel. "The son of man is come to seek and to save that which was lost." I am not among those who think that nothing noble, generous, or lovely, remains in humanity. Man, though fallen, retains a greatness even in his ruin. His nature has been terribly marred and defaced, but there is still some remaining excellence. Dig among the ruins of those noble cities which the foot of time has trodden down, and you will find there outlines of streets, and edifices, and columns, and statues, and many traces of former greatness. Search in like manner into sunken humanity, and you will also find many a mark and relic of original magnificence and glory. But, Babylon in ruins, is no longer the "great Babylon" of the Assyrians' pride; and no man is now the exalted creature who ate of Eden's fruits, and stood as lord of earth amid the beauties and harmonies of Paradise. There has been a fall —a dreadful degeneration. All history declares it.

All consciousness bears witness to it. And he has not expressed himself too strongly, who says, "a man must be a fool, nay, a stock, or a stone, not to believe it. He has no eyes, he has no senses, he has no perceptions, if he refuses to believe it." And in this fallen, degenerate condition, man is *lost*. Darkness, which he cannot dissipate, is around him. Stains of guilt, which he cannot wash out, are upon him. The curse of condemnation stands written against him, beyond his power to expunge it, or check it off. A foul disease is fretting through all his nature, against which there is no earthly antidote or remedy. Death and decay are on him, and cling to him as part of himself, and he cannot cut loose from them. Eternity itself, so far as his own strength goes, can bring him only sorrow and despair. But God comes to us in this desperate estate, and proffers, through Christ, an eternal deliverance. For darkness, he proposes to give us light. For sin, he holds out to us the means of an effectual cleansing. For condemnation, he tenders to us a present and full reprieve. For all our ailments, he engages to work for us an abiding cure. And for our corruption and death, he offers us glory and immortality. In one word, he proposes to *save* us. Restoration — complete restoration — is now proclaimed from the heavens as the portion of those who will receive it through Jesus Christ. It is a blessed proclamation. It is, indeed, *Good news—glad tidings of great joy*. And this proclamation is the Gospel.

Turning, then, to this Third Book of Moses, called Leviticus, what do we find to be its contents? Here and there we have a few records simply and purely historical; but what is the great burden and scope of the book? From beginning to end, everything bears the one pervading purpose, of showing the transgressor wherewithal he might come before the Lord, and obtain justification and peace. It is a great system of salvation by priestly mediation and bloody sacrifices. Apart from any relation to the New Testament, the prescriptions here given dwindle down to a burdensome round of uninviting and unmeaning ceremonies, unworthy of so high an origin, or so solemn a method of inculcation. We are, therefore, driven to take them as connected with the one and only system of redemption, which is through Christ, and to reverence and study them as God's own pictorial illustrations of the Gospel, as a system of practical hieroglyphics of his plan of salvation through the blood of Jesus.

Now, God has taken many ways, and employed many methods, of teaching men his Gospel, and of impressing it upon their understandings and their hearts. Sometimes he presents it in plain and simple narratives, or in easy parables, and then again in epistles of classic elegance, filled with close analysis and logical profoundness. One apostle is sent as the apostle of love, whose words melt gently in upon the heart, fragrant as scented dews; and another is sent as the apostle of faith, with his great arguments deep laid in the truth of God. The prophets are made poets also, to attract and move us the more by the smoothness of their words and the brilliancy of their inspirations. Moses, though else so calm and majestic, now and then breaks out in exalted song. David takes his harp, and utters himself in sweetest minstrelsy. Isaiah stands up to prophesy, and his lips are touched with a coal from the celestial altar, and his words carry us into the highest heavens of poetic sublimity. Jeremiah comes forward in song, mighty as "a lion from the swellings of Jordan, coming up against the habitations of the strong." And a whole constellation of lesser prophets pour forth the light of heaven in scintillating streams of melody and poesy. Gorgeous symbolization has been called into requisition. We look on Ezekiel's visions and seem to be lifted by the hair into the midst of the scenes of God's mysterious doings. Daniel's golden-headed image, and beasts of power, and stone of glory, move before us in significant grandeur. The skies themselves part, and the very secrets of eternity open upon us, in the Apocalypse of John. And even visible nature around us has been transmuted into a living array of pictures and emblems of Jesus and his saving grace. We lift up our eyes in the daytime, and encounter the bright, glad, and golden beams that pour forever from the great orb of heaven. It is the symbol of that bright "Sun of Righteousness," whose rays are the light and healing of earth, and the joy of eternity. We go out with the Psalmist to consider the glories of the starry night; and the brightest of all those glittering and fiery gems—the one which heralds the morning and ushers in the day,—is the appointed picture of that "bright and morning star" who shines with ever cheering radiance in the eyes of Zion's watchmen, and gives tidings of the promised approaching day of Israel. We walk into the fields among the flocks and lowing herds; and that meek-eyed lamb, reposing on the clean sunny bank, is to us a remembrancer of that unspotted "Lamb of God which taketh away the sin of the world." We take our stand by the gushing spring on the mountain side, and gaze upon the glad waters as they leap forth in their crystal purity to cool the thirsty lip, and refresh the parched ground, and wash away the dust from the worn traveller. It is the joyous symbol of that "fountain opened to the house of David and the inhabitants of Jerusalem for sin and uncleanness." We turn our eyes to the tall cedar, that pride and glory of the mountain, stretching up its great limbs into the blue sky; and we see there an emblem of that "Branch of the Lord, beautiful and glorious," whose name is, "THE LORD OUR RIGHTEOUSNESS." We gaze round on that craggy precipice, extending its bald brow to the lightnings and the storms, on whose top the young eaglets sleep in the warm sunshine, and under whose broad shadow the shepherd reposes in safety with his peaceful flocks. It is earth's grandest token of that "Rock of Ages," on which frail man finds his salvation, and in whose cool shade this world's weary ones are blessed. We contemplate that great root of yon mountain oak, which has penetrated the fissure of the rock, and opened its way down to drink up the moisture from the heart of the hill. It is God's emblem of that "Root of David" which hath prevailed to open the seals, and forced a way to the fountain and waters of life. We listen to the roar of the great lion in the thicket, before whom all the beasts of the field crouch or fly in terror. It is the symbol of that "Lion of the Tribe of Judah," who has sent consternation and dismay among all the hosts of hell, and raised the fallen sinner from his "dead level" to his feet again We look upon the flowers as they spread open their beauties to the sky, and pour from their thousand censers their incense offerings to their

God; and that lily there, the most fragrant of all, and that rose yonder, the most deeply colored of all, are meant to tell of "the Rose of Sharon and the Lily of the valleys," which God has planted in this bleak world to gladden the eye and revive the heart of drooping man, and to be a soothing balm to his many, many wounds. We sit down in the arbor, and admire the vine which covers it with robes of green, and has hung it with fragrant clusters; and that too is one of nature's ten thousand images of Jesus and his grace; for he is "the true Vine," and his Father is the husbandman. The visible world scarcely contains one object of glory, beauty, or good, which God has not in some way appropriated as emblematic of his Son Jesus Christ, and of his mercy to sinners through him. He has even made prophecy of history, and written his purposes of grace and good in the very acts and lives of men and nations. And here, in this third book of Moses, in the ceremonial system which it records, there is still another plan adopted to set forth the redemption that is in Christ Jesus. We have here a system of life-pictures and practical allegorical types, in which the Gospel receives a sort of living pictorial incarnation. It treats of the slaying of goats and calves, of meats and drinks, and divers washings, all ordained of God, that in these things men might have a tangible exhibition of the offering of Him who was "delivered for our offences, and raised again for our justification." It presents a solemn ritual of blood and butchery, "imposed until the time of reformation," but meant to be "*a figure*," complete and lively, of those better things which have since been revealed in Jesus Christ. It is only another of those "divers manners" in which God has chosen to deliver to us an idea of the necessity, nature, application and effects of "the common salvation" of which the prophets prophesied, and the apostles wrote. And viewed in this light, so far from being repulsive and profitless, this book of Leviticus at once gathers around it a most attractive interest, and becomes invested with a radiance, which must needs enlist, edify and inspire every attentive Christian heart. It is a torch given of God, and lit with sacred fires, to illuminate redemption's framework, and light us into those profounds of grace, of which the prophets searched and inquired, when they testified beforehand of the sufferings of Christ and the glory that should follow.

But some may ask, Why go back to these ancient types, when we have everything so plain in the writings of evangelists and prophets? Why stop to contemplate a picture when we have the original? Why linger in the twilight when we have the perfect day? Many reasons might be given. Among other things, I may say, that a good part of the light which makes up the brilliancy of gospel day, comes through these ancient institutes. Had it not been for them, gradually preparing the eye of man for intenser light, and opening his mind for moral and spiritual ideas, we would have had no day at all. The very language of evangelists and apostles, which we now think so plain, is all derived and moulded from these ancient rites, and proceeds so fundamentally upon ideas generated by them, that, without them, it would be exceedingly obscure, and, in some things, wholly unintelligible. These typical rites thus hold a place in the economy of revelation, from which they cannot be spared. "Whatsoever things were written aforetime, were written for our learning, that we through patience and comfort of the Scriptures, might have hope." The New Testament is necessary to a right understanding of them, but equally necessary are they to a right understanding of the New Testament. And instead of putting them aside, as we do the toys of childhood, it is our duty to God and to ourselves, and ought to be our delight, to give them a share of our attention, and to do what we can to trace out their glorious meaning.

And, then, who does not know the increased power of pictorial illustration? Who has not felt the additional force imparted to truth by its being clothed and set forth in well-chosen images? Who has not again and again been more touched, moved and convinced by the simple parables of Jesus, than by all the eloquence and massive reasonings of Paul? A thing is not necessarily obscure and difficult because it is typical or figurative. On the contrary, there is nothing which so interests and impresses us. Pictures and images help to simplify truth, and open the mind to receive it with more facility, and write it with greater vividness upon the heart. As Tyndale says, "Similitudes have more virtue and power with them than bare words, and lead a man's understanding further into the pith and marrow and spiritual understanding of the thing, than all the words that can be imagined... There is not a better, a more vehement, or mightier thing," says he, "to make a man understand with all, than an allegory; for allegories make a man quick-witted, and print wisdom in him, and make it to abide, when bare words go but in at the one ear and out at the other." Only give to people something in the shape of pictures, parables, allegories, fables, fictions, stories, and you are much more likely to arrest their attention and reach their hearts, than by any other form of address; as if there were something in the very nature of man to which such forms of communicating truth are better adapted than any other. There is, perhaps, not another book in the English language, the Bible excepted, so popular, or so useful, as Bunyan's "Pilgrim's Progress;" and yet, what is it but a sort of typical story, allegory, or dramatic picture, of great truths which underlie it? There is nothing more natural than types. Nature itself is but a system of types — the translation of what is invisible and divine into material forms. The visible is not the real, but only a shadowing forth — a type of it. And in all the material world, there are ten thousand "links and ties and silent harmonies" connecting it with the spiritual and the true, making one the illustration of the other, and rendering both beautiful and welcome to him who loveth instruction. Not without good reason, therefore, has Tauler, of the olden time, said, "There be some men who take leave of types and symbols too soon, before they have drawn out all the truth and instruction contained therein." Let us not be among them.

There is one thought to which I will refer, and with that I will close this introductory lecture. It is generally agreed that the delivery and arrangement of this Levitical system, as contained in this book, occupied about one month. Forty days had been previously occupied in directing Moses how to make the tabernacle; here, at least thirty more are added in directing him how to arrange its services; and yet only *six* days were employed upon the great work of creation. This, at first, may seem a little strange, and yet it is suggestive of important truth. Redemption is the most glorious of God's works, and is deserving of the most attention. It is of more consequence for man to have his sins forgiven and his soul saved, than to have a fine world to die in, and be lost forever. It is more important for us to understand the laws of grace than the laws of nature. God has devoted only six days, and two chapters of his word to the one, whilst he has devoted a multitude of days and more than fifty, or five hundred chapters, to the other.

Philosophers of this world tell us to study nature — study nature; and praise the knowledge of nature as the perfection of all knowledge. They seem to think that if we only understand nature well, and obey her teachings, we have about enough for all the purposes of life, peace and piety. But, if this were really so, I take it that God would have said more about nature in his word. Instead of confining his account of the heavens and the earth, and all that in them is, to two chapters, I would look to see volumes freighted with it, and would expect Genesis to be geology, and Exodus natural history, and Leviticus medicine, and Numbers mathematics, and Deuteronomy chemistry, and Joshua psychology, and Judges natural law. I certainly could not reconcile it with the fact that he has suffered those great works of Solomon to perish, in which "he speaks of trees from the cedar-tree that is in Lebanon even unto the hyssop that springeth out of the wall, and of fowl, and of creeping things, and of fishes."

Now, it is useful to study nature, and a grand thing to understand nature. It is a dignified and a serviceable work to survey her elements, shapes, motions, and adaptations; to examine the springs, and balance-wheels, and cogs, and bands, and pins, and jewels, and sublime mechanism, and operations, of the universe, so wonderfully set in order by God's wisdom, and kept in everlasting activity by his almighty power. It helps to expand our nature, to exalt our conceptions of the eternal Contriver, and disposes us to reverent awe, and aids us in many of the outward relations and duties of life. But what can it do for those deeper, urgent, moral, and spiritual wants of man, to which the Gospel addresses itself? How vastly better is the knowledge of grace and salvation! God meant that we should study nature, and know something of nature, and look through nature up to nature's God. Nature is the grand handwriting of his power, by which he has spelled out to us the letters that compose his ineffable name; and it is his will that we should read that record, and trace his glory in the heavens, and his wonders in the great deep. Otherwise, he would not have written about the creation in his word, nor have commanded us by his Son to consider the ravens or the lilies of the field. But he means that we should "*give the more earnest heed to the things which we have heard, which at the first began to be spoken by the Lord, and were confirmed unto us by them that heard him.*" Science can tell of God, and trace his footsteps everywhere; but it can tell of no remedy for sin, no Savior for the soul, no peace for the guilty. And in all our attentions to earthly wisdom, let us not forget that six days to science, with thirty or seventy given to the revelations of grace, is about the apportionment and relative importance which God in his word has indicated with reference to these things. *How shall a man be just with God?* is the great question, which is answered only in revelation and Christianity. Christ only hath the words of eternal life. And if we would be wise with that wisdom which is unto salvation, we must, above all things, attend to what he has written to us in his law, and meekly sit down as humble learners at the feet of prophets and apostles, whom he has sent to instruct us in the mysteries of his holy truth.

> Sad error this, to take
> The light of Nature, rather than the light
> Of Revelation, for a guide. As well
> Prefer the borrowed light of earth's pale moon
> To the effulgence of the noon-day sun.

God hath spoken to us from the heavens — mercifully spoken — spoken to the intent that we might be saved; and whilst we do not refuse to listen to him in his works, let us ever give a reverent attention to him in his words.

SECOND LECTURE.

THE BURNT-OFFERING.

LEV. CHAP. I.

It is a little surprising, upon first view, that God should appoint or sanction rites and services of worship, the observance of which would make his sanctuary look so much like a solemn slaughter-house. But, where sin is stayed and quenched, there must be blood. Blood is the substance of life; and as sin involves the forfeiture of life, "without shedding of blood there is no remission." Hence, "almost all things are by the law purged with blood."

These bloody rites, however, did not originate with "the law." It is a question with learned men how they did originate. Some refer them to some primitive enactment of God, and others regard them as the natural outgrowth of man's consciousness of sin, and his desire to appease the Divine anger felt to attend upon it. It is certain that they are nearly as old as man. They date back to Noah, to Abel, to Adam himself. They have been found among nearly all nations. And when God gave commandment to Moses concerning them, they already formed a part of the common religion of the world. They are not here spoken of as a new institution, now for the first time introduced; but are referred to rather as an ancient and well-known element of man's worship, to which the Divine Legislator meant only to affix a more specific ritual. That offerings would, and ought to, be made, seems to be taken for granted, whilst these new commands relate only to the manner in which they were to be made. "If," that is, in the ordinary course of things already familiar, or, "*when*, any man of you shall bring an offering to the Lord, ye shall bring" so and so.

There is a worship, at least a disposition to worship, which has descended upon all serious men from the very beginning. If man is not naturally a religious being, there is something in this universe around him, or something which he drinks in with his mother's milk, which does infallibly impress and move him with religious feelings and desires. There is in all, at some time or other, some motions towards the idea of a God — a groping and searching, and unquietness of soul, as if struggling to feel its way to some acquaintance with its Maker, and to render some sort of homage to him. There is a theology even in Nature, and a faculty of worship or religiousness which is somehow natural unto man. Revelation does not deny this, but takes it for granted, and often appeals to it, and proceeds upon it as its original ground-work. It does not propose to engraft a religious department on man's constitution, but recognizes such a department as already in existence, and proposes merely to assist, and guide, and guard it against falsehood, idolatry, and superstition. Natural religion, in the present degenerate and corrupt condition of humanity, is not adequate to its original purpose. "Nature, left to herself, and unassisted by Divine teachings, certainly wanders into mazes of perplexity, involves herself in error and blindness, and becomes the victim of folly, full of all sorts of superstition." So said the knowing leader of the glorious reformation; and all the records of time attest the truth of his statement. Man needs to hear a voice from heaven — a supernatural word — to guide him successfully to the true God, and to the right worship of that God. Nature may dispose him to make offerings, and a common religious consciousness may approve and sanction them; but it yet remains for God to say what sort of offerings are proper, and how they are to be acceptably presented. And the whole system of revelation and grace is aimed, not at the creation of something wholly new, but simply at the renovation, improvement, and guidance of what already exists. The saint is only the sinner cleansed of his sins, and set right before God. The new man, generated through grace, is only a holier product from a holier seed on the same original soil, where once grew the base overgrowth of iniquity and vice. The "new earth," which is to be through the mediation and reign of Jesus, is only the same earth, renovated and reclaimed, which has been from the beginning, and which always will be. The Gospel was not given to supersede Nature, but to restore, renew, and exalt it.

You will notice, in the delivery of the laws and enactments contained in this book, that, although they were designed for the whole Jewish people, they were first given to Moses alone. The record says, "The Lord called unto *Moses*, and spake unto *him*," and commanded *him* to "speak unto the children of Israel." The people themselves had previously requested this, and prayed that God might not speak directly to them, lest they should die. There is an awful terror in the natural conscience at being brought face to face with the Almighty. The sinner wishes to avoid God all he can. As soon as Adam became a transgressor, he could no longer endure the voice of the Lord, and so tried to hide himself among the trees of the garden. When the voice of the Mighty One was heard upon the quaking mount, and the Lord came down upon Sinai, Israel was afraid, and cried out with terror. And at the face of Him who sitteth upon the throne, in the scenes revealed in John's Apocalypse, even the kings, and great men, and rich men, and mighty men of the earth, pray to the rocks and mountains to fall on them, that they may only be hidden from Him. To bring the sinner and his God harmoniously together, a mediator is necessary. There must be a daysman betwixt us, to lay his hand upon us both. And some such mediator was Moses between God and the ancient Hebrews. The Lord treated with them through him. They could listen to him, when they could not endure to hear God himself. He was a brother man, and him they could approach, when, to stand face to face with Jehovah, seemed to threaten death itself. And if ever we are to be brought into peaceful communication with heaven, it must be through some mediatorial personage, in whom there is a modification of the consuming fires of the divine glory, and with whom we can treat on terms of fraternal confidence and affection. "There is one God, and one mediator between God and man, the man Christ Jesus."

Another peculiarity in the delivery of these laws and ordinances, was, that the Lord spake them "*out of the tabernacle;*" from the mercy-seat. He had previously spoken from the burning mountain, but in this case he spoke from the tent of propitiation.

THE BURNT-OFFERING.

This itself is significant of the nature of the ceremonial system. It was a system of remedies for sin, and hence a proclamation of mercy and good to the guilty. The moral law was an expression of God's wrath upon transgression. It contained not one ray of hope for the offender. It was therefore delivered in connection with its appropriate symbols of terror and indignation. The ceremonial economy was a remedial institution. It connected with the ministration of life and peace to fallen man. It was therefore given in a gentler form, and was made to proceed from the seat of mercy. The law given from the mountain is a minister of death. It is holy, just, and good; but its whole aspect is dark, imperious, threatening, and destructive to every offender. The Gospel is equally uncompromising with sin, and in like manner presents death as the just penalty of disobedience, and holds up blood as the only extinguisher of transgression; but, at the same time, it is a system of divine mercy, in which Jehovah comes down from the mountain of his wrath to make friends with repenting sinners over the blood of sacrifice. It "bringeth glad tidings, and publisheth peace."

The first seven chapters of this book treat of *Offerings*. It begins with the *bloody* offerings, and with that particular kind of bloody offerings, which was the most complete and significant of all the Hebrew sacrifices — the *holocaust*, or *whole burnt-offering*. This wholly burnt sacrifice, lying, as it does, at the very threshold of the typical institutes, serves as a solemn proclamation to Jew and Gentile, that every man is deeply guilty before God, and never can approach him or secure his favor except by bloody and consuming expiation. Blood — *blood* — BLOOD — is the perpetual and exacting cry of the law against every violator of its precepts; and until that cry is hushed, and that demand satisfied, no one can see the face of God, and live. This holocaust, therefore, comes before us, as a practical type or illustration of that sacrifice by which sin is expiated and covered, as also of the portion awaiting those offenders for whom that sacrifice does not avail. In this light, then, let us proceed to consider it.

I. Consider the sort of victim required for this sacrifice;—a bullock, or a sheep, or, in case of great poverty, a young pigeon or dove—the very purest, cleanest, and best of creatures—nothing else would answer. And even these had to be the finest and most desirable specimens. If a bullock or a sheep, it had to be "*a male without blemish*"—the most perfect of its kind. It is impossible to induce purity by anything impure. No imperfect being could become a perfect sacrifice, or effect a perfect righteousness. And when a victim was needed to atone for the world's guilt, none would answer but the very Chief of all the flocks of God. The meek dove had to be brought from the pure olive groves of heaven, and the prince of the herd from the blessed pastures which are laved by the waters of life. Pure and perfect as the bright world from which he came, Christ, our sacrifice, "was holy, harmless, undefiled, and separate from sinners"—"a Lamb without spot" —the first, the purest, the gentlest, and the best in all the domain of the great God. He was the very Prince of creation, who knew no sin, neither was guile found in his mouth.

II. Consider next what was done with the victim selected. If a bullock, the divine command was

THE BURNT-OFFERING. 35

"Kill it before the Lord, and flay it, and cut it into his pieces." If from the flock, the word was "Kill it on the side of the altar northward, and cut it into his pieces." Who was to do this, is not clearly specified. Any one, good or bad, priest or private, the worst or best, may become the executioner of the divine sentence. When Jesus was made an offering for us, earth and hell joined in the infliction of the sacrificial stroke. But whoever laid hands upon the victim, it was to be slain and cut into pieces. If a bird, the word of the Lord was "Wring off his head, and pluck away his crop with his feathers, and cleave it with the wings." Fit picture this of the end which awaits the unforgiven, and of what actually befell the blessed Savior who "was once offered to bear the sins of many." The plucking and tearing off of the skin was to show how naked the sinner is, and how completely he is exposed to the fires of divine wrath, and how unprotected Jesus was when he submitted to bear our sins in his own body on the tree. The cutting into pieces was to show what a complete undoing of the sinner it is for him to have his sins visited upon him. It is like the severance of every joint, the dislocation of every limb, the tearing asunder of every member. What, then, must have been the anguish of Jesus as he stood in the sinner's place and received the strokes of the sacrificial blade upon him, the same as if it had hewn him into fragments! The victim was to be separated "*into his pieces.*" There was a certain order to be observed in the awful mutilation. All the tender openings of nature were to be followed. There is not an avenue to pain through which God's judgments will not strike in upon the finally condemned. There was not a tender susceptibility in the Savior which was not made to feel the edge pressing into it when he stood as the offering for the sins of men. There is no telling how deeply "he was wounded for our transgressions."

But in addition to this terrible mutilation, the victim was yet to be put upon the altar and burned The command was "*the priest shall burn all on the altar.*" And a particular method was also to be observed in this burning. First the head and the loose fat were to be placed upon the fire; the head from without, and the fat from within. After that the legs and the entrails were to be given to the flames; the outward and the inward together. Man has a double nature; and in all divine services, and under all divine inflictions, both departments fare alike. We cannot give our bodies to God and reserve our hearts, nor serve him in the spirit without bringing that service out into controlling influence over the flesh also. The whole man must go, or nothing. Nor is the ultimate doom of sin a mere bodily suffering, or the mere consuming of the exterior members; nor yet mere mental wo and spiritual grief. As the Savior says, it is the destruction of "*both body and soul* in hell." Christ as our sacrifice, suffered not only in the outer man, but in his whole inner and outer nature conjoined. The nails, and thorns, and thongs he did not more feel in his flesh than the pangs of unutterable grief in his inmost soul. True, only his "*body* was broken;" but as no part of the victim was saved from burning, so every part of Christ's mysterious nature came under the curse which he bore for us; the prophet is witness that God also made "his *soul* an offering for sin." It was the whole Christ that suffered for us; and if his body only was broken, he himself said that his "soul" too was "exceeding sorrowful, even unto death." And just so every sinner who turns away from forgiveness in Christ, shall be subjected to the fires of divine indignation; and his whole nature, stripped, lacerated, dismembered, shall lie and consume in unquenchable flames. For so it is written, "The wicked shall perish, and the enemies of the Lord shall be *as the fat of lambs, they shall consume; into smoke shall they consume away.*" Ps. 37 : 20.

III. Consider further what was to be effected by the presentation of this particular kind of sacrifice. If the man who brought it would lay his hand upon its head, and so acknowledge it as that by which he hoped and prayed and trusted to be forgiven, the Lord said "*it shall be accepted for him to make atonement for him.*" That is, the devoting of such a victim to death and fire was to answer as a substitute for the death and burning of the sinner himself. The word rendered *atonement*, primarily signifies *to cover;* especially in the sense of an adhesive covering, as with pitch or plaister. From this original meaning came its metaphorical signification of *appeasing, pacifying*, covering over anger or wrath. "Its predominant usage," says Bush, "is in relation to the reconciliation effected between God and sinners, in which sense *atonement for sin* is the *covering* of sin, or the securing of the sinner from punishment. Thus when sin is pardoned, or its consequent calamity removed, the sin or person may be said to be *covered*, made safe, expiated, or atoned." The English word *atonement*, or *at-one-ment*, clearly expresses the idea. It involves such a removal or covering of the cause of offence or variance as to produce reconciliation and friendly relations. The idea here is, that the sinner who should bring the prescribed offering, and lay his hand on it in humble confession, should thereby be absolved, forgiven, exonerated, saved from the consequences which would otherwise follow his transgressions. What a beautiful illustration of our reconciliation to God through the death of his Son! People sometimes revolt at this Gospel doctrine of substitution. Some dispute its possibility, and some quibble at the justice of it. But God's thoughts are not as our thoughts. There are many fields of contemplation into which man has not yet looked, and many principles of jurisprudence which he has not yet fathomed; and why should we set up the poor deductions of our weak reason against the revelations of an economy as deep and broad as the mind of God. By whatever laws of right or love the victim was procured, by whatever principles of justification the innocent takes the place of the guilty, or by whatever juridical metonomy the sufferings of Jesus become the payment of the penitent sinner's forfeitures, so it is written, and such is the very nerve and marrow of the Gospel, that "he was wounded for our transgressions, and bruised for our iniquities; the chastisement of our peace was upon him, *and with his stripes we are healed.*" We may start back, and affect to lift up our hands in horror at the thought of a transfer of our guilt to the immaculate Christ; yet, the Holy Ghost is witness, that "The Lord hath laid on him the iniquity of us all," yea, and "*made him to be sin for us, who knew no sin, that we might be the righteousness of God in him.*" Let man's philosophy cavil, and unbelief vaunt itself, it

THE BURNT-OFFERING. 39

is the word of God's inspiration, that "*Christ hath redeemed us from the curse of the law, being made a curse for us.*" He was "delivered for our offences, and raised again for our justification." So that he is the true holocaust, upon whom, if the sinner will penitently lean, he is saved from condemnation, and reconciled to his offended sovereign. Be his sins as numerous as the sands, or deep-dyed as the robes of the mother of harlots drunk with the blood of the saints, if he contritely and obediently take Jesus as his sin-offering and his hope, his iniquities are *covered*, and *at-one-ment* between him and the Father is made.

IV. There yet remains one other particular to be noticed with regard to this atoning offering; and that is, the perfect freedom with which any and every one might avail himself of its benefits. It was confined to no special time, and demanded no specific juncture of affairs. It was as free at one season as at another, and could be resorted to whenever any one felt himself moved in that way. If the worshipper could not bring a bullock, a sheep would answer. And if too poor to furnish either, a dove or pigeon was just as acceptable. There was no reason why any one should not come and share the benefits of a full expiation through the burnt-offering of atonement. All that a man wanted was the consent and determination of his own heart — the motion of "his own voluntary will." Now this was not accidental. It was meant to set forth a great Gospel truth. It tells of the perfect freeness with which one and all may be saved, if only there is the proper effort made. It was the lifting up of the voice of mercy even in that remote antiquity, crying, "*Come; whosoever will, let him come.*" Jesus is the turtle-dove for the poor as well as the lamb for the rich. And there is no reason why any sin-burdened soul should bear its guilt one single day or hour longer. If you are thirsty, and anxious to draw near to God; the altar of sacrifice, and the house in which he dwells, is before you. If you are in need of a victim; there is one close at hand, even the choicest of the flock of God. "Say not in thine heart, Who shall ascend into heaven, that is to bring Christ down from above; or, Who shall descend into the deep, that is to bring Christ up again from the dead. The word is nigh thee, even in thy mouth and in thine heart; that if thou shalt confess with thy mouth the Lord Jesus, and shalt believe in thine heart that God hath raised him from the dead, thou shalt be saved." Whatever be the peculiar nature or weight of the sin, your effectual offering is before you, ready to bear it all away. Just believe on the Lord Jesus Christ; put your hand in humble confession upon his holy brow; lean upon him as your sacrificial lamb; and God hath said, "It shall be accepted for you, to make an atonement for you"—your peace is made with your offended Maker.

> No mortal has a just pretence
> To perish in despair.

Such, my friends, is a brief sketch of the burnt-offering according to the word which the Lord spake unto Moses. What startling significance gathers around the spectacle of its presentation! Draw near, ye children of Adam, and survey it yet again. Behold that bound victim led to the slaughter—the prince of the pastures seized for immolation—the meek dove torn from its peaceful nest to die. Behold the fires kindling into flame, and the knife of the sacrificer warming with blood. See the noble creature transmuted into a mass of disjointed bones and mangled flesh. Not its pitiful look of despair, nor its last cry, or struggle, or quiver of wo, could relax a muscle of the strong executioner, or abstract a jot from the terrors of the strokes or the fires. Its joy, and its peace, and its hope, are gone — clean gone for ever. The flames are feeding on its beauty, and consuming all its tender parts. Its end has come! What meaneth this scene of anguish and fierce infliction? What is it, but another version of the pathetic story told in the last chapters of Matthew, Mark, Luke and John? What are we to see in it but the blessed Savior expiating the guilt of man? What is it, but God's own fact-picture of the breaking of the body and shedding of the blood of Jesus for us and for many for the remission of sins?

Draw near, then, oh Christian, and see what thy Lord hath done for thee. Thus did he come down from the great fields of heaven, and bow his head to the sacrificial knife. Thus was his blood spilled, his flesh laid bare, and his whole nature torn, disjointed, and given to the burning flames of penal condemnation, that thy soul might live. Thus was he marred, and mangled, and consumed on Calvary, to avert eternal death from thee. Look, and let thy heart be melted into grateful, penitential joy; for, as thou believest and leanest on his mysterious immolation, thy sins are cancelled and remembered no more. Read there the cost of thy salvation writ in blood, and that the savory smoke which ascends to call thy pardon down is fed by the torn body of thy dying Savior. Oh, rejoice, and be glad, that Heaven has thus thought on thee, and expended so much on thy good, and never let thine heart turn again from him who has thus loved thee, and given himself for thee. Thou art bought with blood; and let thy humble gratitude never cease to ascend for what thy Lord and Life has done for thee.

But let the sinner also come and look on this bloody scene. The rites of the burnt offering have also a solemn lesson for him. Fearfully do they prophesy of the turpitude and damning heinousness of sin. Some think that sin is nothing; that God never will concern himself about it; and that he is at any rate too good and merciful to punish it. Let such answer, then, why he has chosen such awful illustrations of his consuming wrath upon it? Why has he himself ordained so much blood, death-agony, and burning, as the only means of covering it? And, above all, why did he leave his own Son to such unspeakable suffering when found in the room and stead of the guilty? Did God fail to love his Son in that dreadful extremity? Did he take pleasure in those bitter pangs which so oppressed his only begotten in the garden, and so completely consumed him on the cross? If too merciful to punish sin, had he forgotten to be gracious at that dreadful moment when the shafts of his violated law went forth to drink up the life of the darling of his bosom? Ho, ye morning stars, who sung in your joy over the world at its birth, and ye elders of the heavenly ages, who beheld the sun blaze its first light, and have kept the celestial records for uncounted years, when, where, or how, could there have been a more overwhelming testimony of God's abhorrence of sin, or of his unfaltering determination to punish it to the utmost?

Had he condemned criminals enough to crowd the pit, and reddened a thousand worlds with the blood of slain offenders, it would not have been an expression of his holy indignation at sin at all commensurate with this one solitary example of the sacrifice of his only Son as an atonement for it.

There was once a Roman governor, who made a law prescribing death as the penalty for a certain crime. To some the enactment seemed somewhat harsh and unnecessarily severe, and it was questioned whether he really would enforce the law. But presently a circumstance occurred which forever swept away all doubt upon that point. It happened that his own son was the first offender. The boy whom he had carried in his arms, and dandled on his knee, and upon whom his heart was set with bright hopes, stood before him as the culprit. It was a case to tell all that was in that sovereign's heart as to his sincerity when he made the law. If he did not mean to execute it, here was an instance in which the fact must be revealed. If ever there were to be any relentings or relaxations of the law's rigor, they would here make their appearance. If there should be no yielding now, what offender could ever afterwards dream of impunity or escape? And when all the tender and softening affections which worked in that father's heart towards his own son failed to move him from his integrity as a law-giver, and the darling object of his love and pride received the immolating sentence unmitigated from his lips, it not only laid a sublime capstone upon the monument of Roman virtue, but gave to the law a sanction and a seal undoubtable. It was parental affection writing down in the life-blood of its own offspring the stern adherence of sovereignty to the terrific sentence, "THE SOUL THAT SINNETH, IT SHALL DIE." And when God spared not his only Son when found in the sinner's place, but launched upon him the law's full penalty, and put him under a curse at which the world shook and trembled, what unforgiven sinner can ever think of going unpunished? To reach sin, to kill sin, to satisfy justice and right in their demands against sin, God did not turn back when his only begotten was the victim! Whom then will he spare? In whose case will he turn back? O what an alarum is rung into the ears of a drowsy world from Calvary! Come, thou careless one, at rest in thy prayerlessness and sin, and dreaming of peace and safety, come, survey this ritual scene again. And with thine eye upon the suffering victim, within sight of its agonies, within sound of its groans, let me ask thee, *If God did not spare his own Son from an immolation like this, how can he spare thee in thy impenitence and unbelief?*

And then, thy doom, if thou art unsaved! Who shall tell it? Who can fathom the Saviour's agonies? Read his anguish in the garden, when his great soul itself was ready to expire under the pressure. Read his wo upon the cross, which brought from him a cry at which creation shuddered. Consider the strength of that wave which could thus overwhelm the Prince of all God's hosts. And, "if they do these things in a green tree, what shall be done in the dry?" If the stroke invoked by sin so overwhelmed the soul of Him whose voice could hush the storm and stop the ocean's billows, yea drive out devils and raise the putrid dead; what shall be *thy* portion, helpless mortal, when that stroke comes to be visited on thee!

Oh! think of this, and repent thee of thy follies. The great Lord asks, "*Why will you die?*" Haste thee, O! sinner, to thy refuge in the great offering made for thy redemption. Forgiveness, peace and life are within thy reach. Christ has been offered to purge away thy guilt. Embrace him then as thine, lest eternity should find thee in thy sins and in thy blood.

THIRD LECTURE.

THE MEAT-OFFERING.

LEV. CHAP. II.

THERE are some differences between the offerings here prescribed, and those treated of in the preceding chapter. Those were animal; these are vegetable. Those were bloody *sacrifices;* these are unbloody *oblations.* Those were wholly consumed upon the altar; these were to be burned only in part, and the remainder made the property of the priests. Those were altogether *propitiatory* — intended to expiate sin; these are essentially *eucharistic* — expressions and returns of gratitude and thanksgiving.

And as these differ from the preceding in their nature, so do they also in their application and meaning. Both refer to Christ, and to the sinner as represented in Christ; but in other attitudes. The former presented the Savior in his character as "a propitiation for our sins;" in these he is exhibited as our model and sanctifier, through whom we ourselves are offered to the Lord. The one relates to *justification*, or the mere forgiveness or atonement of sin; these relate to *sanctification*, or our conformity to Christ's holiness. In the one we behold penitence laying its hand on the head of the innocent sufferer, and praying to be spared for that sufferer's sake. In those now before us, we behold gratitude making its living return for the unspeakable gift obtained through the former. The one, however, is not to be separated from the other. The holocaust, or whole burnt-offering of the first chapter, and the meat, or rather *bread*, offering, are but two parts of one great transaction According to the twenty-ninth of Exodus, it was not allowable to present a holocaust without accompanying it with a meat-offering. The fifteenth of Numbers also connects the two, as in some sense parts of each other.

The holocaust goes first. This is the foundation of the whole process. A man cannot be sanctified, or made holy, without first having his past sins covered and forgiven. But mere forgiveness, without something more to follow it, is not salvation. There must be reformation, and a moral change, additional to the atonement, or we shall soon find ourselves again just where we were before. Hence followed the meat-offering, as a sort of essential consequent and filling out of the holocaust, indicating the grateful surrender of the sinner to a life of obedience. The relation between the two is intimate and essential. To separate them, would be to put asunder what God hath joined together — a vitiation of the Divine arrangement. If we have effectually laid hold upon Christ as the sacrifice for our sins, we must needs go on to glorify him in our bodies and our spirits, which are his. No attempt to be holy shall ever succeed before God, unless founded upon atonement by blood. From the days of Adam, bloody sacrifices and meat-offerings went together; and until the day of doom, justification through the blood of Christ, and sanctification, must remain connected and inseparable. Abel brought of the firstlings of his flock, and so looked for acceptance through blood; "and the Lord had respect unto Abel and to his offering." Cain refused to offer the sacrifice of blood; and though he brought the fruit of the ground — the meat-offering — God had no respect to him, or to his offering. The one embraced the doctrine of atonement by blood, and thus became pleasing to God, and a holy and patient martyr. The other expected to be sanctified without atonement by blood, and with all his meat-offerings, he remained under the curse, and became a persecutor and a murderer. Sanctification by the Spirit is built upon justification by the blood of atonement. And it is only when we have received Christ in his character of a sacrifice for our sins, that we are in a condition to render ourselves a living sacrifice, so as to be acceptable to God. The meat-offering illustrates *the second great step* in the process of salvation. Let us, then, look at it somewhat more in detail.

I. Let it be observed, that the Jew, for the substance of his meat-offering, was directed to bring *fine flour*, or cakes or wafers of fine flour, or fine flour baked on a plate, or fine flour fried in oil, or the first fruits in advance of the harvest beaten out of full ears dried by the fire. Either wheat or barley would answer; but the requirement reached the very best grain, either whole, as in the case of the first fruits, or in its very finest and best preparations. Thus are we to offer our very best to the Lord — our bodies and souls, our faculties and attainments — and in the highest perfection in which we can bring them. Christ is the very finest of the wheat and flour, as well as the chiefest of the flock; and both as the one, and as the other, he was completely given to the Lord. From the silence of far eternity, his voice was heard, saying, "Lo, I come, to do thy will, O God!" When on earth, it was his constant protestation, "I came down from heaven, not to do mine own will, but the will of him that sent me." And up to his last hours, when the clouds of his great agony began to settle heavy upon him, he still held out to this: "Father, if thou be willing, remove this cup from me; nevertheless, not my will, but thine, be done." "Being found in fashion as a man, he humbled himself, and became obedient unto death, even the death of the cross." There was no selfish reservation in him. He freely surrendered everything, even to the laying down of his life in crucifixion. This he did, not only as our burnt-offering, but also as our meat-offering, "leaving us an example, that we should follow his steps." And if we are to be identified with him to the forgiveness of our sins through his blood, we must also be identified with him in a living exemplification of his spirit by walking "even as he walked." "I have given you an example," says he, "that ye should do as I have done." To our faith in him as our sacrifice, we must, therefore, add a devout imitation of him as our model. We must submit ourselves to God, as he submitted himself; and give ourselves entirely up to do the whole will of the Father, as he gave himself. "For if any man have not the spirit of Christ, he is none of his." Holiness is not the mere saying of a few prayers; or the paying of a few weekly visits to the sanctuary; or the giving of a few pennies, now and then, for the Church or the poor. It is the rendition of fresh grain and fine flour to the Lord, our God and benefactor. It is the presentation of our entire selves a living sacrifice, holy, acceptable unto God, which is our reasonable service.

II. It is also to be observed, that *oil* was to be poured upon, or mingled with, the flour of the meat-offering. This was not common oil, but *the oil of unction*, or holy oil. It was a peculiar composition, made according to divine directions. It was made of "pure myrrh," "sweet cinnamon," "sweet calamus," "cassia," and "olive oil," "compounded after the art of the apothecary." It was a material used in consecrating, or setting apart. It refers to the Holy Spirit, and the operations of that Spirit in setting apart whom he pleases. It typifies that "*unction of the Holy One*," of which John speaks so largely. No offering of ourselves to God, no true sanctification can occur, without the oil of divine grace, the principle of holiness and sacred power which is poured upon the believer by the Holy Ghost. Even Jesus had to be thus anointed, or *christed*, before he was fully set apart to his work, or could become our acceptable oblation. And in this also he is our example. No consecration is complete without this holy unction and anointing of the Spirit. It is not the mere surrender of ourselves to the Lord that makes us holy, but the accompanying oil of the Holy Ghost, working in and through us, mellowing and softening everything to the divine will, and making our whole being fragrant with love, gratitude, reverence, and every gracious disposition. "The fruit of the Spirit is love, joy, peace, long-suffering, gentleness, goodness, faith, meekness, temperance, and such like." These are the graces in which the Spirit manifests its presence and operations. These are the myrrh, and cinnamon, and sweet calamus, and cassia,

THE MEAT-OFFERING.

and olive oil, which are to perfume and lubricate the fine flour which we bring to the altar of God. And without these, or the sincere effort to have them accompany our gifts, we fail in our oblation, and are not accepted before the Lord.

III. You will notice here another peculiarity in the meat-offering. There was *frankincense* to be put on it. The frankincense, or *olibanum*, was a resinous gum, obtained from a tree of the turpentine bearing kind, which, when put upon the fire, or a hot plate, sent forth very fragrant vapor. In the case of the meat-offering, it was to be wholly burnt on the altar. This circumstance identifies it at once with the burnt-offering, or holocaust. That burnt-offering, as we saw in our last, represented Christ as the sacrifice for our sins. The frankincense therefore plays the part here, of representing the mediation and intercession of the Savior — the grateful fragrance which comes up before God from the altar of burnt sacrifice. Our consecration to God, even with the gracious operations of the Spirit, could not be acceptable, except through Christ, and the sweet intercessorial perfume which arises from his offering in our behalf. It is remarkable how particular the Scriptures are, in making everything connected with our salvation depend upon Christ and his suffering in our stead. The meat-offering is based upon the holocaust; our consecration to God is on the ground of our justification through the blood of atonement. And even then it is nothing, except through the appeals and grateful intercessions which continue to rise and plead for us from the cross of Calvary. With all our forgiveness, and all our consecration, and all our spiritual graces, we should still fail to approve ourselves unto

God, but for the incense that rises from the burned lamb. It is all through the mediation and merit of Christ, that our services for his honor and glory, our gifts to his priests or his poor, our works of faith and love, or any of the best deeds of the best saints, "come up as an odor of a sweet smell, a sacrifice acceptable, well-pleasing to God." It is a comforting thought, that our poor services and prayers, if sincere, are acceptable to the Lord — that our tears for the desolations of Zion are all treasured in his bottle — and that our efforts for good are things in which he delights. But it is all owing to the sweet frankincense of the Savior's righteousness and atoning sacrifice. To him we are indebted for it all. As a sweet flower over which the passing traveller stoops down to regale himself with its fragrance, so does the Father delight in the mediation work of his Son. This is "the mountain of myrrh, and the hill of frankincense," to which he betakes himself "until the day break, and the shadows flee away." And so should all Christians seek to dwell amid the Redeemer's righteousness, that, like the maidens of Ahasuerus, they may be fragrant with sweet odors for the bridegroom's coming.

IV. Another peculiar regulation in the case of this meat-offering is, that it was to be kept clear of *leaven and honey*. The record says, "No meat-offering which ye shall bring unto the Lord shall be made with leaven: for ye shall burn *no leaven, nor any honey*, in any offering of the Lord made by fire."

Leaven indicates corruption. Its principle is a species of putrefaction. It tends to spoil and decay. We can be at no loss to ascertain the moral meaning of its prohibition in this case.

THE MEAT-OFFERING. 53

"Leaven is a well known emblem of pride and hypocrisy. These swell the heart, and puff it up with self-importance and self-deceit. This was especially the leaven of the Pharisees, who made their prayers, and gave their alms, and did all, to be seen of men."

"Leaven is also used as an emblem of malice and wickedness, as we learn from the words of the apostle, 'Let us keep the feast, not with old leaven, neither with the leaven of malice and wickedness, but with the unleavened bread of sincerity and truth.'" (*Bush in loc.*)

By forbidding the use of leaven, then, God meant to set forth the truth, that our offering to him must be pure, and accompanied with a charitable heart. Any insincerity, hypocrisy, selfishness, malice, or wickedness cherished in the soul, will corrupt, vitiate. and destroy any man's piety or consecration to God We must be honest in these sacred things, and in real earnest, and not deal deceitfully with others or with ourselves. If there is anything to be abhorred, it is the man who seeks to promote his own selfish ends by pretending to be devout and good. Not too much did the indignant poet say, when he charged such a man with "stealing the livery of heaven to serve the devil in." If we would be Christians indeed, we must purge out the old leaven of hypocrisy, and let it not so much as touch our sacred offerings. It is a foul and putrefying thing. And so also with "the leaven of malice." It must be put away far from us. It is a dreadful corruption to be bearing enmity and hatred. It unfits for everything good, and sullies the soul in which it dwells. We must be forgiving. What saith the Savior? "If

5 *

thou bring thy gift to the altar, and there remember that thy brother hath aught against thee, leave there thy gift before the altar, and go thy way; first be reconciled to thy brother, and then come and offer thy gift." "And when ye stand praying, if ye have aught against any, forgive; that your Father also which is in heaven may forgive you your trespasses: but if ye do not forgive, neither will your Father which is in heaven forgive your trespasses." We must purge out the old leaven of malice. It will taint any offering, however perfect and pure otherwise.

But why keep away *honey?* Simply because it is a fermenter, a corrupter, and carries in it the principle of putrefaction. And as leaven represents the ugly, offensive, sour elements of depravity, so honey is the emblem of such as are sweet and attractive to the taste—"the lust of the flesh, and the lust of the eyes, and the pride of life." Sensual indulgences and worldly pleasures, as well as hypocrisy and malice, will corrupt and destroy our best oblations. God does not mean that we should become cynics and eremites. The good and the blessedness that is in the world, is here for his friends, and not only for his enemies. He has not placed us in connection with the grand physical economy around us, just to torment us with the sorry efforts of trying to cut loose from it. He has not given us these five senses, just that they might be five grand avenues of vexation and torture by depriving them of the very gratifications for which they were made. I cannot so conceive of God, or of his ways. Nay, how does the Christian's charter run? "*All things are yours;* whether Paul, or Apollos, or Cephas, or the world, or life, or death, or things present, or things to come; ALL ARE YOURS." Would God deprive me of what is mine by solemn charter under his own seal? No, never. What is it, then, that he does demand? It is simply that we "use this world *as not abusing it*"— that we make it *our* servant, and not ourselves *its* servants. Most men love and serve the creature more than the Creator. They know no God but pleasure. They honor no king but self. They live only to the flesh. They are not only sinners, but take pleasure in their sins. And this is that putrefying honey proscribed and prohibited by the Lord— "the members upon the earth" which we must "mortify." "Fornication, uncleanness, inordinate affection, evil concupiscence, and covetousness," will make any offering an abomination unto the Lord, and must be wholly and forever avoided, if we would have the favor of God upon us or our services. There dare be no honey with the meat-offering—no sensuality or licentiousness along with our consecration to Jehovah.

V. Notice still another particular in this very significant service. *Salt was to be used in it.* The command was, "Every oblation of thy meat-offering shalt thou season with salt; neither shalt thou suffer the salt of the covenant of thy God to be lacking from thy meat-offering: with all thine offerings thou shalt offer *salt*." What did this mean?

Salt is just the opposite of leaven. The one corrupts, the other preserves. The one taints and hastens putrefaction; the other purifies and keeps wholesome. It was the custom in ancient times to ratify and confirm nearly every important bargain or contract by the eating together of the parties. This of course required the use of salt as an article invariably present on all such occasions It thus, or in some other way, came to be regarded as a symbol of agreement and pure abiding friendship. God's covenant is called "a covenant of salt;" because it is a covenant of sincere friendship, which is to endure. "The salt of the covenant," is the emblem of the honesty and incorruptible character of the covenant.

The salt of the meat-offering, then, tells of agreement; of real, mutual, happy agreement. If we are true in presenting ourselves to God, we come into harmony with God. We become *his* friends, and he *our* friend. As we move to him, he moves to us. As we come to terms with him, he comes to terms with us. We agree to be his obedient and loving children, and he agrees to be our protecting and loving Father. We give ourselves up to be his people, and he brings himself down to be our God. There is a complete concord and union—a welding together in a holy compact never to be broken. And without this *salt*, the offering is faulty and of none effect. We must throw down all our rebellion and selfishness, and cheerfully submit ourselves to God. We must join ourselves to him in friendly and inviolable bonds. We must covenant with him as he covenants with us, in "a covenant of salt;" that is, in an everlasting covenant of love and faithfulness.

But this same salt tells also of a pure, healthful, pervading savor of virtue and grace. It was the principle of savory purification to the sacrifice; and so the Savior requires of us to "have salt in ourselves." As every Christian is to be a living sacrifice—an accepted oblation unto God, he must comply with the law of sacrifice, and "be salted with salt;"

that is, made savory and incorruptible by being pervaded with unfaltering principles of righteousness. His speech must be "always with grace, seasoned with salt;" that is, he must be a man of pure lips, not allowing corrupt communications to proceed out of his mouth. And no one can ever be a steadfast and accepted Christian without having in him the savory salt of good principles — honest intentions, and decided virtues. "With all thine offerings thou shalt offer salt."

How clearly and beautifully does all this set forth our sanctification in Christ Jesus! Many have debated, and wondered, and argued as to what sanctification is. Here is the answer. It is the willing and cheerful presentation of ourselves and our best to the Lord. It is the oil of the Holy Spirit pouring over us, and mixing through and through us, softening and consecrating every part and particle of us, and working in us the sweet fruits of grace. It is our poor but best endeavors perfumed and made acceptable by the rich frankincense of the Savior's immolation. It is the purging of ourselves of the corrupting leaven of hypocrisy, malice, wickedness, and all the deceitful honey of sensual sweetness. It is the binding of ourselves to God in "a covenant of salt" — a covenant of perfect friendship and everlasting compact — a covenant ever to be actuated by pure motives and good principles. This is religion —piety—holiness. This is what God means that we should do and be, and for which he has made every necessary arrangement in the construction of the Gospel system. With this we are his friends, his chosen ones, his children, and heirs of all his glory. "Happy are the people that are in such a case; yea, happy the people whose God is the Lord!" "They shall abide under the shadow of the Almighty."

VI. There is yet one particular respecting this meat-offering, to which I will call attention. I refer to its *eucharistic* nature. It was not so much a sacrifice as an oblation of praise. It was something of a thanksgiving service — a grateful return for forgiving mercies—a devout acknowledgment of deep and lasting indebtedness to God for his unspeakable goodness. When the pious Jew came with his sheaf or lubricated flour, his heart glowed with the sentiment of the Psalmist, "What shall I render unto the Lord for all his benefits towards me!"

Many are the obligations by which we are bound to present ourselves as living sacrifices unto God. Viewed in whatever light, it is our "reasonable service." But of all the great arguments which bind and move us to this surrender to our Maker, none stand out with a prominence so full and commanding as that drawn from "the mercies of God." When the apostle Paul looked around for considerations to persuade men to make the necessary offering of themselves to the Lord, he at once seized upon "the mercies of God," and began to beseech "by the mercies of God." *The mercies of God — the mercies of God* — this was argument enough. By these are we shut up and bound in to a life of holy consecration by walls and incentives which no man ought ever to wish to break, and which no good man will ever ignore or disregard. "*The mercies of God!*" who shall tell their excellence, their multitude, and the deep and mighty obligations with which they bind us to grateful and cheerful obedience to our Maker! Many a fond affection has glowed in the

THE MEAT-OFFERING. 59

human heart, beautifying the circle of friendship, blessing the quiet home, dropping flowers along the pathway of life, and awakening reverence and attachments as strong as death; but none so unfaltering or so munificent in good as "the mercies of God." We were wrapped up with them in our Creator's thought before our life began. They were present, breathing their blessings with our very substance, when we were fashioned into men. Before our appearance in the world, they had been at work preparing many fond affections for our reception, and arranging many a soft cushion to come between this hard earth and our youthful tenderness. They have tempered the seasons for our good, and filled the horn of plenty to make us blessed. Every day is a handful of sunbeams, kindled and cast down by the mercies of God, to gladden the place of our abode, and to light us to the paths of peace. Every night is a pavilion of the same making, set around us to give us rest, whilst God touches his fingers to our eyelids, saying, "Sleep, my children, sleep." These living natures, by which we are distinguished from inanimate clods —these thinking, reasoning, moral powers, by which alone we rise above the brutes of the field—this beautiful creation by which we are surrounded—this earth, so admirably fitted up for our residence, carpeted with green and flowers, waving with pleasant harvests and shady trees. gushing with springs, gladdened with laughing brooks, lined with winding rivers broad and silvery, varied with hill and valley, girt round with the majesty of ocean, and arched over with a starry canopy which is the pavement of heaven—these varying seasons, youthful spring with life bursting out under all its dewy steps, autumn with its mellow glory and harvest songs, winter with its snowy vestments and joyous firesides—and living nature in ten thousand forms, singing, and dancing, and rejoicing before us forever; whence is all this? To what mysterious authorship is all this good and blessing to be ascribed? Ask from the angels who looked on when the world was made — ask of the morning stars which sang together when it rolled forth into its place in the circuits of the sky—ask of the sons of God who shouted for joy as it went wheeling over its everlasting course — ask of the floods that clap their hands, and of the mountains and the hills that never cease their singing — ask of the winds that drive the chariot of Deity, and of the years that mark the revolutions of its wheels; one answer comes from all: "THE MERCIES OF GOD!" And yet the half has not been told. Why is it that any sinner is out of hell at this moment? Why was he not cut down in his first fit of passion, and sent to the judgment long ago for his sins. Why has not the earth yawned under him and swallowed him up as an ingrate rebel against the majesty of heaven? Why have not the thunders of eternity leaped forth and consumed him forever? Why does the voice of salvation come to him again and again, inviting to an everlasting home far in the peaceful sky? Why do the holy agencies of immortality throng around him to woo and win him from the ways of death? Why do redemption's hopes still visit him as loving angels, and plead so earnestly for admission into his guilty soul? Consider, O man, the goodness of thy Maker. Turn over the leaves of the great volume of his mercies, and read. Survey those mighty depths of love. Sum up the records of his compas-

THE MEAT-OFFERING 61

sion. Thrust out a little into the ocean of his loving kindness, and say whether there is not something to move thee to lay thyself at once upon his altar, and to cry with thankful penitential joy —

> Here, Lord, I give myself away,
> 'Tis all that I can do!

There was once a calm Lord's-day evening, when the little band of Christ's first disciples had quietly locked themselves into a private room for meditation and prayer. The night had hushed the busy world to rest, and solemn soberness was on the silent waiting worshippers. The door was securely shut, and all was still as the chamber of death. Suddenly there stood among them a mysterious stranger, and said, "*Peace be unto you.*" He showed them his hands, with great gashes cut through them by strong nails. He unwound his mantle, and pointed them to a great opening torn up into his side. And he breathed on them, and said again, "*Peace be unto you.*" It was one that had been dead. It was one who had been crucified. It was the risen Jesus, showing to his friends the marks of what he had borne for them, and proposing to them the rich purchase of his sufferings and death. It was an impressive scene, which made even the skeptical Thomas cry out, "*My Lord! and my God!*" But that same mysterious personage is here, in this solemn assembly, at this very moment, as really as in the place where he met the waiting disciples of old. Jesus is here; for he says "Wherever two or three are gathered together in my name, there am I." We see him not, but he is here. Here he stretches forth his pierced hands, and uncovers his torn side, and says, "See, what I have endured for you! Thus was my body broken, and my blood shed, for you! Thus have I suffered for you, and bled for you, and given myself up to death for you, and gone through the very woes of hell for you! But I have now made peace by my cross, and taken away the sentence of wrath, and purchased eternal life, and am come to offer to you a home in the mansions of my Father! You have given me many a cold neglect, and harsh word, and cruel thrust, by despising my Gospel, and turning away from my love; but I forgive it all for ever, and offer you my peace! Take it, and you will soon weep no more, and sorrow no more. Take it, and my angels shall be your companions and friends. Take it, and my Father will be your Father too. Take it, and my own hands shall minister for ever to your joy. Only *"take my yoke upon you, and learn of me, and ye shall find rest for your souls!"* O, the mercies of God! The mercies of God! Who is not moved by the mercies of God! Who can refuse to say,

> Here's my heart, Lord, take and seal it —
> Seal it from thy courts above!

FOURTH LECTURE.

THE PEACE-OFFERING.

LEV. CHAP. III.

We have here another class of offerings, differing from either of those which we have thus far considered. Like the first, they are of a bloody nature, but still having peculiarities of their own.

In the first class, treated of in the first chapter, only a bullock, or a lamb, or a dove, of the male kind, could be taken. In this class, the offering might be a bullock, or a sheep, or a goat, whether male or female, only so that it was without blemish. All bloody sacrifices, of course, always represent Christ, in his character of an expiation. The reason for the allowed difference in the victims here, is, that this class of offerings fixes more upon the results, impartation, and reception of Christ's sacrifice, than upon the precise manner of it. The holocaust is *the picture* of the Savior, as the propitiation for sin. This is more especially a picture of his offering *availing for and conveyed to* those who believe.

The offerings of the first chapter were holocausts; that is, they were to be burned entirely upon the altar. But such is not the case with these peace-offerings. The only parts of these to be burned, were the suet pertaining to the inwards, the two kidneys with their fat, the "caul" (sacking, or whatever it was,) of the liver, and, in the case of the sheep, the large fat tail, which, in Syrian sheep, was a most remarkable and highly prized part of the animal. These the priest was to take away, and burn upon the wood on the altar. It was the Lord's part, an offering made by fire of a sweet savor unto the Most High. The breast and shoulder became the property of the priests, to be eaten by them. All that remained belonged to the offerer, to be eaten by him, his family and his friends, in a joyous sacred festival. This peculiarity settles the point to which I have just adverted, that these peace-offerings refer mainly to the benefits and blessings of Christ's sacrifice as distributed and feasted upon by his people. To this also answers their name.

This particular kind of offering is called *the peace-offering*. The word *peace*, in the language of the Scriptures, has a shade of meaning not commonly attached to it in ordinary use. With most persons it signifies a cessation of hostilities, harmonious agreement, tranquillity, the absence of disturbance. But in the Scriptures it means more. Its predominant import there is, *prosperity, welfare, joy, happiness*. The original Hebrew word includes both these meanings. The old Greek version renders it by terms which signify *a sacrificial feast of salvation*. This, perhaps, comes as near to the real import of *shelamim* as we can come. The Scriptures elsewhere mention the peace-offering under a name which denotes victims slain for banquets, especially for sacrificial banquets. The idea of great blessing, prosperity, rejoicing, evidently enters into the designation. We may therefore confidently take the peace-offering as a joyous festival, a solemn sacrificial banqueting, illustrative of the peace **and joy** which flows to believers from the atoning work of our Lord Jesus Christ, and our sanctification through his blood and Spirit.

Religion is not a thing of gloom, but of gladness. It is not a sullen sourness, requiring a dull and morose kind of life, barring all delight, all mirth, all pleasant cheer. It mingles with it a never-failing stream of true, pure, and steady peace. The first Gospel word that ever was uttered upon earth, was a joyful promise, kindling fond expectation and cherished hope. The angel who came down to announce the fulfilment of that promise in the birth of the long-expected seed, said, "Behold, I bring you glad tidings of great joy." God is to his people "the God of peace" — a fountain of consolation — a dew of freshness and joy. He cheerfully smiles upon them with his favor, and anoints them with the oil of praise, and throws around them the sunshine of his loving kindness, and stretches forth his own paternal hand to wipe away their tears. Laying our hands in humble confession upon the holy brow of his Son as our sacrificial Lamb, and presenting ourselves a living sacrifice, holy, acceptable unto him that same altar becomes to us a source of blessing and furnishes us substance for a happy festival "Being justified by faith, we have peace." "The kingdom of heaven is righteousness, peace, and joy 'n the Holy Ghost." A gloomy, dull, unsocial, dark-spirited Christian, is a very imperfect Christian. He has not entered into the full experience of his calling and prerogatives. He yet needs to bring his peace-offering. It yet remains for him to fulfil the command, — "Be joyful in the Lord." Whatever some may say, Christianity is meant to be a feast—a great royal banquet for every invited guest — as well as a penitential confession, and a living sacrifice. "Light is sown for the righteous, and gladness for the upright in heart."

Let us look, then, at some of the peculiarities and relations of the Christian's happiness, as it is pictured to us by God himself in the rites which he prescribed for the ancient peace-offering.

I. *The peace-offering was a bloody offering.* Everything in Christian life, justification and sanctification, the forgiveness of our sins, and the acceptableness of our services, our hopes and our spiritual festivities, run back into Christ's vicarious sufferings, as their fountain and foundation. If he had not submitted to be slain and offered for us, we could not be forgiven; and if not forgiven, we never could be holy and acceptable; and without being holy and acceptable, we never could have peace. There is not a spiritual joy which the believer has, but must be traced back to atonement by blood. This is the centre from which all Christian doctrine, and all Christian experience, radiates, and into which it ultimately resolves itself. Without this, Christianity dwindles down into a cold, flat, and powerless morality, with no warming mysteries, no animating sublimities, no kindling and melting affections, no transforming potencies. Without this, the soul languishes and droops like a plant excluded from the sunshine, or flourishes only in its own disgrace. The sinner must have it, or he sinks into a dead and gloomy Deism, or into a mere idolatry of self, with his highest and tenderest affections shrivelled, crisped and destroyed. If we would have peace, it must be founded upon blood. If we would rejoice, our sacrifice must die.

If we would have a feast of fat things, the provision must come from the altar of immolation.

II. *The peace-offering comes after the meat-offering.* We must present the "fine flour" of our best affections, and the fresh first fruits of uncorrupted obedience, before we can come to feast upon the rich provisions of the altar. We must surrender ourselves to God, and give up to him in a "covenant of salt," before we can taste of the "peace-offering," or be happy in the Lord. There is a strong disposition in the human heart to reverse this divine order. People wish to have some comforting assurance that they are accepted and pardoned, before they start out upon the work of obedience. They stand aloof from swearing allegiance to God, decline to offer themselves wholly to the Lord, refuse to join themselves unto the people of Jehovah, and draw back from the appointments of the church, until they have satisfactory proof that they are "*converted*," as they say. They want to have some spiritual consolation first, to assure them that they are right. They wish to experience the redeeming love of God before they will venture to do all the will of God. They desire to put the peace-offering before the meat-offering. And many people, in their ignorance, work themselves into the persuasion that all is well with them, that they are now God's people, that the happiness they feel is the sweet peace of a well-founded hope, before they have even so much as made up their minds to join the Church at all. Nor do I doubt the reality of their alleged happy state of mind. But, I do say, that such a peace is a delusive peace. It is not the divine feast which comes from the altar, and which the Scriptures warrant. Before you can taste of the peace-offering, you must present the meat-offering. You must first give yourselves to God, and be fully made up to do all his will, and surrender every possible reservation, and yield your whole being a living sacrifice to him; or your joy is a delusive joy, and your hope, a hope that shall perish. Many very sincere people will recoil at this doctrine. They will say, "I know that I am a Christian, because I am so happy. I know that my God is reconciled, and that I am his adopted child; for I feel it. True, I am not a member of any church; I never go to the communion table; my business and some of my dealings with my fellow-men are not in all respects considered reputable; but God certainly is my God; I cannot be mistaken in it; I have the evidence of it in my own heart; I know it, for I *feel it;* I am so happy." How often do we meet with persons just of this class? And what are we to say to them? It is not pleasant to disturb people in their joys; but I tell you that such individuals are deceived. They are miserably imposing upon themselves. They must give up to do all God's will, or their joy is not the solid peace of true Christianity. As long as they are content to stand aloof from God's Church and sacraments, or to harbor grudges against this one and that one, and to deal dishonorably towards any of their fellow men, they fail to surrender themselves wholly to the Lord, they have not yet brought their meat-offering; and, with all their raptures and ecstacies, they are yet "in the gall of bitterness, and in the bonds of iniquity." They may say, "Lord, Lord;" but he knows them not; he never knew them. They may cry *"Peace, peace!"*

but there is no peace. The **meat-offering** must go first.

III. *The peace-offering was so arranged, that the most inward, the most tender, and the most marrowy part of the sacrifice became the Lord's part.* The inner fat of the animal, the kidneys, the caul of the liver, and, if a sheep, the great fatty outward appendage, were to be burned on the altar, a sweet savor unto the Lord. God must be remembered in all our joys. Especially when we come to praise and enjoy him, and to appropriate to our hearts the glad provisions of his mercy, must we come offering to him the inmost, tenderest and richest of our soul's attributes. It was thus that Jesus was made a peace-offering for us. Every deep affection, every tender emotion, all that love could feel, all that desire could yearn over, did he give, when, "through the Eternal Spirit, he offered himself to God," to make our peace. It was upon these that the fire fed as they flashed forth from the face of indignant heaven. But he hesitated not to yield them up to all the consuming heat of wrath. And as he devoted every rich thought, every strong emotion, every intense feeling, for us, we must now send back the same to him without stint or tarnish. We may love our friends; but we must love Christ more. We may feel for those united to us in the bonds of domestic life; but we must feel still more for Jesus and his Church. We may be moved with earthly passions; but the profoundest and best of all our emotions must be given to the Lord. The fat, the kidneys, and the most tender and marrowy parts, are his. To withhold them, or to expend them upon friend or self, would be desecration, robbery of God, violation of his law and a total vitiation of our offering.

IV. *The peace-offerings were sacrifices of gratitude and praise*—a species of joyous, thankful banquetings. When the Jew came to make a peace-offering, it was with his heart moved and his thoughts filled with some distinguished mercy. Any remarkable favor was a call for a peace-offering. When Hezekiah succeeded in abolishing idolatry, and saw the true worship restored, he had the people to join him in a peace-offering. When Manasseh was brought back from his captivity and restored to his kingdom, "he sacrificed peace-offerings." And if any one had been the subject of some great deliverance, or had been remarkably preserved or prospered, or had achieved some noble object, he gave expression to his grateful joy in a peace-offering. The true Christian has been the subject of wonderful favors. He has had deliverance wrought for him, to which he may ever refer with joyful recollection. Frightful dangers once encompassed him. All the fierce artillery of heaven was once aimed at him as a rebel and a traitor to the righteous government of God. Perdition's fiery floods were rolling under the very ground on which he walked. The frown of terrific condemnation was on him, and hell from beneath was moved to meet him at his coming. And when all was dark and desperate, the loving Savior rushed between him and destruction, and snatched him as a brand from the everlasting burning. He considers the length, and breadth, and depth, and height of that love which thus interposed for his rescue — the mighty woes which the Lord endured for him — the secure ground upon which he now stands in Christ

Jesus — and his soul overflows with tremulous gladness. He is melted, and yet is full of delight. He is solemnly joyous. What to say or do he hardly knows. He weeps, and yet exults while he weeps. He smiles with tears. He rejoices in awe. And the burden of his soul is, "O magnify the Lord with me, and let us exalt his name together. I sought the Lord and he heard me, and delivered me from all my fears. This poor man cried, and the Lord heard him, and saved him out of all his troubles." The whole thing to him becomes a feast of profoundly solemn joy, in which he would gladly have all the world to participate.

V. *But the feasting of the peace-offering was on sacred food.* The people might have feasts at home, and have other banquets; but they were not peace-offerings. And so the Christian may have feasts and viands apart from the sacred food furnished directly from Christ. There is much virtuous enjoyment in this world of a merely secular sort, from none of which does Christianity exclude us. Talk of the enjoyments of learning and science; the Christian, as well as any other man, may tread those inspiring walks, and hold converse with nature and the past, and trace the footsteps of Omnipotence in the rocks — his finger-prints in the heavens — his praises in the rolling spheres — and his wisdom and goodness in everything. Talk of the happiness of domestic life, and the fond associations of friendship and love, and the silken cords which bind the household into a bundle of happiness; there blooms not a flower by the hearthstone, the beauty and fragrance of which the Christian may not enjoy; nor is there a chain of tender and noble attachments in which he may not be a link. Talk of the pleasures that spring from refined art — of the sublime creations of the past, the musician, the painter, the sculptor, and the curious artificer; it is enough to say, that God made his prophets poets, and has commanded us to praise him with songs and with harps, with stringed instruments and organs; and that Jesus himself went with his disciples to view the temple, to "see what manner of stones, and what buildings" were there. And as to the beauties of the physical world, where has ever Jehovah forbidden man to consider the lilies of the field, how they grow — or the heavens, the work of his fingers — or the deep broad sea, in which are things innumerable — or the massive mountains, which proclaim his majesty — or his great waterspouts which shake the world and brew the thunder — or the sharp lightnings which go as his messengers, and say: "Here we are!" Nay, the Christian, above all men, is the best qualified to enjoy life in its real substance, and to draw from nature her ten thousand oracles of truth, good, and beauty.

But all these are mere home-feasts on common viands. The food that was eaten in the joyous feast of the peace-offering fell from the altar. It was holy. No defiled person or stranger was allowed to touch it, or to partake of it. And so, above and superadded to the common joys of ordinary life, the Christian has a feast with which the stranger dare not meddle — a feast of fat things, of which the pure only can taste — a banquet of holy food proceeding directly from the altar at which his sacrifice was made. Of worldly comforts and bliss, some may be providentially deprived; but Christianity carries with it a consecrated good — a spiritual peace — a holy meat

— the same for the rich or the poor, the sick or the well, the living or the dying. Whosoever will come penitently to God, and present himself as a willing subject of Divine grace, shall from the altar receive a portion with which he and his house may be glad

Let us briefly review some of the faithful Christian's peculiar joys. Let us follow him a little into the sources of his consolation, and see of what sort his feast is.

And when I speak of the faithful Christian, I picture to myself a man who has gone through all the various services and experiences adumbrated in the Hebrew ritual as far as we have now considered it. I picture to myself a man who has brought his whole burnt-offering unto God, by a true confiding faith in Jesus Christ as the Lamb slain for the expiation of his sins; who has presented his meat-offering by the entire surrender of himself a living sacrifice, holy, acceptable unto God; who has brought his peace-offering with the distinct consciousness that he owes everything to the blood that was shed for him on Calvary, and who is now fully pervaded and absorbed with the redeeming mercies of the Lord. Let him be what the world calls a learned man, or not; let him be what we would call a man of taste, or not; let him be a minister at the altar, or an humble laborer at his daily toil, unnoticed by the gay multitude; it matters not. He is a happy man. He has a feast with God.

First of all is the great and cheering conviction of his heart, that THERE IS A GOD; that the universe is not an orphan, but has a righteous, almighty, and loving Father, who sees all, and provides for all, and takes care of all. Whatever disorders other men may see, he knows that the Lord reigneth, and is superintending all for good. Injustice and oppression may rise up before him, and trample innocence to the dust; but he is not overcome with fear. He knows there is a hand which will soon requite iniquity, and rectify all inequalities. He knows that "the triumphing of the wicked is short, and the joy of the hypocrite but for a moment;" and that the time is coming, when righteousness shall be brought forth as the light, and judgment as the noonday. He may have misfortune, but he knows that it is guided by a Father who pities his distresses, and loves him with an everlasting love. He knows he has a Friend mightier than the powers of evil, and he sings in spite of his adversities — "The Lord is my strength and my shield, my heart trusteth in him, and I am helped: therefore my heart danceth for joy, and in my song will I praise him!"

The next is the joyous light that shines upon him from God's revelation, relieving his native perplexities, comforting his heart, filling him with pleasant wisdom, and kindling radiance along all his path. Here the riddle of life is explained to him, his duty made plain, and his conscience put to rest. Here is food for delightful meditation, and living water for his thirsty soul. Drinking ever from these wells of salvation, he repeats again the grand experiences of the ancient saints. He becomes another Enoch walking with God, and a Moses on the Mount, and a Noah outriding the waves which flood and overwhelm the unbelieving world. He is Isaiah, filled with visions of God, the living temple, and the everlasting throne, where seraphs in their worship cry, — "Holy, Holy, Holy!" He is John, leaning on his Savior's breast,

THE PEACE-OFFERING. 75

drinking in lessons of truth and grace warm from the great Teacher's lips, or exulting amid the stupendous scenery of Apocalyptic visions. He is Paul, caught up to the third heaven, lost in the contemplation of things which man may not utter. He is Stephen, gazing into the gates of glory upon the Son of God in his celestial home, where the angels attend upon him. He is Simeon, ready to depart in peace, for his eyes have seen God's salvation. He is Elijah in the bright chariots of the Almighty, ascending without knowing the bitterness of death.

Along with these, are the gifts and graces of a present redemption. Though penitently sensible of his sins, Christ has borne their penalty for him, and he stands justified before his Lord. Though according to his earthly nature he is very weak, and blind, and erring, he has grace to help in every time of need, the Spirit to enlighten him, and the truth to guide him. The burden that once weighed upon his conscience is gone. The apprehensions of dread with which he once anticipated death and the judgment, have been hushed to peace by the soothing voice of his Savior. His heart, once so unruly and corrupt, has been brought into subjection, released from the reign of cruel passion, and fashioned to the Spirit of Jesus. Though once an alien and a stranger, he is now a member of the family of heaven, a Son of God, and an heir of eternal life. Though penniless here, he has treasures which shall never perish, reserved for him on high. Though friendless here, he has a home and friends to whom he is going, to be for ever at rest. Though a sufferer here, he is accumulating thereby "'a far more exceeding and eternal weight of glory." He is in the goodly fellowship of the saints; he is in the noble army of the martyrs, he is united with the glorious company of the apostles; he is allied to angelic orders; he is a Son of the ever-living God.

And beyond all present experiences, he is authorized to look forward to still higher and greater things in the future. The present is only his seed-time, which is yet to yield an unspeakable and eternal harvest. His Redeemer has gone to prepare a place for him, the glories of which cannot now be conceived. Let the earthly house of this tabernacle be dissolved; he has a building of God, a house not made with hands, eternal in the heavens. Even his body, now so full of aches, and ills, and symptoms of decay, shall be touched with the healing hand of God's Almightiness, and fashioned into a glorious and unfading tenement. He is a pilgrim now; but he is on his way to an eternal rest. The dust of earth is on him now; but it soon shall be brushed off, that he may shine as an undying star of light. Lifting up his eyes, and pointing away beyond the sky, he says, with tears of joy,—

> "Yonder's my house and portion fair;
> My treasure and my heart are there —
> And my abiding home!"

And everlasting love and power are pledged by the oath of God to bring him safely to that "home," where the last sorrow shall be over, the last tear dried, and the last taint of sin and folly for ever washed away.

> Oh! how happy are they, who their Savior obey,
> And have laid up their treasures above!
> O what tongue can express, the sweet comfort and peace,
> Of a soul in it's earliest love!

> O the rapturous height, of that holy delight,
>   Which we feel in the life-giving blood!
> Of the Savior possessed, we are perfectly blest
>   As if filled with the fulness of God.

Such, then, is the Christian's feast of joy and thankfulness, as symbolized by the ancient peace-offering. Indulge me yet with a few inferential observations, and I will leave you to your own reflections.

And first, let me say, that this subject entirely does away with all ground for that common feeling on the part of non-Christian people, that to be religious and good would be an abridgment of their comforts and their joys. It is not so. To be gloomy, ever sighing, ever dull, is not piety. Joining one'sself to Jesus, is not like joining a nunnery, or a total casting away of all the pleasures and enjoyments of life. "Wisdom's ways are pleasantness, and all her paths are peace." The Bible requires nothing morbid or morose. Christ demands nothing incompatible with the highest possible earthly good. His whole system breathes peace, joy, cheerfulness, and love. If religion were that leaden and sombre thing which deadens and paralyses every gush of youthful feeling into a stupid and lifeless monotony, it would be unfitted for many, and could hardly be sustained as of God. But the Savior never meant to graft the demure gravity of age upon the laughing brow of childhood and youth. The natural temper of young people is proverbially joyous and cheerful. Untouched as yet by the cares and sorrows of life, it belongs to their years to be buoyant, sunny, and gay in their spirits. Youth is the period of glee. God himself has made it so. Nor was religion ever meant to make it otherwise, or to tie down the young heart to solemn cant or slavish bondage. It was intended to moderate youthful lust, intemperance, and vanity. It forbids wild and unreasonable excesses. It draws the check-reins upon idolatrous extravagance. It will not allow levity to be carried on to madness, or pleasure to degenerate into impurity, or the gay heart to rush on without a balance for boisterous exuberance. But it does not disallow the common joys of life. With the rest of its offerings, it presents its feast of gladness. No, no; we do not ask you to cease to be happy, when we ask you to be pious and good. We only ask you to cease sinning, and by ceasing to sin, to cease sowing for a harvest of inevitable misery.

Finally, let us be admonished how incongruous it is for Christians to be all the time sad, sorrowing, and desponding. Who have so much cause for cheerfulness and joy as they? God is their Father; Christ is their faithful Savior; heaven is their covenanted home; and why should they go bowed down with gloom? The commonest birds will sing when the sun shineth; and the ugliest weeds will stretch up their arms, and spread open some pleasant flower when the summer is around them; and why should we be depressed when the radiance of celestial love is flowing down upon us, and everything invites to joyousness and praise. Ask thyself, dejected disciple — "Why art thou cast down, O my soul? and why art thou disquieted within me? Hope thou in God: for I shall yet praise Him, who is the health of my countenance and *my* God!" Jesus says, "Let not thy heart be troubled, neither let it be afraid." The word of Jehovah is, "Let them that put their trust in the Lord rejoice; let them ever shout for joy."

THE PEACE-OFFERING.

"Let the saints be joyful in glory; let them sing aloud; let the high praises of God be in their mouths." "Let Israel rejoice in Him that made him, let the children of Zion be joyful in their King." "Let the righteous be glad; let them rejoice before God; yea, let them exceedingly rejoice." "Sing unto God, sing praises to his name; extol Him that rideth upon the heavens."

And now, let glory be to the Father, and to the Son, and to the Holy Ghost, as it was in the beginning, is now, and ever shall be, world without end Amen.

FIFTH LECTURE.

THE SIN AND TRESPASS OFFERINGS.

LEV. CHAPTERS IV. V. VI.

It has been very correctly observed, that, in doctrinal substance, the first three chapters of this book closely resemble the first chapter of first John. They portray the universal sinfulness of mankind, and point to the only remedy for sin, and set forth that "eternal life" which was manifested in Christ Jesus, and declare unto us the way of peace, "that our joy might be full."

But not less do the chapters now before us resemble the second chapter of that epistle. If the first three were meant to show the way up to communion with God, and to the fulness of joy in Christ Jesus, the succeeding three were written "that we sin not, because our sins are forgiven us for his sake." If the former present the sinner justified, sanctified, and happy in believing; these now, with equal beauty and clearness, exhibit him in what appertains to a life thus consecrated to the Lord. And as we have seen the offender in humble confession and penitence laying his hand upon the head of the atoning Lamb, and thereby obtaining release from his past sins; then gratefully offering himself a living sacrifice in return for his deliverance; then joining with the pure in a rich feast upon the provisions of redeeming love; we now are called upon to contemplate him in connection with those weaknesses and infirmities which still cling to him even in his justified and consecrated estate.

With all the blessed experiences which have thus far come under review, man is still a dweller in the flesh, surrounded by a perverse and vexatious world. Though pardon has been obtained, and sin is dethroned in his heart, he has not yet clean escaped from all its relics, influences, and effects. A soul in the first raptures of reconciliation, and filled with the enthusiasm of a new-born zeal, is prone to think that now the victory is complete. It is so full of God's glory and the Savior's love, that it can see no lack, and no possibility of coming down again to sin. It sometimes occurs in Christian experience, that God brings us so near to him, and into such heavenliness of fellowship with himself and his Son, that we feel ourselves quite beyond all the power of evil or temptation, and incapable of those bad affections which have so often sullied our peace. When the ancient Hebrews had gotten safely out of the land of their oppression; when they saw the strength and pride of their haughty pursuers overwhelmed in the sea; when the living thought first came thrilling through them, that now they were *free;* it woke up their joyous exultations. "Then sang Moses and the children of Israel, saying, I will sing unto the Lord, for he hath triumphed gloriously; the horse and his rider hath he thrown into the sea." It was all right. The occasion called for it. But their troubles were not all over yet. Some that now overflowed with gladness, would very soon murmur in bitter complaint. Pharoah and his hosts were gone; but Amalek remained. The hard masters of Egypt were gone; but a Korah, Dathan, and Abirim, were among themselves. The tasks of the brick-yards had been left behind, but the guile and treachery of Balak were before. They had been triumphantly delivered; but as yet they were by no means near or settled in their final rest. And so with the man rejoicing in his first experiences of the redeeming grace of God. He may feel as if heaven itself had come down to him, or as if no powers of death or hell could ever shake his faith, or cast a suspicion on his love; but he is nothing but a poor frail erring child with all. To his burnt-offering for past guilt, and his meat-offering of personal consecration, and his peace-offering of communion with God, he must yet add his sin-offering for failings through ignorance, and his trespass-offering for his defections in charity.

I. There are, then, some lingering defilements and trespasses adhering to man, even though he be justified, consecrated, and in fellowship with God. This is the first point of doctrine which I gather from the chapters now before us. The most firm and conscientious Christian has roots of evil still remaining in him, though there may be times and seasons when their existence is neither felt nor suspected. By the converting grace of God, and the renewing power of the Spirit, the dominion of sin is broken in every believer's soul, and its tyrannous sway completely overthrown, and now and then may seem entirely dead. He may be so much under the influence of faith, and so absorbed with things divine and eternal, as not to feel or know that there is a treacherous rebel in his heart. He may be so fully taken up now with God, and his love in Christ, as to be quite beyond all temptation to transgress. But there never yet was "a day when the sons of God came to present themselves before the Lord, but Satan came also among them;" nor a mere man so holy, but when he would do good evil was present with him. Let him be a Moses in the mount, with his face radiant from divine communings, and joyfully pressing the tables of the law to his bosom; when he comes down to the camp, he shall find strange feelings stirring in his heart, and a chance if that law is not dropped and broken before he has had time to think. Let him be that man of Uz, who, in the sunny days of his prosperity, "was perfect and upright, and one that feared God and eschewed evil;" the dark night of his trial shall move him to curse the day of his birth, and he shall yet have reason to abhor himself, and repent in dust and ashes. Let him be that rapt apostle caught up into the midst of heaven; no sooner shall he touch the earth again, but a vexatious thorn is in his flesh, and sharp contentions with brethren spring up to mar the picture of a perfect love, and Paul himself is left to lament that he had not yet attained — that he is not yet perfect. With all his efforts, prayers, and joys, the best Christian is still very faulty.

Many estimable Christians hold a different doctrine; and I would be glad to agree with them if I could. But having listened often to their conversations, and read their books, I have found nothing in them, or in their arguments, to convince me in their favor. They are honest, no doubt, but they are mistaken. God's commandment is exceeding broad and holy. It is the only rule which the angels know, or by which seraphs are so excellent and good. And to suppose that law completely fulfilled in the heart or life of any mortal, seems to me a great degradation of it, and a putting of the goodness of earth on an equality with the goodness of heaven. Christ has taught us to pray daily, "forgive us our trespasses;" but why continue praying for forgiveness, if we have not continual trespasses to be forgiven? I know and preach that "the blood of Jesus Christ cleanseth from all sin." That is a precious truth to me. But did he not continue a priest for ever, daily presenting his atoning blood anew in our behalf, we should most certainly come into condemnation. It is only because "he continueth ever," that he is "able to save them to the uttermost that come unto God by him, seeing he ever liveth to make intercession for them." If he did not ever live to make intercession for us, we could not stand for a single day. The reason that we have a character for innocence before God, is, that our "sins are not imputed to us." Christ's blood comes in between them and the law, and by virtue of that blood we are held as innocent. But were it not for that blood availing afresh for us every day, we certainly should be very obnoxious to condemnation, and could not be saved. And the fact that Christ continues in heaven ever offering and pleading his atoning blood in our behalf — ever interceding for us — is proof that we continually need the application of his cleansing blood, and are not perfectly sinless. If we were not continual sinners, we would not need this perpetual atonement.

I know, too, that "whosoever is born of God doth not commit sin, and cannot sin, because he is born of God." But it is the intention, the motive, the principle. of the man, that is here in contemplation. and not the actual perfection of the life. He has in him the seed of holiness. He has been recovered by grace to the dominion of virtue. He has put off the old man with his deeds. All his aims, purposes and desires are directed to obedience and purity He has been renewed in the spirit of his mind. He has become deadened to sin, so that he cannot live any longer therein. It is contrary to his whole feeling, wish, and calling. He can no longer consent to it for a moment. His new experiences have made him its perpetual foe. And in this sense it is impossible for a Christian to sin. The whole bent of his renewed nature is antagonistic to all known wrong. If it is not so, he is not born of God. But this does not prove, that, contrary to his purpose and efforts, no imperfections shall ever occur in his life, or no defects attach to his endeavors. A man may run from a gathering storm, and be terribly shocked at the idea of being caught in it, and exert all his wisdom and his power to escape it, and yet may be made to feel its force; and though a good man's whole being is averse to sin, and he can have no more fellowship with the unfruitful works of darkness, it can argue nothing against a remaining weakness subjecting him every day to lacks and failings which would undo him but for the pleadings of his Savior's blood. Though his face and heart are fully turned away from sin, it proves nothing against his liability to be "*overtaken* by a fault." Nay, this same apostle, in this same Epistle, says, "If we say that we have no sin, we deceive ourselves, and the truth is not in us." Yea, "what is man that he should be clean? or he that is born of a woman, that he should be righteous?' Let men speculate as they please, when we come to inspect earthly goodness in the light of heaven, we shall find ourselves just where the apostle places us when he says, "*In many things we all offend.*"

II. And these lingering imperfections and defects are *real sins*. This is the second point of doctrine which I deduce from these chapters. People are prone to think that an offence committed unintentionally or unawares, cannot incur the charge of guilt. Men do not scruple to plead their ignorance, their infirmities, their natural and habitual propensities, in excuse for their misdeeds. But the law of God acknowledges no such plea. "If a soul shall sin through ignorance against any of the commandments," he must bring his sin-offering, and atone for his sin by blood, the same as for those old wilfu transgressions in which he once lived. If a man becomes contaminated, even though it should be through accident, or commits any of those things which are forbidden, even "though he wist it not, yet is he guilty, and shall bear his iniquity;" and can only be cleansed and delivered by atoning blood. So saith the Lord, and no man can annul it.

There is a school of moralists, who make a difference between sins. They tell us that while some are mortal, and carry after them the certain judgment of God, others are only *venial*—mere imperfections, to which no serious guilt attaches. But, I find no such distinctions in the word of God. Sin is sin; and guilt is a part of its essential nature wherever found. True, in their effects upon the perpetrator, or in their influences upon society, some are worse than others; but in their relations to God and his holy law, they are always the same, always evil, abhorrent, and damning. Men may talk of "little sins;" but God never does. Let them be never so little, they are big enough to sink the soul to everlasting death, if uncancelled by the Savior's blood. It is not in all respects as wicked to sin only in ignorance and infirmity, as to sin knowingly, intentionally, and presumptuously; but to sin in any way, needs to be atoned for by the shedding of blood. All sin therefore is intrinsically mortal. And there is not a Christian on earth, however eminent, who does not, every day he lives, accumulate guilt enough to ruin him for ever, were it not that he has "an Advocate with the Father, Jesus Christ the righteous."

All this is very forcibly portrayed in the rites of the sin and trespass-offerings now under consideration. As to sins of ignorance, if the guilty party were a priest, he was to offer "a young bullock;" if a judge or magistrate, he was to offer "a kid of the goats," of the male kind; if one of "the common people," he was to offer "a kid of the goats," of the female kind, or a lamb. And so in the case of trespass, the guilty one was to offer "a lamb or kid;" or, if poor, two doves or young pigeons; or, if poor, and unable to procure the doves or pigeons, an offering of fine flour might be substituted as the representative of the animal or bird which could not be procured, but was to be looked upon, not as a meat-offering, but as a "sin-offering," the same as if it were a living animal. These offerings were then to be slain and burned, and their blood presented as the only adequate expiation. And from the nature of the expiation we are to learn God's estimate of the offence. Though committed in ignorance, or no more than a trespass, or an accidental contamination, it required blood and sacrifice to cover it.

Now, I can easily conceive how the taste of some may be offended with these continual displays of blood, blood, blood. And there are men of a skeptical turn of mind who rail out against all this ceremonial slaughter and burning, as unworthy of God and repulsive to man. They are terribly shocked at it, and cast away from them the book that prescribes it, and the God who could sanction it. But, how is it, that these same men are such enthusiastic admirers of the polished taste and refined attainments of the Greeks and Romans of other days? How is it, that they can dwell with so much complacency and approbation upon the philosophies and religions of ancient heathendom? They had similar sacrifices and like bloody rites, yet with vastly more barbarous concomitants and offensive ceremonies. This appears in every chapter of their history, and on almost every page of their poetry. People can tolerate, and admire, and gather instruction from this; but as soon as the hand and authority of God are manifested in such bloody ordinances, then they are disgusted, and the thing becomes intolerable. Of this one thing, be assured, that it is not so much the rites themselves with which such people are offended, as God in those rites. "The carnal mind is enmity against God," and wherever he shows his holy authority, there is an immediate revulsion of that carnal mind, and it draws back, and reviles, and blasphemes. Let the heart be right, and God's appointments will be right, beautiful, impressive, and good. It is in man that the fault lies, and not in God, or in the appointments

of God. Though there be a constant recurrence of
blood, it is full of mighty significance. It tells of
guilt, and of death and ruin merited by that guilt.
It tells of our condemnation, and of the way in
which that condemnation is removed in Christ Jesus.
It shows us the awful penalty which we have incurred,
and how our Savior undertook to bear it in his own
body on the tree. And when we see Jehovah annexing
these bloody expiations to sins of ignorance, accidental contaminations, and trespasses against the law
of charity, we are to see and know that these are
really *sins* from which we never could be saved, were
it not for the ever efficacious blood of that Lamb of
God who was slain for us.

III. There is also a noticeable gradation in these
sins of ignorance. Though they are all sins, so that
blood only can atone for them, they are yet more
serious and offensive in some persons than in others.
When a priest or ruler sinned in this way, a more
valuable sacrifice was required than when one of the
common people thus sinned. The more prominent
and exalted the person offending, the more flagrant
was the offence.

There is a very serious augmentation of responsibility going along with high station. A public man
is like a town clock; upon which much more depends
than upon private time-pieces. When a man's watch
gets wrong, it is only he that is misled; but when
the great public clock gets out of the way, multitudes are deceived, and a whole community is led
astray or thrown into confusion. Hence the necessity
for greater care and attention with reference to the
one than to the other. Every official personage is
responsible beyond a common individual, for the

reason, and to the extent, that his office or station represents others beside himself. A parent is responsible beyond a child, because he acts for, influences, and represents the child. A minister is responsible beyond one of his congregation, because he in a measure acts for, influences, and represents those who attend upon his ministrations. A judge or ruler is responsible beyond the ordinary subject, because he acts for, influences, and represents those who are under his jurisdiction and legislation. And among the Jews, the priest was the most responsible of all, because he was the most exalted man of the whole people, acting for, influencing, and representing them to a greater extent, and in more important matters, than any other official of the nation. An error in him, was the same as an error of the whole nation, for he represented the whole nation ; and so his fault could only be atoned for by a sacrifice which was required in case of the whole nation's sin.

A sin in a public man is a sin to the sinning of others ; and it is peculiarly aggravated, first, because it is presumed that he understands his office and knows its duties, before entering upon it; and, second, because it is a precedent and pattern which will be copied by others, and be thought right because it has the sanction of greatness. A public character is like the "copy" set by a schoolmaster at the head of the page, which feebler hands will imitate to every letter, and curve, and line, and dot; and if the copy is wrong, of course all the imitations are wrong, and that by reason of the mistake of him who set the copy. The master is thus accountable for the error of the pupil, the parent for the child, the preacher for the church member, the ruler for the subject, the priest for the people. And a sin in high life is a greater offence than the same sort of sin in the humbler walks. It is more mischievous in its effects, it is committed under more solemn responsibilities, and it requires a heavier atonement.

Some people are very feverish and ambitious for place. They wish to be conspicuous, influential, and prominent. They covet office. They long for power. They will do almost anything for an exalted position. But they seldom sufficiently consider the increased responsibilities involved in the fulfilment of their desires. It is the mere flare and glitter of station by which they are captivated, without laying to heart the additional jeopardy which it imposes. And there are some who seem to consider office a full license for them to do just as they please. They forget with what a jealous eye God looks upon those invested with public influence and trust. A misstep in them is no common offence in his sight. Abuse of power, is with him the worst of all abuses — a sin more aggravated than ordinary sins. What in other men might be considered trivial, in them is held to a most rigid accountability. Let public men consider this, and tremble when they lay hold of the helm of power. Office is a solemn and awful thing. It is a momentous trust. It is a fearful charge. And it is to be entered into reverently, discreetly, and in the fear of God. Over its portals are written this inscription, in letters of flame: *Let him who enters here beware, for a jealous God is within.* And if any would enter upon office, let him read that inscription, and tread softly, lest it should prove to him the gateway of death and perdition.

IV. But whilst we are treating of these defects and

failings which are to be found in Christian life, let us not overlook the principal point of the text, that *there is an adequate remedy for them.*

I once heard of a man, a bishop I believe, who gave it as his objection to the protestant religion, that it made no provision for sins after baptism; and with this as one of his principal grounds, he became a pervert to Romanism. Deluded man! How had Satan blinded his eyes to the truth! *We have a remedy for sins after baptism,* the same as for sins before baptism. We have a great atoning sacrifice, provided of God, to which we may ever betake ourselves in penitence, and find a full salvation. For so it is written —" *If any man sin, we have an advocate with the Father, Jesus Christ the righteous: and he is the propitiation for our sins; and not for ours only, but also for the sins of the whole world.*" When the cleansed and consecrated Jew sinned through ignorance after his consecration; or through accident, inadvertance, or infirmity, became contaminated after his cleansing; there was a plain way for him to get back again to his former purity; and that way was essentially the same as the way by which he secured forgiveness at the first. He had to return to the same bloody sacrifice which he had offered in the first instance. The chief of the herd or of the flock had to die and burn, and have its blood put upon the horns of the altar. Its fat, and its kidneys, and the caul of its liver, had to be laid upon the fire; and every remaining part had to be carried forth without the camp unto a clean place, and consumed there in the place of ashes. What did all this mean? "The blood of bulls and of goats could not make him that did the service perfect, as pertaining to the conscience;" wherefore, then, were they required to be thus slain? The apostle has given the explanation. "It was a figure for the time then present"—"a shadow of good things to come." It pointed to a holier sanctification 'with better sacrifices than these." It was God's own prefiguration of the way of forgiveness in Christ. For just as "the bodies of those beasts are burned without the camp, Jesus also, that he might sanctify the people with his own blood, suffered without the gate." Away from the holy place, driven from the mercy-seat, beyond the bounds of the holy city, on Calvary's hill, outcast and forsaken, the criminal's veil hung over him for three hours of darkness, a spectacle to all that passed by, his face more marred than the face of any man, the fires kindled around our holy Lamb, and flashed through him, and drank up all his substance, and left him a mere pile of ashes in Joseph's tomb in "the place of ashes"— the ashes of the dead. "Let us go forth therefore unto him without the camp," says the apostle. Let us contemplate him in those tragic scenes. Let us view him in those awful fires as suffering for us. Let us penitently stretch forth the hand of faith, and lay it on his devoted head. Let us behold in those mysterious transactions the payment of our debts, and the meeting of our penalties. This is enough. If we have sinned, this secures our forgiveness. If we have offended, this cancels all the guilt. If we are defiled, this purifies us, and makes us clean. If we are deficient and unworthy, this covers whatever may be lacking. Here we have pardon, not only for this once, to cancel the past debt, and then leave us to manage the future as best we can; but daily, hourly, continual pardon—a pardon that ever flows without interruption or exhaustion — a pardon that is ever fresh and ever availing, as often as the sin-burdened soul will sue for it, and cast itself anew upon its Savior.

"No provision for sins after baptism!" How ridiculous! How false! How little must he know of the resources of those who take the Bible for their guide, who can give to such a thought one moment's entertainment! What! are we to be told that Christ's infinite atonement is that shallow thing, that the first draw of the sinner upon it quite exhausts its virtue, and leaves all subsequent sins to be disposed of by the wicked farce of the confessional, the fires of purgatory, and the mumbled prayers of man-made priests? Are we to be told that Christ "ever liveth to make intercession," and for this reason "is able to save unto the uttermost," and yet that there is not virtue enough in his mediation to cover a few sins of ignorance and infirmity in Christian life? Are we to behold the priest of a typical economy, with the mere blood of beasts upon his fingers, obtaining a full remission for the Jew, and yet believe that our great High-priest in heaven, bearing the scars of deadly wounds endured for us, is unable to secure mercy for those struggling saints of God, who, in hours of surprise or weakness become entangled again in guilt, of which they heartily repented the moment it was done? O, foolish bishop, how camest thou to forget, that "*the blood of Jesus Christ cleanseth from all sin?*" Give us this, and we want no pontifical absolutions, no penal inflictions, no purgatorial fires, to make us acceptable to God. Let us but know that Jesus has entered heaven as our surety and advocate, to appear for us, and to plead our cause there, and it is enough to satisfy us for ever.

> Five bleeding wounds he bears,
>   Received on Calvary;
> They pour effectual prayers,
>   They strongly speak for me;
> Forgive him, O forgive, they cry,
> Nor let that ransomed sinner die.
>
> The Father hears him pray,
>   His dear anointed One;
> He cannot turn away,
>   Cannot refuse his Son;
> His Spirit answers to the blood,
> And tells us we are born of God.

From this general subject we are now led to reflect:—

First, what a holy thing is God's law! It finds guilt, not only in the sins which are deliberate, known, and presumptuous; but even in the mistakes of ignorance, the contaminations of accident, and the short-comings of the holiest saints. Where our dull reason would not at all suspect anything criminal, it detects and marks iniquity, for which the death of Jesus alone can atone. Yet, this law is but a transcript of God himself. How awful then is his holiness! How terrible is his jealousy of sin! Who are the prayerless and the wicked, that they should stand in his sight, when even the failings that cleave to his best saints are so offensive to him as only to be purged by blood! We may think lightly of sin, and sometimes esteem it sweet; but not so does it look in the wounds and agonies of Jesus. It has an ugliness, even in its lightest forms, which shows unto heaven, and wakens indignation in the very heart of God. He cannot look upon it with the least degree of allowance. Well may the seraphs sing, "Holy, holy, holy, *is the Lord of hosts!*"

Second, what reason have we to cultivate the modest virtues of Christian life — to be moderate in our pretensions, humble in our spirit, charitable in our censures, forgiving under injuries, lenient towards offenders, pungent in our self-examinations, hearty in our repentance, watchful in our walk, constant in our prayers, and deeply anxious to be firmly rooted and grounded in the true faith? I care not how good we may be, we are still great offenders, and much worse than we think we are. Every time we search and weigh ourselves, we ascertain new deficiencies, and sins come to light where we had not supposed them to exist. And if we could just see ourselves as God sees us, and estimate our goodness just as it stands in the eye of his pure law, we should behold a spectacle which would sicken us perhaps to death. Every day but adds new vileness to us, which calls for new forgiveness.

Finally, how precious is the mercy of God in Christ Jesus! We sin every day. "We do nothing well. If we pray, it is with cold and wandering thoughts; if we hear, it is with distracted and forgetful minds; we are continually surprised, continually overtaken, continually turned aside by the current of temptation, that runs so strong against us, when perhaps we cannot convict ourselves of one indulged or deliberate sin." And even at the best, our righteousness is nothing, and our imperfections very great. But we are not without recourse. If we daily and hourly sin, there is provided a daily and hourly forgiveness. Our sacrifice has been slain. Our Priest is ever in the temple holding up the blood that was shed for us. "We have an Advocate with the Father," whose intercessions never cease. Our Lamb is ever before God. Those dying agonies of his can never fail to move Jehovah's pity. And if we have unwittingly or inadvertently offended, we have only to recur to his offering on Calvary, and his sufferings without the gate, and vengeance is stayed, forgiveness is complete, and we are still the children and heirs of God. O, precious, precious mercy that we poor sinners have in Jesus! We need only come in sight of the cross, and the load is removed. If we only look upon the face of that meek sufferer, as our Lord, our sins, however great or many, are remembered against us no more. Hither, then, let us ever come, and kneel, and look, and pray, and trust. In the shadow of the cross let us build our tabernacle, and say, "*Here will I dwell.*"

> Here I'll sit — forever viewing,
>   Mercy streaming in his blood:
> Precious drops, my soul bedewing,
>   Plead and claim my peace with God.

SIXTH LECTURE.

SUPPLEMENT TO THE LAW OF OFFERINGS.

LEV. CHAPTERS VI. VII.

We begin, this evening, in the midst of the sixth chapter. The first seven verses belong to the chapter which precedes, and ought not to have been severed from their proper place. They treat of the same subject with that chapter, whilst the eighth verse commences a new strain of discourse and quite another theme.

I need hardly say, that the Bible was not originally divided into chapters and verses. In the early Christian ages, the sacred text had no divisions but the various books, and those books consisting of short unbroken paragraphs, according to the sense of the writer, or the subject of discourse. All beyond this has been the work of editors, publishers and printers, of comparatively modern times, who had no claims to inspiration, or any superior knowledge; and who, in some instances, have made sad havoc with the sense of the sacred record. As furnishing facilities for reference, it is well that we have these divisions; and their usefulness in this respect may compensate for their occasional mutilations, and dislocations, and obscurations of the holy record. But there is no crime in correcting them, or in calling attention to the plain mistakes which have been made in them.

We do no irreverence to the inspired word by paying no attention to them. It is merely saying that we have as good a right to read the Bible *our* way, as the monk Arlott, or the Canterbury bishop Langton, of the thirteenth century, or the Jew, Mordecai Nathan of the fifteenth, or the French printer, Robert Stephen, of the sixteenth, had to read it *their* way. And amid all the increased light and learning of our day, it would be strange if the devout biblical student and critic now could not read it as well as any of the monks or even bishops of the dark ages, or any printer who lived in 1551.

Leaving the first seven verses, then, as properly belonging to the preceding chapter, our present observations will embrace the remaining part of the sixth, on to the close of the seventh, chapter, which concludes the first grand division of this book. All that precedes relates to the law of offerings as applicable to "the children of Israel" in general; what we have here, is a sort of supplement to that law, intended for the direction of the priests, and addressed specifically to "Aaron and his sons." It is a section of God's word which does not seem to be of much account, or to promise anything very edifying to us. And yet, we ought not to despise it, or to pass it as totally barren. All Scripture has its use, and may yield us profit under proper culture. True philosophy never neglects or despises anything which God has made; and true religion will cast nothing aside as unworthy of its attention and study, which God has said. Let us see, then, what we may learn from this supplement to the law of offerings.

I. Verses 8 to 14, treat of the whole burnt-offering, or holocaust, and tell how Aaron and his sons were to proceed in presenting it. All true Christians are priests, ordained to show forth the praises of him who hath called them out of darkness into his marvellous light. And what was required of these ancient priests in offering the sacrifices of the law, is the type of what is required of us all in the offering of those "spiritual sacrifices, acceptable to God by Jesus Christ." As the ancient priests were required to attire themselves in pure linen garments, so John tells us " the fine linen is the righteousness of saints," in which we must needs be arrayed in order to be accepted priests of God, or to serve in holy things at his altars. As Aaron and his sons were carefully to gather and bear forth the ashes of the burnt-offering, so must we take up Christ, crucified and consumed to dust as our holocaust, and bear him with us in purity and reverence. As they were never to allow the fire to go out upon the altar, so are we ever to see the holiness and justice of God flaming unquenchably against all sin, and consuming forever whatsoever may have sin to answer for.

II. Verses 14 to 24, give directions concerning the second kind of offerings. Whether everything here detailed is typical, I know not. As there is often more in the antitype than in the type, so there is oftentimes more in the type than in the antitype. The two do not always quadrate in every minute and unimportant particular. It is not necessary that they should. The main drift is clear. God means that we should be priests, and that with our other offerings should be eucharistic offerings. We are to "sacrifice the sacrifices of thanksgiving, and declare his works with rejoicing." And, in so doing, a goodly portion shall fall to us from the altar at which we serve, on which we may satisfy ourselves forever

III. Verses 24 to 30, inclusive, describe things to be observed in the sin-offering. There is here a remarkable provision. "Whatsoever shall touch the flesh thereof shall be holy: and when there is sprinkled of the blood thereof upon any garment, thou shalt wash that whereon it was sprinkled in the holy place. But the earthen vessel wherein it is sodden shall be broken: and if it be sodden in a brazen pot, it shall be both scoured and rinsed in water." Well may it be said, "How awful is atoning blood! Even things without life, such as garments, are held in dreadful sacredness if this blood touch them. No wonder, then, that this earth, on which fell the blood of the Son of God, has a sacredness in the eye of God. It must be set apart for holy ends, since the blood of Jesus has wet its soil. And as the earthen vessel, within which the sacrifice was offered, must be broken, and not used for any meaner end again; so must this *earth* be decomposed and new-moulded, for it must be kept for the use of him whose sacrifice was offered there. And as the *brazen vessel* must be rinsed and scoured, so must this earth be freed from all that dims its beauty, and be set apart for holy ends. It must be purified and reserved for holy purposes, for the blood of Jesus has dropped upon it, and made it more sacred than any spot, except where he himself dwells. *My holy mountain*, is the name it gets from himself, when he is telling how he means to cleanse it for his own use." (*Bonar in loc.*)

IV. Chap. 7 : 1–7. We next have sundry directions for the trespass offering. These differ very little from the requirements in case of the sin-offering, with which the trespass offering is very closely related. Both were intended as remedies for the sins of infirmity attending upon life still subject to the trials and temptations of this world. One point of difference between them was in the mode of disposing of the blood. Both were bloody offerings, but the blood in one case was to be put on the four horns of the altar, and in the other it was to be sprinkled "round about upon the altar." In all these rites there was an ample display of blood. The Psalmist sings, "How amiable are thy tabernacles, O Lord of hosts!" But the appearance of those sacred courts was very different from what we might naturally fancy upon hearing such expressions. Approaching those admirable courts, our attention would have been attracted on all sides with marks of blood. Before the altar, *blood;* on the horns of the altar, *blood;* in the midst of the altar, *blood;* on its top, at its base, on its sides, *blood;* and tracked along into the deepest interior of the tabernacle, *blood!* Such a display would be calculated, some might think, to make us exclaim, "*How sanguinary!*" rather than "*How amiable!*" But he who has learned to look at things interiorly, and to see in that blood the letting forth of the forgiveness and grace of God to lost sinners, will know how to appreciate it. The preaching of Christ crucified is to the Jews a stumbling block, and to the Greeks foolishness; but to those who know what sin is, and what is implied in redemption from it, will ever hail the announcement as the sublimest tidings that ever fell upon the ear of earth. "The natural man perceiveth not the things of the Spirit of God; they are foolishness unto him, neither can he know them, for they are spiritually discerned."

V. The remaining portions of the seventh chapter go back over much the same ground again, presenting sundry directions with reference to the various kinds of offerings. It would seem as if the Lord could not weary in repeating and explaining his will respecting these ancient sacrificial rites. They are typical displays of a work upon which his great heart has been let forth in universal glory. They tell of his love for sinners, and still more of his love and interest in that well-beloved Son whom these figures were meant to set forth, and that it is grateful to him to linger among them, and to dwell upon them. What a shame ought this to be to those professing Christians, who are hoping for immortality and heaven through Christ, and yet weary in one hour, and often show disgust, with the theme of his immolation for their redemption! All heaven is moved at the spectacle of Calvary, and angels bend from their lofty thrones to inquire into it; yet man, for whose good it was displayed, and for whom it was meant to secure eternal life, often turns away from it as insipid, spiritless, and disgusting! What a commentary on earthly taste and wisdom!

VI. In the 8th verse you will find a singular regulation. You will remember that the victim for the burnt-offering was to have its skin taken off. It is here said that this skin was to belong to the priest who officiated at the offering. God says, "the priest shall have to himself the skin of the burnt-offering." Our minds at once revert to those early days of man, when our first parents received from the Lord's hand "*coats of skins*," in place of the poor fig-leaf aprons which their own hands had made. The first animals slain for man were slain in sacrifice; and the skins with which Adam and Eve covered their nakedness, were the skins of the victims slaughtered by them by order of the Lord, as types of the great atonement to be made in the fulness of time. As Adam was the first sinner upon earth, so he was the first priest upon earth, who officiated in the offering of sacrifices for sin. And as a priest, God gave him the skins of the victims to clothe him. And so Christ has covering for every naked soul called to serve at his altars — a good and effective covering, obtained from his own sacrifice. What saith the Savior: "Buy of me white raiment that thou mayest be clothed, and that the shame of thy nakedness do not appear." This is that "wedding garment," and "clothing of broidered work," and "covering of silk," and "raiment of fine linen," which is the portion of all those who serve the Lord as his true priests. The very altar they serve shall furnish them all necessary covering, that they may be clothed with everlasting honor. "Blessed is he that keepeth his garments, lest he walk naked, and they see his shame." (Rev. 16 : 15.)

VII. There is another significant provision in the 15th verse, where the Lord says of the peace-offering, that it must be eaten the same day it is made, otherwise it would vitiate the offering, and no benefit would result from it. "The flesh of the sacrifice of his peace-offerings for thanksgiving *shall be eaten the same day that it is offered;* he shall not leave any of it until morning." The feast of salvation in Jesus Christ has its day. In that day we must eat of it, if ever we are to eat of it availingly. In the general, that day is the day of Gospel tidings. In a more restricted view, it is the day of man's natural life. To most people the door of salvation stands open till their last moments. There is nothing to prevent them from finding Jesus a ready Savior even in the hour of death. But to some, this day is even shorter than life. There are times of visitation and days of grace which some sin away with so stout an arm and so obdurate a heart, that their doom is sealed long before the sun of life sets. If ever, then, we are to come to the joys of redemption, we must come and eat the feast ere the day closes. What may be left for the morning shall be unavailing and full of condemnation. This is the day of our peace-offering, and to-day we must eat it.

> There are no acts of pardon passed,
> In the cold grave to which we haste;
> But darkness, death, and black despair,
> Reign in eternal silence there.

Bestir thee, then, O sinner, and haste to thy sacred altar-feast. Thy sacrifice has been slain, and thy portion is ready. This is thy day, waste it not. "Behold, now is the accepted time! Behold, now is the day of salvation!"

VIII. But there is, in the 20th and 21st verses, an additional requirement, well worthy of our attention. God says, "the soul that eateth of the flesh of the sacrifice of peace-offerings, *having his uncleanness upon him*, even that soul shall be cut off from his people." The Gospel is a *holy feast*. It cannot be shared in by those who continue in their impurities. He that would enjoy it, must be careful to depart from iniquity. Only "*the meek* shall eat and be satisfied;" that is, such as humbly surrender themselves to God's requirements, and are really made up to forsake all known sin. There is a *morality* in religion, as well as faith and ecstasy. Grace does not make void the law. And faith without works is a dead and useless faith. Though we are redeemed by blood, and justified gratuitously by believing in Christ; yet, that redemption obligates us just as much, and still more, to a life of virtue and moral uprightness, than the law itself. "We are not under law," as those are under it for whom Christ's mediation does not avail; but still, we "are under law to Christ," and bound through him to a practical holiness, the pattern of which he has given in his own person and life. If his blood has purged us, it is, that we might "serve the living God." If "we are God's workmanship, created in Christ Jesus," it is "unto good works, which God hath before ordained that we should walk in them." A pure life must needs go along with a good hope. "Faith, if it hath not works, is dead, being alone." "A good tree cannot produce evil fruit." And for a man to believe himself an accepted guest at the Gospel feast while living in wilful, deliberate, and known sin, is a miserable antinomian delusion. The plain Gospel truth, upon this subject, is, that, although we cannot be saved by our works alone, we certainly dare not hope to be saved without them, or without being heartily and effectually made up to do our best. Wherever grace is effective, a well-ordered morality must necessarily follow. And all this idea of justification without repentance — of religion without reformation —of forgiveness without purity—of faith without morality — is a libel upon the economy of God, and a Satanic cheat to ruin immortal souls.

Nor need we be in doubt as to what true Christian purity or holiness is. Many foolish fancies have been indulged on this point, and many well-meaning people have gone far astray. The reason has been, that men listened more to human philosophizing and sickly romance, than to the oracles of God. Some have supposed the highest moral excellence to consist in seclusion from the cares and business of the common world — in retirement to caves and dens of the rocks to spend life in fastings, vigils, prayers, and meditations. There was a time when he who spent his days in the cell of the hermit, had his name written in the calendar, his praises chanted in the churches, and his bones carefully gathered after his death and laid up in golden altars, whither mitred bishops and high officials came kneeling to touch them in solemn devotion. And there still are those who locate the highest sanctity in the celibate, and point for man's sublimest goodness to the cloisters of monks and the prisons of nuns. But this also is delusion. God does not mean that we should be morose and misanthropic eremites, but bold and active confronters of the trials and evils of life—men and women who shall act well our parts in the common relations in which he has created man, and earnest copyists of the example of that Holy One "who went about doing good." Jesus did not flee to the solitudes, and keep aloof from intercourse with men. He remained among his fellows. He visited their habitations; he gave attention to their tears and distresses; he wept with them when they wept; he rejoiced with them when they rejoiced. He came "not to be ministered unto, but to minister." His whole life was one ever-blooming charity. The atmosphere he breathed was love. And the spirit that was in the Master, is that which constitutes the most heavenly goodness in his followers. "*Love thy brother;*" "*Love thy neighbor as thyself;*" "*Do unto others as ye would that others should do unto you;*" these are the comprehensive precepts of Gospel morality. "He that saith he is in light, and hateth his brother, is in darkness even until now." "He that loveth not his brother abideth in death." "Love is of God; and every one that loveth is born of God, and knoweth God." An injury done to a fellow man, is an injury done to one's own soul and immortal hopes; and "to him that knoweth to do good, and doeth it not, to him it is sin." There is no higher moral excellence than a pervading charity. "Love is the fulfilling of the law." There may be gifts of tongues, equal to those of Pentecost; but it is only empty sound and tinkling, without charity. There may be gifts of understanding, forecast, and great knowledge; but it is nothing without charity. There may be faith enough to take up mountains from their seats; but it is useless without charity. There may be self-sacrifice even to beggary and martyrdom; but if the pure spirit of love and beneficence be wanting there, it can profit nothing. Whether there be prophesying, it shall fail; whether there be tongues, they shall cease; whether there be knowledge, it shall vanish away; but charity abideth for ever. It is the grand substance of all virtue. It is the essence of the law of all worlds and all time. It is said of the good old apostle John, the man who had lain the closest on the Savior's heart, that when aged, blind, and feeble, he would still have himself carried to the assemblies of the Church; and when he could say nothing more, he would still tremulously repeat to them these words: *"Little children! love one another."* "LITTLE CHILDREN! LOVE ONE ANOTHER." And without purging out the old uncleanness of malice and wickedness, whatever else we may boast of, we shall be cut off from the Lord's people. "For this ye know," says the apostle, "that no whoremonger, nor unclean person, nor covetous man, who is an idolater, hath any inheritance in the kingdom of Christ and of God." (Eph. v. 5.)

IX. There is another specification, in the 29th and 30th verses, which is suggestive of another very important fact in Christianity. The Lord said, "He that offereth the sacrifice of his peace-offerings unto the Lord, shall bring his oblation: . . *his own hands shall bring the offerings."* The worshipper could not do the work by proxy. He had to come in his own person, and bring his offerings in "his own hands." Indeed, this is a feature running through all these offerings. If any one wished to have the benefit of the holocaust, he had, "of his own voluntary will," to bring the offering to the door of the tabernacle, and there put his own hand upon its head, before it could be "accepted for him to make an atonement for him." If any one desired the advantages of the meat-offering, he had himself to bring the flour or first fruits, and put the oil and frankincense upon it, and give it over into the hands of the priests. If any one wished to enjoy a peace-offering, he was required himself to present the victim, and lay his hand upon its head, and kill it at the door of the tabernacle, and eat the portion which fell to him.

And so in the case of the sin and trespass offerings. The man had to go for himself, and present the sacrifice himself, and lay his hand upon its head, and confess, and eat, all for himself.

There can be no transfer of religious obligations—no substitution in the performance of religious duties. Of all things, piety is one of the most intensely personal. It is the intercourse of the individual soul with its Maker; just as much as if there were no other beings in existence. As each must eat, and die, and be judged for him or herself, so each must repent, and believe, and be religious for him or herself. I do not depreciate the importance of social relations, compacts and organizations. I believe that religion is very greatly dependent upon them. Had we never been placed in a Christian land, or been related to Christian parents and friends, or been brought into contact with the Christian Church, we never could have become Christians. But when it comes to the real activities and experiences of piety, they relate as directly to ourselves as individuals as if we alone existed. Association must place the means of piety around us, and may greatly dispose us to be pious; but the making of that piety our own, is a work which never can be done without our personal concurrence and activity.

It is a great thing to have pious friends. The prayers of a godly mother are like soft silken cords around the heart of her son, which draw upon and check him in his wildest wanderings and his maddest passion. The rude sailor on the deck, or the hardened culprit in his cell, is melted and subdued at the mere remembrance of a sainted mother. The soldier who stands up with steeled nerves upon the field of com bat, unshaken by the fury and thunder of deadly battle, is touched to tears when he comes to muse upon the pressure of his good mother's hand upon his head, as he knelt by her knee and said — "Our Father, who art in heaven!" But, though that mother be as good as the virgin mother of our Lord — though she nightly bathe her pillow with tears of supplication for her boy — though her daily prayers go up for him fervent and pure as those which dropt from the lone Jesus in the Mount of his devotions, — it shall avail nothing to the salvation of her erring child, unless he himself shall move to turn from his follies, to bend in penitence, and to submit himself to God. True religion demands one's personal and individual action — the putting forth of one's own hand. No man or angel can do it for us. Preachers and pious friends may prompt, direct, encourage and pray for us, but that is all. They can do nothing more. No minister, or priest, or bishop, or pope, or saint on earth, or virgin in heaven, not even a mother with all her prayers and undying solicitude, can so unlock the door of heaven to any man as to exempt him from the necessity of going through the work of devotion and godliness for himself. We ourselves must pray, and set out to obey the calls of mercy, and come to the door of the sanctuary meekly trusting in the Savior's mediation, or all the sermons, masses, supplications, and godly associations in the world cannot save us. We must individually and for ourselves believe on the Lord Jesus Christ, or be lost. There is no other alternative.

A very expressive gesture was required of the Jew to signify all this. He had to put his hand upon the head of his sacrifice when he presented it. **He thereby** acknowledged his sin, and expressed his personal dependence upon that sacrifice. The Hebrew word is still more suggestive. "He shall *lean* his hand upon the head of the offering." It is the same word used by the Psalmist, where he says, "Thy wrath *leaneth* hard upon me." Sin is a burden. It is ready to crush him upon whom it is. And with this burden the sinner is to *lean upon* his sacrifice for ease. He could not lean with another man's hand; he must use "his own hand." The ceremonial worshipper used the outward hand; we are to use the hand of the soul, which is *faith*. Much is said about faith; but when we come to extricate it from the entanglements of metaphysical discussion, it is the simplest of all our mental operations. You have important business which will involve you without prompt and careful attention. Sickness overtakes you, and unfits you to do what is required. A friend engages to take your place, and to attend to it in your name. You scan his competency and integrity, and are willing to trust him. You agree that he shall act and check, receipt, accept, and sign in your place, the same as if it were yourself. He attends to the business. He returns to you with tidings that everything is safe and turned to your great advantage. You are convinced that he is a truthful man, and does not mean to deceive you. You take his report as reality. And with a heart overflowing with gratitude, you rest from your anxieties on that subject. And what is it that you have done? You have simply *believed*, and done with reference to your earthly friend and business what is required in the securement of your eternal good. We are all spiritually sick. Great interests are in jeopardy by reason of our disability

Jesus is the friend who agrees to take our place, and to manage all for our benefit. What, then, is faith? It is the persuasion that Christ is competent to do what he proposes. It is our hearty consent that he shall act for us in the case. It is our confidence in his fidelity to the interests which we have placed in his hands. It is our belief of the report he brings us that all is safe and well if we only abide by what he has done. This is faith. It is this that identifies a man with Christ, and makes him an heir of salvation. But it is a personal act—the most intensely personal. No other being could perform that act for us. We must perform it ourselves, or we never can be saved.

X. Thus far, we have been contemplating man as an individual. We have been looking only at the isolated offerer, and his individual relations to his offering. But, as there are numerous individuals continually passing through the same experiences, there is also a social aspect presented as they come thus to be related to each other. Nor was this wholly overlooked in these typical arrangements. The trespass-offering, which is the last in the list or series, contemplates the worshipper for the most part as a social being — as one of a common brotherhood of men of equal rights with himself. It provides for sins growing out of social relations—for breaches of the law of charity, injuries done to a neighbor, faithlessness in partnerships and trusts, &c. It thus brings up the idea of *community*. This comes in very beautifully at the conclusion of the law of offerings. It is like the adding up of a column of figures, which gives us the ultimate product of the various items, and preserves the logical connection of these types unbroken. So many individual sinners, personally applying and appropriating the great remedy for sin, and undergoing all the hallowing experiences adumbrated in what we have thus far had under review, necessarily form a congregation of justified, sanctified, and holy people. And thus, step after step, through the blood of offering after offering, we have finally reached a point, at which the whole doctrine of *the Church*, its nature and composition, bursts full-orbed upon our view.

There is much inquiry and discussion now-a-days about the Church. People are wading through tomes of patristic writings, and studying creeds, and dragging through the dark places of history, to find out what, and which, and where, is the Church. Did they consult their Bibles more, and the Fathers and their own imaginations less, they would come to a truer, if not speedier, conclusion. *The Church is simply the congregation of the justified and clean.* Bishops do not make the Church; liturgies do not make the Church; particular holy days or ceremonies do not make the Church; but God makes the Church, by absolving men through faith in his Son Jesus Christ, and joining them into a common union by a common trust and obedience in a common Savior.

Some have very singular ways of inquiring whether they are members of the true Church. The moment they think of the question, they begin to revolve in their minds what denomination they belong to, how its ministry is constituted, what sort of a history it has, and what specific modes of service they have submitted to. But all this does not touch or even approach the vital point. The inquiry is not whether we are Lutherans, Episcopalians, Catholics, or Baptists, or which of these can make out the best denominational claim. The point is, Have we presented our holocaust, by coming to Christ and leaning upon him by a confiding trust as the propitiation for our sins? Have we presented our meat-offering in the grateful surrender of ourselves a living sacrifice unto God, to meet, and obey, and abide by his will? Have we presented our peace-offering, by making Jesus and his salvation the great feast and rejoicing of our souls? Have we made our sin and trespass offerings, by resting upon him and his perpetual intercessions as our only availing righteousness and support amid the infirmities of life? If so, we belong to the congregation of the justified, and have come to the general assembly and Church of the first-born, whose names are written in heaven; and if not so, we are yet "aliens from the commonwealth of Israel, and strangers to the covenants of promise, having no hope, and without God in the world," be our denominational relations what they may. Simon the sorcerer belonged to the Apostolic Church, and received baptism from apostolic hands, yet had he "neither part nor lot in this matter." The reason is given: his heart was "not right in the sight of God." It is not forms and sacraments then, but real heart-union with Christ our Savior, by which men come into the true brotherhood of saints, and have membership in the true Church. Outward acknowledgment, of course, goes along. The Jew could not bring and offer his sacrifices in secret; no more can a real Christian escape the confession of Christ before men. "No man lighteth a candle and putteth it under a bushel, but on a candlestick;" but it is not the putting of it on the candlestick that lights it, or that makes it a candle. It is personal contact with

Jesus, and the moulding of our whole nature to his own, that puts us into the holy fellowship of those who are "the light of the world."

What a beautiful thing, then, is the real Church! There all are brothers by a sacred interior birth to holiness and good. There all are one, though seas roll and mountains rise between them — linked together by invisible but indissoluble bonds. In all that great congregation, there is not one but reflects the image of Jesus, and holds citizenship in heaven. Blessed assembly! "How goodly are thy tents, O Jacob, and thy tabernacles, O Israel! As the valleys are they spread forth, as gardens by the river's side, as the trees of lign-aloes which the Lord hath planted, and as cedars beside the waters!"

SEVENTH LECTURE

AARON AND HIS CONSECRATION.

LEV. CHAP. VIII.

In entering upon this chapter, we pass from the consideration of sacred *things*, to sacred *persons* — from offerings, to the priests who were to officiate at their presentation. All religions are founded upon some sort of priesthood. All people, of whom we have any record, have had their priests. To say nothing of Adam, Abel, and Noah, we read in the days of Abraham of "Melchisedek, priest of the Most High God;" and a few generations after him, of one Potipherah, priest of On, whose daughter Pharoah thought a fit match for his chief favorite, Joseph, whom he had made ruler of all his house. After these, we read of Jethro, priest of Midian, who became the father-in-law of the illustrious Moses Then came the long line of Aaron's order, as insti tuted in the chapter before us. Nor need I speak of the Hierophantæ of Egypt, the Magi of Persia, the Sacerdotes of Greece and Rome, the Druids of Gaul, the Caliphs, and Mufties, and various religious orders of other nations, to show how universally this system of priesthood, or attorneyship in sacred things, has pervaded all ages. Indeed, it is essential to religion. It enters into the very substance of inter- communication between God and fallen man. Of this no one can doubt who understands God, or our moral and religious relations to him.

Man is not now what he was originally made. His whole nature has come under a disastrous eclipse, a gangrenous disturbance, a deep disorder. He has turned aside from his Maker. He has strayed as a sheep into dangerous wilds. He has become greatly alienated from goodness. He has been betrayed into wicked rebellion against his rightful Sovereign. He has become guilty, corrupt, ignorant, faint, and afraid. He is not in a condition to be acceptable to God; he has lost his affection for God; he has sunk away from a right knowledge of God; he knows not how to get back into communion with God; and what spiritual consciousness still adheres to him, serves only to make him dread and fly the further from God. This picture is not too highly colored. It exhibits the real estate of man apart from priestly mediations. And on the other hand, God cannot desert his own law, or be untrue to his holiness, justice, and word, by conniving at sin, or looking complacently upon rebellion. A righteous sovereign may feel for and pity his convicts, but he dare have no fellowship with them without compromising his own character for righteousness. Here, then, is a chasm between man and his God. The fallen one goes on sinning, and the wronged Sovereign must go on maintaining his righteous administrations. Man cannot of himself come to God, and is only terrified when he thinks of his presence; and God cannot sacrifice his sovereignty or tarnish his throne by advancing with favors to those who continue to trample everything sacred under their feet. The whole bent and drift of man's native affections are against God, and the whole divine nature and commitments are against all thus opposed to what is good. It is not in man to turn or change himself; and God cannot reverse his own immutability, or retire from his eternal constitution of right and holiness. Some have thought that the combined influence of nature, conscience, and reason, is competent in the end to bring man to the knowledge of the truth, and to restore him to right affections for his Maker. But no instances of this have ever occurred. Amid all the varieties of circumstances in which man has lived for six thousand years, no case has ever come to light of such a transformation by the forces of nature alone. And God, in his word, declares that no such case ever has occurred, or ever can occur. "*They that are in the flesh cannot please God.*" Jesus says, "*No man cometh unto the Father, but by me.*" The mere powers and workings of nature, then, can recover no man from sin. Nay, even when men had a right knowledge of God, these natural forces were not competent so much as to keep that knowledge alive in them. For "when they knew God, professing themselves to be wise, they became fools, and changed the glory of the uncorruptible God into an image made like to corruptible man, and to birds, and four-footed beasts, and creeping things; changed the truth of God into a lie, and worshipped and served the creature more than the Creator." This is Scripture, and it is history. Nor is it difficult to trace the philosophy of it. It requires only a little attention and analysis of our commonest and most inward impressions and experiences under the workings of nature.

"No man hath seen God at any time;" and the

power which is unseen is terrible. Fancy trembles before its own picture, and superstition clothes it with dark imagery. The voice of the thunder is awful; but not so awful as the conception of that angry Being who sits in mysterious concealment, and gives it all its energy. In such sketches of the imagination, fear is sure to predominate. We gather an impression of nature's God, from those scenes in which nature threatens and looks most dreadful. With all the parade of scholastic demonstrations, the theology of every man's actual *feelings* is as here represented. God is most present to our imaginations when nature is most terrific—when winter with its mighty elements sweeps the forest of its leaves, and the rushing of the storm is heard upon our windows, and man flees to cover himself from the desolation that walketh over the face of the earth. From the dreadfulness of nature's elements, we feel how dreadful must be that mysterious and unseen Being who sits behind the elements he has formed, and gives birth and movement to all things. Our souls are awed and frightened at the mystery in which he is shrouded. Terror and wrath become the mantle in which our fancies robe him. And the outcry of conscience is, "*Let not God speak with us, lest we die!*" Instead of being drawn to him we are repulsed. Like Adam, we are impelled to seek for some place to hide from his presence. And so the natural and inevitable results of these awakenings and promptings of nature are, to induce us to worship God only in symbols and representations which soon must assume our own corrupt attributes, or else to drive us to expel all thought of him from our minds, and resign to a dark and grovelling atheism. Hence nature cannot bring us into peaceful relations to the true God. (*See Chalmers on Job*, 9 : 33.)

How, then, may God and man be brought harmoniously together? How shall man have the veil of terrific and repellant mystery lifted off of Deity, that he may have hope in returning to his Maker; and how shall God show himself in any other form to rebels and traitors? There is but one way. There must be a Days-man—a spiritual attorney—between the two, who can lay his hands upon both. There must be some competent one to mediate from God to sinners, and from sinners to God. There must be some great officer (of the character shadowed forth in the various orders of priesthood), who shall, in his peculiar qualifications and office, bring God down to the right apprehension of men, and bring men up in some acceptable form to God. The idea of priesthood, then, and the exercise of priestly functions, enter into the very heart and substance of religion. Paul, in his masterly appeal to the Hebrews, takes it as one of those deep essential principles upon which his whole argument is built. It is presupposed in the whole framework of the Christian system. It is the root trunk, and sap of the tree of Life—the very spine, marrow and soul of the Gospel.

Previous to the institution of this Levitical ritual, the offering of gifts and sacrifices for sins, and the priestly functions in general, were much like prayer —the right and duty of all, without much distinction. They were not specifically entrusted and confined to any one order or class of men. Cain and Abel, even in the lifetime of their father, seem to have officiated for themselves. So far as one performed sacerdotal duty for another, perhaps more from the natural proprieties of the case than from any divine regulation, the work usually devolved upon the father of the family, or the prince of the tribe. Noah and Job officiated for their respective families, and Melchisedek was a king as well as a priest; and may have been a priest, in part at least, because he was a king. But, unless Melchisedek, of whom we know but little, is to be regarded as an exception, there were no divinely constituted priesthoods—no established sacerdotal orders, previous to the appointment and consecration of Aaron and his sons. And the fact that this office was at first free to all, and then gradually narrowed down, first to the father or chief, then to the tribe of Levi and the house of Aaron, and then to the great High Priest whom all former priesthoods foreshadowed, may have been designed to show, that the longer the race went on, the more unworthy and unfit man became to approach God. The moral history of mankind, from beginning to end, presents the appearance of an inverted arch, bending downward from Adam to Christ, and then gradually upward again to the time when holiness shall once more be the inheritance of earth. Adam began the work of degrading his species. In Eden, the balance between good and evil began to dip the wrong way. Sin became more facile and deep-colored with every generation; till the scale came heavily down. Depravity was at its depths, and all the hopes of the world settled upon Jesus.

There is no authentic priesthood now, but that which has its centre in the "great High Priest that is passed into the heavens, Jesus, the Son of God." He alone of all earth's generations—he alone of all the heavenly principalities—is THE ONE selected, ordained, invested and set forth to mediate between God and man, to effect at-one-ment between the righteous Sovereign and the guilty rebel. More holy than an angel, more Divine than a seraph, more deeply pervaded with Godhead than anything that ever took form, and yet more tenderly human than any mere man, the world has looked for him, the ages have prophesied of him, and in the fulness of time God sent him, to fill the breach between earth and heaven, to bring the unknown God to man's understanding and affection, and to bring man up to God's acceptance and approval. For this he was conceived by the Holy Ghost, born of the Virgin Mary, put to death under Pontius Pilate, raised from the dead by Almighty power, received up to heaven amid the devout acclaim of angels, and now appears in the presence of God for us to the wonderment of celestial orders, and to the everlasting redemption of those who believe. And from the nature of things there is no real priesthood but his, and no true priest but himself. Whatever other priesthoods God may have appointed, or approved, or even tolerated, resolve themselves into this one, and have been or are only prophecies, types, pictures, foreshadowings, or subordinate distributions from this sublime and only original.

Entering, then, upon a survey of the Levitical priesthood, we must take with us the thought, that we are about to look upon what was meant to set forth a higher priesthood than that of Aaron. It is not so much with the Levites that we have to do, as with Christ, of whom these Levites were the living hieroglyphics. In the earthly we are to see the heavenly. From the typical we are to rise to the contemplation of the real. Aaron and his sons constitute the subject, and yet, Jesus and his people are the theme.

The chapter before us gives a description of the ceremonies by which the priests were consecrated, and formally inducted into their high office. These ceremonies were, for the most part, the same for Aaron and his sons; but it is the case of the high-priest more particularly that I propose to present now. The case of the common priests is reserved for another occasion.

I. Fixing attention, then, upon Aaron, as about to be set apart for the high-priest-hood, the first thing I notice is the publicity with which the consecration was performed. The whole congregation of Israel had to be gathered together to witness the solemn transaction. The creation of so high an officer for the whole people, required to be done in open daylight, and in the view of all concerned. And the scene presented an imposing spectacle. In the background stood Mount Sinai in solemn silence, terrible yet in the imaginations of the people, for the fires that had so lately enveloped it, and the holy law that came thundering down its gorges. In long bending lines through the valley at its base, stood the white tents of Israel. In the centre hung the cloudy pillar, stretching high into the heavens, its shadow resting upon the holy tabernacle. The princes of Jacob were there arranged about the door of the sanctuary in devout expectancy. In view of them all came Aaron and his sons, and Moses, the man of God, thoughtful and solemn, and half-trembling in their steps. The very breezes seemed to hush their soft whispers, and the sun himself to stand still in the sky. A breathlessness was upon all the witnessing hosts; for the priests of the Lord were entering into their great office!

But, through this scene in the Hebrew camp, I ascend at once to the contemplation of a more glorious spectacle. There rises up before me, in awful grandeur, the mount of Almighty Holiness. Around it, in seried orders, lie the princedoms and principalities of heaven. Myriads of holy ones, who looked on when the world was made, stand in compact throngs to watch in solemn silence the development of that new thought which has been thrown into their celestial contemplations. The four-and-twenty elders, with their crowns of gold glittering in the sublime effulgence of the great white throne, wait in impressive seriousness; when out upon the glassy sea, spanned by emerald bows, and radiant in jewelry of Godhead, steps the blessed Son, saying, "LO! I COME TO DO THY WILL, O GOD!" "I WILL REDEEM THEM FROM DEATH: I WILL RANSOM THEM FROM THE POWER OF THE GRAVE!" and the Father from his everlasting seat lifts up his hand in solemn oath and says, "THOU ART A PRIEST FOREVER AFTER THE ORDER OF MELCHISEDEK!" What saith the Scripture? "Christ glorified not himself to be made an high priest;"—he did not ambitiously or clandestinely obtrude himself into this momentous office—"but was called of God, *as was Aaron;*" and all the congregation of heaven were witnesses to his rightful investiture and consecration.

II. The first thing to be done after the appearance of Aaron before the congregation as the designated priest, was to wash him with water. There has always been more or less washing connected with priesthood. The Egyptian priests washed twice **a** day in wate. ; the Greeks had their sprinklings; the Romans also had numerous lustrations; and the Church of Rome still retains a shadow of the old rites in the use made of what is called "holy water." All this I take to be the distorted remains of what God himself appointed at the institution of his ancient ritual, and the consecration of his ancient priesthood. They are the traditional relics of what had a glorious significance once, but having neither dignity nor meaning in any of their modern associations. The water applied to Aaron was a token of cleansing and purity, without which no man can approach the holy and sin-hating God. It was meant to impress the idea of cleanness in **him who was to act as an attorney** between man **and his Maker.** And Aaron in his outward purification shows us our great High-priest in the sublime purity which he brought to his mediation-work. Jesus "was holy, harmless, undefiled, separate from sinners." It was partly in token of this pureness and separation that John, as another Moses, baptized him in Jordan vale. He needed no cleansing. He always was pure. But, to indicate this purity, and to enter upon his priesthood in the regular way, he consented to be washed, as was Aaron. His baptism was part of his priestly installation. It is one of the items of proof that he meant to be and is a priest. And it was done in the presence of thousands of Israel.

III. The next thing done for Aaron's consecration was, the putting of the sacred vestments upon him. The priest was to be endowed with grace and glory as well as purity. He had to be clothed in righteousness and girt for active obedience He needed covering for those shoulders, which were to bear the people's guilt, and for that brow, which was to be lifted up in confession. A rich, curious, graceful, and imposing suit was therefore provided for him — a suit which received its pattern from God, and was made according to specific divine directions.

The first article was "the coat," elsewhere called "the ephod;" a sort of frock, thrown over the shoulders, and extending down to the ankles, made of pure fine linen. This was the innermost part of the priest's vestments, It had sleeves to the wrists It was the symbol of grace and righteousness in the hidden as well as visible man.

The next article was "the girdle," a narrow, long band or belt of linen, tied around the waist to confine the ephod close to the body. The priest was not only for show, but for service, and all his graces and endowments of righteousness were to be held subservient to his office. He had to be girded up for work.

A third article was "the robe," or "robe of the ephod," a seamless garment, curiously embroidered with blue, purple, scarlet, and gold. Its lower border was ornamented with a row of red pomegranates and little golden bells, encircling the entire robe in alternate succession. It was a garment which extended from the shoulders to a little below the knees. This was a robe altogether peculiar to the High-priest. Its tinge was heavenly. It had about it the greatest intensity of ornament. And it bespoke an exaltation and glory beyond anything worn by common priests.

Next came "the embroidered coat" of fine linen,

with sleeves, and extending about half the way down the skirt of "the robe of the ephod."

Over this coat, and wound several times around the waist, was "the curious girdle;" a piece of fine twined linen, embroidered with blue, purple, scarlet and gold, tied in front of the body, with the ends left hanging nearly to the feet.

Then came "the breastplate," with "the Urim and Thummim." This was a fabric about nine inches square, set with twelve different jewels, large and well arranged. Its two upper corners had gold rings, by which it was connected with jewelled shoulder pieces, with wreathed chains of gold. At its lower corners it was fastened to the girdle with blue ribbons. The twelve jewels stood for the twelve tribes of Israel, and each jewel had upon it the name of its tribe. They were the most precious things belonging to the priest's attire. They were called "Urim and Thummim;" that is, Lights and Perfections. Some say that the law was written upon them, and that it was to the law as seated in these pure and precious gems, flashing with light and glory, that the Psalmist alluded when he said, "the law of the Lord is *perfect*"—"the commandment of the Lord is *pure, enlightening the eyes.*" This breastplate was at any rate an exceedingly sacred thing, glorious in appearance and full of stirring suggestion. A thrill of deepening interest must have run through the congregation of Israel as they beheld this jewelled heart-piece put upon their priest.

The seventh item was the putting of "the mitre upon his head." This was a kind of turban, made of fine linen, somewhat resembling the diadems of ancient kings It was a fit and imposing crown to the other parts of the priest's dress, and doubtless brought a shout of admiration from Israel when they saw it adorning the brow of Aaron, fronted as it was with a plate of shining gold, in whose glittering sheen appeared the solemn inscription — "HOLINESS TO THE LORD."

Thus did God direct for the clothing of his ancient priest "for glory and for beauty." No man can approach God uncovered. The very seraphim cover their faces and their feet before his terrible majesty. And as Aaron was to serve before the Lord in the priest's office, this was to be his glorious covering when on duty. A noble object he was to look upon as he stood that day before the congregation of Israel. Fold upon fold of pure linen enveloped his person. His breast, and his shoulders, and his brows, and even the girdle and hem of his robe, blazed with costly jewelry and gems. All native deformities were hidden in glory and beauty.

But, from the picture we lift our thoughts to the original. Aaron in his robes and jewels is but an earthly type of our great High-Priest arrayed in the sublime glories of his everlasting righteousness. True, Isaiah says, "he hath no form nor comeliness; and when we shall see him, there is no beauty that we should desire him." But it is his appearance to this world's carnal and perverted taste of which the prophet there speaks, and not his appearance to minds and hearts capacitated to appreciate him. This same prophet elsewhere tells of a vision which he himself had of this blessed one. "In the year that king Uzziah died," says he, "*I saw the Lord.*" There was no absence of dignity and glory in that vision. "A throne, high and lifted up" was there, and upon it sat our royal High-Priest, the mere train or skirt of whose glorious robe was like "the fulness of the whole earth." Around him stood the seraphim in rapt admiration, crying one to another, "HOLY, HOLY, HOLY, IS THE LORD OF HOSTS: THE WHOLE EARTH IS FULL OF HIS GLORY!" until the very door-posts moved at the power of their words. It was more than the prophet could endure to look upon. He fell down upon his face and cried, "*Wo is me! for I am undone: for mine eyes have seen the King, the Lord of hosts!*" At another time this same prophet, contemplating the magnificence of Jesus and his achievements, breaks out with the exclamation: "Who is this that cometh from Edom, *with dyed garments from Bozrah,* GLORIOUS IN HIS APPAREL, *and triumphing in the greatness of his strength?*" A glorious High-Priest is Jesus. Fold upon fold of glory and beauty encompass him. With round upon round of heavenly excellency and celestial praise is he girded. Purity, and holiness, and power, and grace, and majesty, and ten thousand indescribable attractions, cluster upon him, and surround him with flames of perfection and light, which only the most costly jewelry can typify, which angels bend to contemplate, and which archangels cannot find words competent to express. Even the Eternal Father looks on him with delight, and says, "*This is my beloved Son, in whom I am well pleased!*" Fit is he to draw near to God, and worthy of our holy adoration—"chief among ten thousand, and the one altogether lovely"—"holy, harmless, undefiled, separate from sinners, *and made higher than the heavens;* who needeth not like those high-priests to offer up sacrifices for his own sins: for the law maketh men high-priests which have infirmity; but the word of the oath which was since the law, maketh the Son [an High-priest], who is *perfected for evermore.*" (Heb. 7 : 26–28.)

> O! could I speak the matchless worth,
> O! could I sound the glories forth,
> Which in my Savior shine!
> I'd soar and touch the heavenly strings,
> And vie with Gabriel while he sings,
> In notes almost divine.

IV. The next thing in this impressive service was the holy chrism, or the anointing with oil. This was not common oil, but the sacred, fragrant, and costly compound used only in solemn consecrations. It was "precious ointment on the head, that ran down upon the beard, even Aaron's beard, and went down to the skirts of his garments," enveloping him in aroma as grateful to the smell as his garments were to the eye. It was the symbol of divine gifts and unction. It pointed to that solemn chrism or *christing* of Jesus, by the pouring out upon him of the Holy Spirit and energy of God "without measure." Our great Highpriest was not only *washed* in Jordan, but he was also immediately after solemnly *anointed* by the visible descent of the Spirit upon him. It was that, that constituted him THE CHRIST; that is, *the anointed one.* It was by that unction that he was endowed from on high with the rights and powers, with the gifts and graces, of his blessed priesthood. From that time forward he was installed forever in the sublime office of mediatorship between God and man. From that time forever, the command of the Father to all the children of men is, "HEAR YE HIM." And if the anointing of Aaron was a thing to be sung about by inspired minstrels, what shall be said of the christing of Jesus and those adorable official powers with which it invested him! We have read of his wonderful gifts of teaching — how the people were astonished at his doctrine—how skepticism stood confounded at his words—how all Judea was moved by his presence—how light, and grace, and blessing gilded and perfumed everything along the paths which he passed—how even the children in the streets lifted up their voices and shouted "Hosanna!" as he rode by—how the poor, and sick, and lame, and blind, and deaf, and palsied, and possessed, came crying to him and were relieved and healed — how he wrestled with Satan in the wilderness, and overcame him, and spoiled his dark kingdom—how he invaded even the territories of death, and brought back the departed to their afflicted friends — how he burst the rocky doors of the sepulchre and ascended up in triumphant power, whilst leaving to his church ample gifts of miracle and grace to overcome all earth's mighty superstitions, and to tread in the same victorious path with himself to glory, honor, immortality, and eternal life. We have learned something of the wondrous might by which he draws men unto himself, and slays the enmity of their hearts, and moulds them to a spiritual life, and connects them once more with a heavenly commonwealth, and reinstates them in the favor of God, and makes his life and teachings live in them, and endows them with joint-heirship with himself to an inheritance which is incorruptible, undefiled, and fadeth not away. We have read how the Father hath committed all judgment to him, that men should honor the Son even as they honor the Father, and how he is gone to prepare a place for us and will come again to take us to himself, that we may live and reign with him in that New Jerusalem whose streets are gold, whose gates are pearls, whose foundations are jewels, whose watchmen are angels, and which blazes forever with the glory of God and of the Lamb. Yet, the consecration, anointing, investiture, and official endowment for all this was performed and given when the Holy Ghost came down upon him on Jordan's banks, filling him with his amazing official fulness as *the Christ*, the Redeemer of the world.

> Great was the day, the joy was great,
> When the Divine disciples met;
> While on their heads the Spirit came,
> And sat like tongues of cloven flame.
> What gifts, what miracles he gave!
> What power to give and power to save!
> Furnished their tongues with wondrous words
> Instead of shields and spears and swords.

What glory, then, is to be attached to the blessed christing of Jesus, of which these gifts and powers to his disciples were only the remote and secondary effects! Blessed, blessed unction of our great High-Priest!

V. But still, Christ was not yet "made perfect." Moses had yet to mark and sprinkle Aaron with the blood of sacrifice; and, as the Captain of our salvation, Christ had to be "made perfect through sufferings." He needed to have upon him the marks of blood. And as he was both the sacrifice and the priest, he had to give himself to death before he could enter the holy place as our availing intercessor. We read that "Moses took of the blood, and put it upon the tip of Aaron's right ear, and upon the thumb of his right hand, and upon the great toe of his right foot. And he took of the anointing oil, and of the blood upon the altar, and sprinkled it upon Aaron and upon his garments." It was the picture of "the blood of Christ, who through the Eternal Spirit offered himself without spot to God," marking our great High-priest with the final touches of his installation as the Savior of the world. Thus "being made perfect, he became the author of eternal salvation unto all them that obey him."

"Holy brethren, partakers of the heavenly calling, consider the Apostle and High-priest of our profession, Christ Jesus." Survey him as these ancient pictures place him before us. From the heights of eternity he looked down upon the breach which sin had made between man and God. He saw our frailty and helplessness, and pitied us in our misery and ruin. And when there was no daysman, he stepped forward in the presence of the congregation of heaven, and said, "*Here am I, send me.*" The Almighty Sovereign answered, "*It is done; go thou and be a priest for ever. A body have I prepared thee!*" In the fulness of time he came. John, like another Moses, was commissioned to wash him for his consecration. By an unspotted life and an ineffable oneness with Godhead, he was adorned and beautified with the sublimest excellence and glory. On the banks of the holy river, the christing unction descended in unmeasured profusion upon him. In the hall of judgment, the thorny crown was pressed upon his head, and marked his ears with blood. On Calvary the nails were driven, and brought out the crimson drops upon his hands and feet. On the cross the victim of the consecration was pierced, flayed, disjointed, all its tender parts given to the fires, and all its substance turned to dust in the place of ashes. In the tomb of Joseph, the Spirit, mingling with the blood from the altar, brought about the final baptism which completed the solemn round of his official investiture. And lo! he stands before men and angels *a perfect High-priest,* "able to save unto the uttermost all them that come unto God by him."

Trembling soul, behold thy Redeemer! This is He, of whom Moses in the law, and the prophets, did write. This is He, of whom it was said from the beginning, *"He shall come."* This is that *"Branch of the Lord, beautiful and glorious,* whose name is, THE LORD OUR RIGHTEOUSNESS." This is He, of whom the rejoicing angels said, "Unto you is born this day, in the city of David, a Savior, which is, *Christ the Lord."* Yea, this is He, of whom the expecting Church for ages sang, "He shall come down like rain upon the mown grass: as showers that water the earth; in his day shall the righteous flourish; and his name shall endure for ever." And let all the congregation fall down at his feet and cry, "Blessed be the Lord God, the God of Israel, who only doeth wondrous things; blessed be his glorious name for ever: and let the whole earth be filled with his glory; Amen, and Amen!"

EIGHTH LECTURE.

THE CONSECRATION OF AARON'S SONS.

LEV. CHAP. VIII

In our comment thus far upon this chapter, we have occupied ourselves mostly with the High-priest — with Aaron, and the Lord Jesus Christ as represented in Aaron. And the High-priesthood, indeed, includes the whole priesthood, and everything that appertains to the work and office of mediation. But it had some inferior and subordinate honors and services, which were distributed among a number of associated, lower priests. Aaron was not alone; his sons were consecrated with him; not to the same high office, not in all things in the same way, but to a lower grade of priesthood, in connection with, and depending upon, the one only High-priest. *There were two orders.* There was the High-priesthood of Aaron, and there was the lower, associated priesthood of Aaron's sons. We have considered Aaron's induction into the one; and it now remains for us to consider the induction of his sons into the other. This, then, is what I propose for the present occasion. (See Verses 6, 13 to 16, 22 to 25, and 30 to 36.)

You will notice in these consecration services, that in many things Aaron and his sons are dealt with alike — made partakers alike of the same rites Apart from his peculiar investments, Aaron occupied a position in common with the inferior priests. This

CONSECRATION OF AARON'S SONS. 137

was not accidental. It pointed to a great fact in the history of our great High-priest that has passed into the heavens. In many things he was a man, the same as other good men. Whatever there was superhuman and divine in him, he lacked nothing that was human. He is "the Son of Man"—the child of Mary. "Both he that sanctifieth, and they who are sanctified, are all of one: for which cause he is not ashamed to call them brethren. As the children are partakers of flesh and blood, he also himself likewise took part of the same. In all things it behooved him to be made like unto his brethren." And it is an affecting thought, that in many particulars, and in all the common constituents and conditions of human life, we occupy a place just as high, and exactly the same as our blessed Savior. If we feel the pressure of this world's woes, so did he. If we are tried with sore temptations, he was "in all points tempted like as we are." If we have the duties of piety to go through with, it is no more than our glorious Redeemer had in common with ourselves. Though he is "the only begotten of the Father, full of grace and truth," "yet learned he obedience by the things which he suffered." Aaron, in a great part, was consecrated by the selfsame services with his sons.

It is also proper to remark here, that these ancient priesthoods had nothing in common with the pretended priesthoods of modern times. The Levitical priesthood embraced *two orders*—no more, and no less—the High-priesthood of Aaron, and the common priesthood of Aaron's sons. The first could never have more than one occupant at a time, who, in that position, represented the Lord Jesus Christ,

The inferior priests, according to divine arrangement, were all of equal dignity, and represented all the people of Christ — his sons by regeneration through his Spirit. Christ having come, and entered himself upon the High-priesthood, there can now be no High-priest but himself; for there could not be more than one High-priest at the same time. And as all the people of Christ are alike priests of God and of Christ, we have the two orders complete, and there is no other priesthood but these two, and even these two are one.

We know certainly that Christ is a priest; that he is a priest now; and that he always will be a priest; for he is "a priest *for ever*, after the order of Melchisedek." In him, then, we have *the High-priesthood*.

And it is equally certain, that all Christ's people, without distinction of laity or clergy, male or female, are also priests; that they are priests now; and that they will ever continue to be priests hereafter. Of old already did God say to all who should obey him — "Ye shall be unto me a kingdom of priests." Isaiah, by the inspiration of God, repeated the announcement — "Ye shall be named the priests of the Lord." Peter, by the same Spirit, says to all the scattered household of faith, "*Ye are a royal priesthood.*" Paul says, "We have an altar." John, in the name of all the saints, ascribes glory and dominion to him that loved us, and washed us from our sins in his own blood, for having "made us kings and priests unto God." And of all who have part in the first resurrection, it is written, "They shall be priests of God and of Christ." All Christians, then, are priests. This is the dignity which God himself has conferred upon them. Here, then, are *the common priests*. We thus identify the present occupants of both orders. The High-priesthood is filled by Christ; the common priesthood is filled alike by all the people or children of Christ. This is the entire priesthood, so far as God has constituted it. Any other priesthood is therefore foreign to the divine constitution, and an innovation upon it. God has not appointed any other, or sanctioned any other, in his word. Whatever claim may be set up for another priesthood, it is a mere device of man, an earthly fabrication, without warrant or authority. If it is really a priesthood, it is antichristian, and an invasion of the rights and honors of Christ or his people; and if it is not really a priesthood, it is wrong to call it so. Aaron and his sons, that is Jesus with his children, as such, are the only divinely appointed priests; and to hold to any other priests, is to pronounce against the institutions of God, and a sin against holy order. Our High-priest is Christ, and all we are common priests alike.

It is further to be noticed, that *common priests were the sons of the High Priest*. Their attainment of this high honor depended upon, and was the result of their filial connection with Aaron. They became common priests, because their father was the High-priest. In other words, their priesthood grew out of the High-priesthood of Aaron, and was based upon it. This fact was also the shadow of a great Gospel truth. We can only become priests, by connection with Jesus the High-priest. Our priesthood proceeds out of his, and can only become ours by virtue of a filial relation on our part to him. If Aaron is not our father, we cannot be God's priests,

We must be "born again"—"born of the Spirit"— born children of the ever-blessed Lord,— or these high honors do not belong to us. Christ must first become our life; we must become members of him, of his flesh and bones and blood; we must be grafted upon him, and united to him, as the branch is united to the vine, as the child to the father, as the wife to her husband; we must become one with him in the bonds of a spiritual sonship; or we are in no way partakers of his glory. There was no priesthood for Nadab, Abihu, Eleazar, or Ithamar, but by virtue of their being Aaron's sons.

And this thought refers us back again to those spiritual experiences and acts to which our attention was directed by the law of offerings. It is by means of those acts and experiences, that a man comes into saving relationship with Jesus, and is made spiritually his son. So here now we have the results of that sonship, a blessed priesthood. I cannot but more and more admire the deep moral, spiritual, logical, and connected history of the sinner in the process of his redemption, that is presented in the order and construction of this Levitical ritual. First we see him helpless, casting about for something wherewithal to come before the Lord, and at length finding a sufficient sacrifice in Jesus the Lamb, upon whose head he leans with his burden, and is released. Next he is presented as offering himself in grateful return a living sacrifice to Him who hath redeemed him with the price of blood. Then we behold him feasting upon the fat things of hope and joy that come to him through his offerings. After that we see him struggling with remaining weaknesses of nature, but still clinging closely to his great Advocate in heaven.

And by virtue of all this, we here come to view him as designed for, and actually being inducted into, the high honors of a glorious and eternal priesthood. It is this sacred inauguration that we are now to consider.

We will first look at some of its surroundings, and then at the particulars of which the transaction was composed.

1. These sons of Aaron, as well as Aaron himself, had been previously and divinely called to be priests. They had not been elected by men, but designated of God. The voice of the Almighty had said to Moses, "Take thou unto thee Aaron thy brother, and his sons with him, from among the children of Israel, that he may minister unto me in the priest's office, even Aaron, Nadab, and Abihu, Eleazar and Ithamar, Aaron's sons." Even so our calling and election to be priests of God and of Christ has come not from any workings of nature, but from the supernatural interposition of Divine grace. God, by his word and Spirit, has come forth, and nominated every one of us to the high service of ministering at his altar. He has sent forth his ministers and commissioned them to set apart all men whom they can reach, to be his priests. There is not one among you, however thoughtless, however wicked, but Jehovah has said of him, set him apart that he may minister unto me in the priest's office. Whether old or young, poor or rich, high or low, male or female, young man or maiden, there is no difference; every individual, of all nations and times, has been divinely singled out and nominated for this holy consecration. The command is, "Go and make disciples of all nations." Not one is left out. All are named, and all

that hear the Gospel are called, elected, and appointed, to enter at once upon this sublime and holy office. And not more really were Aaron and his sons called of God to the ancient priesthood, than you, and I, and all the people among whom we live, have been called of God to the "royal priesthood" of believers in Christ Jesus.

2. Aaron and his sons obediently assented to their Divine appointment. Would to God that I could say as much for all who are called to be priests under the new and better covenant! But it cannot be said. Though God calls, many refuse. Though all are nominated, thousands will not consent to serve. They prefer to be priests of sin and self, to being priests of God and of Christ. They choose rather to minister for iniquity and Satan, than minister at the pure altar of Him who made them. It is a sad, and melancholy, and wicked perverseness, thus to resist heaven's high election to heaven's highest honors; but alas, it is a perverseness which multitudes cherish and glory in. God has commanded us to set them apart to be his priests, but they will not consent; and without their obedient concurrence they never can be inducted into the offices for which they have been named. Like Aaron and his sons, we must agree to be made priests, or we cannot become priests.

3. Aaron and his sons were consecrated according to specific Divine directions. As Moses proceeded to attend to it, he said, "This is the thing which the Lord commanded to be done." No wisdom or ingenuity of man can set apart priests for God. No rites that we can devise, no observances which this world's sages may invent, can ever induct a man into Christian offices. Not even Moses had any right to proceed

a single step, or to do one thing, except as God directed him. And everything which God commanded had to be done. There was to be no adding to, and no taking from the services as God had arranged them. The investment of Aaron and his sons with the dignities of priesthood, was God's work. And he did, in the ceremonies which he appointed, put forth his hand, and lay it, as it were, upon the heads of these men, and himself constituted them his ministers in the priest's office. Nor is it different now. We can only be set apart as priests of God and of Christ by the ceremonies which God himself, by his Son, has prescribed. No rites of human make, no decrees of councils, or commands of earthly sovereigns, in Church or State; no liturgies; no manual impositions; no services, however solemn or dignified; nothing, can avail one feather's weight toward making any one a priest of God. His own clear and specific appointments alone can do this. It must be done by means of God's own unmutilated prescriptions, or it cannot be done at all.

4. The consecration of Aaron and his sons was a public and open transaction. The command of God was, "Gather thou all the congregation together;" and the history says, "the assembly was gathered together unto the door of the tabernacle of the congregation," around the spot where the solemn deed was done. We cannot secretly be inducted into the holy priesthood to which the Gospel calls us. If there is any such a thing as secret discipleship, it is a very imperfect discipleship. People sometimes think they will be good, and prayerful, and holy, and gain for their souls the full portion of the blessed, and do it all without letting the thing be known. They will come to Jesus, but

only like Nicodemus, under covert of the night, and in the secresy of retirement. They wish to be the priests of God and of Christ, but they are not willing to be brought before the congregation of Israel—not willing to submit to a public and daylight consecration. With all their many valuable experiences, they yet have a lingering shame to give themselves up to all God's appointments. They wish to abridge God's own ritual; and are sometimes more than half offended because their way of expecting to get into the holy Christian priesthood is not thought as good as God's way. But, whatever people may think, God's prescriptions for the consecration of his priests involve *publicity*. Christ requires of us to confess him before men. He demands of us an open and unreserved following of him. He exacts submission to all his holy ordinances, some of which are essentially public. He has arranged the way to enter into the sheepfold, and pronounces him a thief and a robber who undertakes to climb in some other way. Let men beware, then, how they undertake to stint and curtail the appointments of God. If he has instituted sacraments, it is our business to attend to them. If he has commanded a public acknowledgment of the faith and identification with his people, we have no right to decline it. And if we are not willing to be openly known as God's consecrated priests, I doubt whether your secret religion is of a sort that will avail in the great day.

We come now to consider the particulars of the consecration itself.

1. "And Moses brought Aaron and his sons, and washed them with water." This was the first item

in the service. And what does it typify, but that "washing of regeneration, and renewing of the Holy Ghost, shed on us abundantly, through Jesus Christ our Savior?" "Verily, verily," says the Son of God, "except a man be born of water, and of the Spirit, he cannot enter into the kingdom of God." Nay, for this very purpose hath Christ given himself for the Church, "that he might sanctify and cleanse it, with the washing of water by the word."

I said a little while ago, that God has sent forth and commissioned his ministers to set apart all men to be his priests. And that same commission prescribes how it is to be done; viz. by "baptizing them in the name of the Father, and of the Son, and of the Holy Ghost." Not merely by the outward application of water to them in solemn religious service; but also "teaching them to observe all things whatsoever Jesus has commanded." Our washing is not a mere external rite, but an inward grace, "the answer of a good conscience toward God." It is not mere water; but water joined with the word of God, in which we by faith receive the cleansing and renewing efficacy of the Holy Ghost. A man may be outwardly baptized, and still be impure, but he cannot spiritually apprehend, appropriate, and enter into his baptism, without becoming a renewed and sanctified man. Nay, his whole spiritual renovation is included in this washing; so that his baptism is virtually no baptism at all, unless attended or followed by the death and burial of the old man of sin, and the planting in the soul of a new, pure and vigorous righteousness. I have no sympathies with the aberrations of Tractarian folly upon this subject. I locate no transforming or renewing power in the mere outward ceremony.

The outward rite is not the substance of the baptism
It is the moral purgation, the inward renovation, the
spiritual experience of the purifying grace of the
Holy Ghost, that fills out the scriptural conception
of Christian baptism. And without this spiritual
cleansing, the baptismal washing is a mere empty
rite, and our baptism is no baptism to us. But if we
have the real faith to lay hold of the grace offered
and proposed to us in our baptism, it becomes to us
the "laver of regeneration"— the burial of the old
man, and the quickening of the new man; "that as
Christ was raised up from the dead by the glory of
the Father, even so we also should walk in newness
of life." And this is the true washing of the Christian priest—the first item of his consecration to the
holy ministry of eternal priesthood. *"Except we be
born of water and of the Spirit, we cannot enter into the
kingdom of God."*

2. "And Moses brought Aaron's sons, and put
coats upon them, and girded them with girdles, and
put bonnets upon them." This was the second item
in the service. After their cleansing they had to be
clothed with ornaments "for glory and for beauty."
The long flowing robe of linen, clean and white,
covering the whole body from the neck to the hands
and feet, the curious girdle, figured with blue, purple
and scarlet, surrounding the loins, and the pyramidal crown upon the head, constituted the beautiful and imposing regalia in which each was arrayed.
But this also was a figure for the time then present.
It was a type of the glory of grace, and the beauty
of holiness, in which we must be enveloped in order
to become priests of God and of Christ; *"for the fine
linen is the righteousness of the saints."* We must be

pure, and we must be holy. Our native deformities must all be covered. We must "put on the Lord Jesus Christ," and be arrayed in his loveliness. His own glorious attirements are to be reflected in ours. The one must be, in its degree, of the same kind as the other. By our own weak endeavors, this never could be. No man is able to work out a satisfactory righteousness of his own. But it was not left to the priests to find their own dress. God had provided it for them. The wedding guest need not bring a wedding garment with him; that is an article furnished by the maker of the feast. And so, our moral equipment in Christ Jesus is given us by him who hath called us to be his priests. Our Savior is our Righteousness. What we lack personally, is supplied by him as our surety. "As by the offence of one, judgment came upon all men to condemnation, even so by the righteousness of one the free gift came upon all men unto justification of life." And "as by one man's disobedience many were made sinners, so by the obedience of one shall many be made righteous." If we are in Christ Jesus, united to him as his sons by faith, he is "made unto us wisdom, and righteousness, and sanctification, and redemption;" that he that glorieth may glory in the Lord. The law contemplates the saints in Christ, and sees them arrayed in his holiness, and accordingly pronounces them acceptable and just. Their faith in Christ secures to them the imputation of the righteousness of Christ. And under the complex workings of grace, this imputed righteousness also takes root in the believer's heart, and works itself into his experiences, so as in part to become a personal as well as an imputed righteousness. "For if we have been planted together in the likeness of his death, we shall be also in the likeness of his resurrection: knowing this, that our old man is crucified with him, that the body of sin might be destroyed, that henceforth we should not serve sin." Every Christian must needs be holy; holy by virtue of relationship to Christ, and holy in the aims, purposes, desires, and efforts of life. And this is the robe of glory and beauty that we must needs put on to be constituted priests of God. As without the wedding garment we cannot partake of God's supper, so without holiness we cannot come into the presence of our Lord to minister in the priest's office. Jehovah hath written on the gates of the everlasting city, "There shall in no wise enter into it anything that defileth, or worketh abomination, or maketh a lie." And unless we have fully given up to be holy and good, we have not yet come to be God's priests.

3. A third item in this consecration service, was the leaning of hands upon the head of the sin-offering. Sin—sin—sin—in everything there is remembrance made of sin, as man's great, ever present, crushing burden, and of the bloody sacrifice of Christ Jesus as its only remedy. Everywhere, even in our holiest moods and most sacred doings, there still flashes out the stern and humiliating accusation — "O man, thou art a sinner! All thy goodness is but abomination apart from Christ! Thy only hope is in him whose body was broken and whose blood was shed for the remission of sins!" There must, therefore, be a habitual recurrence of our minds to this fact. Our hand must be ever kept on the brow of the atoning Lamb. We must never cease to rest

upon Jesus and his offering of himself for us. Here must we

> ——— sit, forever viewing
> Mercy streaming in his blood.

This underlies everything else. There is no heavenly consecration which does not take in this. It is the beginning, and the middle, and the end, of all human sanctification. And without resting upon Christ as the sin-offering, we never can come to the high honors of the priesthood of saints.

4. "And Moses put of the blood upon the tip of their right ear, and upon the thumbs of their right hands, and upon the great toes of their right feet." The whole person is visibly dedicated to the Lord. Every faculty and power is consecrated with the blood of the Lamb. Jehovah touches that blood to the right ear, hand, and foot; as much as to say, "As my priests, all the faculties and powers represented in these parts, from ear to toe, are to be used only for me." The ear is consecrated, that it may be ever open to the gentlest whispers of the Divine word, and listen to nothing but what is of God. The hand is consecrated, that it may never more be stretched out unto iniquity, but ever lifted up in devotion to him to whose service it is set apart. The foot is consecrated, that it may never again be set down in the ways of sin, but ever made to move and carry us in the paths of righteousness. Such is our solemn consecration of the whole man as God's priests. We are no longer our own; we are bought with a price — "with the precious blood of Christ as of a lamb without blemish and without spot;" and forever set apart to glorify God in our bodies and our

spirits which are his. This is the consecration of priests; and unless we have surrendered to be thus devoted to God, we are not partakers of the glorious priesthood to which we have been called.

5. "And Moses took of the anointing oil, and of the blood which was upon the altar, and sprinkled it upon Aaron, and upon his garments, and upon his sons, and upon his sons' garments with him." Even after their setting apart to be priests, they needed to be yet further sanctified as priests. Not only themselves, but their very garments also, were marked as holy. The sacred oil was emblematic of the gifts and graces of the Holy Spirit. And so the Holy Ghost, in conjunction with the blood of the Lamb, sanctifies and endows us for holy services. Sprinkled with these sacred elements — touched with moral unction and constrained by the dying love of Jesus, we become equipped for duty, and qualified "to show forth the praises of him who hath called us out of darkness into his marvellous light." It is not enough that we are installed in the priesthood. It is not the ultimatum of our calling merely to attain the honor and place of priests. Even this honor and place are to be made subservient to something more. Our very priesthood must be consecrated, as well as we to the priesthood. Not for our beauty and glory only does God invest us with our Christian offices and gifts, but for his own praise. We must therefore aim not merely at getting ourselves into heaven, but at being saved for the further purpose, that, as saved men, we may the better glorify God, and set forth the praise of his glorious grace. There is danger that we think too much of the blessings of the Gospel and our portion as believers, as the end,

They are not the end. They are only means to the end. We are not called to be priests, for the mere sake of being priests; but that we may "*minister unto God in the priest's office.*" We are ordained for a purpose beyond our ordination. Our very priesthood must be set apart for God. All the gifts and efficacies of the Spirit and the blood upon our nature, are to be for the everlasting praise of our Redeemer. And as we look forward to that nearing world when our sanctification shall be complete, we must not contemplate it as a mere scene of resting upon our dignities, but as a scene of sublime, noble, and unceasing services, rendered unto God and the Lamb.

6. Still another item in the consecration of God's ancient priests, was, that they had to eat the boiled flesh of the offered lamb with unleavened bread, at the door of the tabernacle. This boiled lamb of course typifies the Savior as offered for our sins. It calls to mind the great sufferings which he endured as our substitute and sacrifice of consecration. Every joint in him was relaxed. He was "poured out like water." We cannot contemplate the scenes of his passion without feeling that "his countenance was more marred than the face of any man." But it was a necessary part of the process by which we are constituted priests of God. Christ had to die, and have all the tender parts of his nature brought under the fires of wrath, and his body given to be food for our souls, to qualify us to come acceptably before our Maker. And now that he is thus made an offering for our sanctification, it appertains to us to put forth our hands, and eat of that offering, as the life and feast of our souls. He is the bread of life, and upon that bread we must feed to be God's priests. For,

"Except we eat the flesh of the Son of man, and drink his blood, we have no life in us." And as our washing is connected with our baptism, so this eating is connected with the sacramental supper. The one points to the birth of the new man; the other points to the nurture and nourishment of that new creature. Merely receiving the baptismal water is not regeneration; and so merely eating and drinking in the holy Supper is not partaking of the flesh and blood of Christ. There is an inward in both, as well as an outward. But as it is only real renewal by the Holy Ghost that takes up and fills out our baptism, so it is only a believing and real appropriation of Christ's body and blood that constitutes a complete and effective participation of the holy supper. It is more a spiritual than an oral eating; nay, it is essentially a spiritual eating, only assisted by means of outward elements and bodily manducation. Faith must do the work, and the external is only a representation on which faith may more easily lean, and receive aid in laying hold upon Christ crucified. Faith is the hand that reaches out to take Christ as our salvation, and faith is the mouth by which we receive him; but the physical hand is extended to grasp the consecrated elements, and the mouth of the body receives them, to give unto faith a greater vigor, and thus aid the inward thought by an outward act. And thus feeding continuously upon our slain and boiled Lamb, we are nourished and strengthened for our spiritual priesthood, and consecrated to serve in it for ever.

7. There is yet one point in these consecration services to which I will call your attention, and then leave the subject to your own management. Aaron

and his sons, having attended to these several particulars, were further required to "abide at the door of the tabernacle day and night seven days," before they could enter fully upon the high offices to which they had been consecrated.

The number *seven* is very often used in the Scriptures as the type of perfection and completeness. The "seven Spirits of God" represent the fulness and perfection of the one Holy Spirit. "The seven stars," or "the seven angels," represent the entire or complete ministry of the Christian Church. And so generally, the number seven is identified with completeness. This is especially true when used with reference to *time*. We read of the "seven days" of the week in which creation was finished; "seven years" as completing a reckoning; and seven times seven years bringing round the grand sabbatic year of jubilee, when things went back and started again afresh. It was a completion of the period. So then, the priesthood of Aaron and his sons was made perfect; it took in the completing number seven — "seven *days*." The consecration *period* was a complete period — a full measure of *time*. It was not only the fact of completeness, but a duration through which this fact was brought out. We are not only to be completely consecrated to a complete spiritual priesthood; but it is to take a complete period of time in which this completeness is to be effected. We are called and consecrated now. We are real priests as soon as we have attended to the sanctifying services of which I have spoken. But we must yet abide "seven days" at the door of the tabernacle before we can go into it. We must yet wait the revolution of a complete period before we can come into the Holy of holies. That complete period can be nothing short of our entire earthly life.

These present days, then, are the days of waiting. Though we are set apart as priests, we have to abide here at the door of the Holy Sanctuary until the days of our consecration be at an end. We cannot yet go in to see God in his glory, and to bend before him where his holy angels adore and wonder. We must wait until the "seven days" are fulfilled. It may seem like an imprisonment. It may often make us feel somewhat impatient. It may tie down and fetter our desires. But it is only to make us perfect. It is necessary to complete our glorious installation, as priests of God and of Christ. And it will soon be over. It is only "*seven days*"—the shortest of all the complete periods of human reckoning. Before we think of it, it will have passed. For some of us, much of it has already gone. Two, three, four, five, six, and to some even a part of the seventh, of these days of waiting, are even now numbered with the past. Presently the whole term will have expired. It will not be long till we all find the period completed.

And what a scene then awaits the elected and consecrated priests of the Lord! Found abiding at the door of the tabernacle when the clock strikes the finishing hour, who shall describe what follows!

> In vain our fancy strives to paint
>   The moment after death;
> The glories that surround a saint,
>   When yielding up his breath.
>
> One gentle sigh his fetters breaks;
>   We scarce can say "He's gone!"
> Before the willing spirit takes
>   Its mansions near the throne

And then begin the everlasting services. Then shal'
we hear the tinkling of the golden bells that herald
the motions of the great High-Priest in heaven.
Then shall we look upon the beauties of redemption's jewelry that hangs in glorious splendor around
his noble form. Then shall we walk in the light of
the golden lamps which fill the celestial sanctuary
with the brightness of wisdom and the warmths of
love. Then shall we eat holy bread in the presence
of God, and wave the golden censers of heaven with
the sweet incense of everlasting praise. Then shall
we hear Jehovah speaking to us from his eternal
seat, and look with adoring angels into the awful
mysteries of his Being, and rejoice in the great
heart of our Father's love pulsating with Almightiness.

> Oh! glorious hour! Oh, blest abode!
> We shall be near, and like our God!
> And flesh and sin no more control
> The sacred pleasures of the soul.

NINTH LECTURE.

AARON IN THE DUTIES OF HIS OFFICE.

LEV. CHAP. IX.

As far as our examinations of this Book have progressed, we have seen the complete arrangement of two important particulars; first, the kind of offerings to be made; and second, the consecration of the persons who were to officiate in offering them. We have therefore seen enough in this ritual to behold it now going into actual operation. Aaron having been ordained, and the days of his consecration having ended, he enters at once upon his priestly functions. The chapter before us, accordingly, shows us *the Levitical system in active exercise.*

The business of a priest is summed up by Paul to be, to "offer both gifts and sacrifices for sins." And as Aaron was a mere man, he had to offer these gifts and sacrifices, "as for the people, so also for himself." Hence, in giving us this account of what Aaron did in his office as high-priest, God brings us again to the contemplation of scenes of slaughter and blood. Redemption by blood is the great theme of the Scriptures, from beginning to end. It ever and again comes up. God will not permit it to remain out of sight for a single chapter. No matter what the figure is, it is made somehow to embrace this. It is repeated at every turn. It stands out boldly at every step. Every imaginable method is taken to write it deep in the soul, to engrave it upon the conscience, to fill the whole mind with it, and to make it the grand centre of all religious thought and belief. I have before referred to the fact, that this peculiarity of the Scriptures is exceedingly repugnant to the feelings of some people. It seems greatly to disgust and offend many, that we have so much to say about *blood*. Some verily seem to think, and some skeptics have argued, that the Bible cannot be what it claims to be, because it represents God as appointing and taking pleasure in such sanguinary arrangements and services. But I have also alluded to the glaring inconsistency of such people in shrinking with abhorrence from the bloody nature of the system which God has arranged for our salvation, whilst they are yet great admirers of the taste and culture of the men and times we read of in the classics. They are charmed with the ancient Greeks and Romans, and are ever putting them forward as our exemplars and guides; and cannot get done talking about their glorious civilization; just as if the Religion of Greece and Rome had no sanguinary rites, or involved no dealing in bloody sacrifices. Never was there a religious system on earth more bloody in its observances, or more shocking in its sacrificial ritual, than those in vogue among these very Greeks and Romans, sanctioned and supported by their laws, and advocated by their greatest men. Every classical scholar knows this. I will not annoy you with details of their sacrifices of dogs, and pigs, and cats, and horses, and hecatombs of cattle, with salaried officers of state, manipulating and inspecting the entrails, to read in sickening filthiness the pretended communications of their gods. Nor were these the worst. They not only sacrificed animals, but *men also*. Their altars flowed, not only with the blood of bulls and of goats, and various unclean and disgusting creatures, but with the blood of human beings, who were annually slain and offered up in religious worship to propitiate their sanguinary deities. In the worship of Zeus Lycæus in Arcadia, human sacrifices were regularly offered for hundreds of years, down to the time of the Roman Emperors. In Leucas, a man was every year put to death at the high festival of Apollo. When their great generals went out to war, they first offered up human victims to gain the assistance of their divinities. Before the battle of Salamis, Themistocles sacrificed three Persians to Dionysius. The city of Athens — the very "eye of Greece" — had an annual festival in honor of the Delian Apollo, at which two persons were every year put to death, the one for the men, and the other for the women, of that renowned metropolis. The neck of the one who died for the men was surrounded with a garland of black figs, and the neck of the other with a garland of white figs, and both were beaten with rods of fig-wood as they were led forth to a place where they were burned alive, and their ashes cast into the air and sea. And Grecian story tells of many parents, who laid violent hands upon their own children, and offered them up as bloody sacrifices to their gods. Nor was it much different with the Romans. In their earlier history, it was the custom, under certain contingencies, to sacrifice to their deities everything born of man or beast between the first day of March and the last day of April. Even in the latest period of the Roman republic, men were sacrificed to Mars in the Campus

Martius, by priests of state, and their heads stuck up at the Regia.

I mention these things, not to vindicate the Levitical rites, of which they were monstrous and wicked distortions and perversions, but to show the miserable inconsistency of those skeptical people who denounce the atoning regulations of the Scriptures, and hold up the taste and ideas of the Greeks and Romans as the true models of what is beautiful, refined, and elevated. I merely wish to have you know and feel, that if the Hebrew ritual is to be regarded as offensive to a lofty aesthetic taste, the ritual of the most polished nations of antiquity was still more offensive, and abhorrent in the utmost degree; and that if the religion of the Scriptures cannot be received as of God by reason of its connection with scenes of blood, there is no system of religion upon earth, ancient or modern, that can be so received; because all others have been equally and still more sanguinary in their services, and that too without any of the deep and affecting moral meaning of this. And I freely confess, that I see nothing in the doctrine of salvation by blood, or in the Jewish rites, which typified it with so much strength and clearness, either to offend my taste, to shock my reason, or the least to interfere with the readiest and fullest acceptation of the Scriptures as the true revelation of Almighty God. True, I behold in it much that humbles my pride — that tells me I am a very wicked sinner — that proclaims my native condition far removed from what God's law requires — that assures me I am undone as regards my own strength — and that holds out death and eternal burning as what I deserve. But all this accords with my conscience, and is reechoed in the deepest convictions of my soul. And with it all, it presents to me a plan of redemption so out of the line of man's thoughts, so fitted to my felt wants, and so completely attested by its moral efficacy, that it is itself a mighty demonstration to my mind of its divine original.

The very fact that the Bible has but one great subject running through all its histories and prophecies, ordinances and types, epistles and psalms — that salvation by blood is the focal point in which all its various lines of light converge — is to me one of the strongest evidences that it has come from God. When I consider that its writers lived hundreds and thousands of years apart; that they were found in all walks of life; and that they wrote in languages foreign to each other; I can find no way to account for the unity which pervades it, but by admitting that these various writers were all moved and guided by the same high intelligence, and inspired of God. No matter who held the pen, whether Moses in Midian when time itself was young, or David in the mountains of Israel, or Ezekiel lying on the river's bank, or Daniel in the palaces of Babylon, or Paul a prisoner at Rome, or John in the solitude of the bleak rocks of Patmos, the records are all essentially the same, and blend together as parts of one great whole. Just as the various notes and chords of the musician's oratorio, express the one great thought of the composer, so the grand hymn of Revelation presents but one central idea; and whatever chords in the harp of inspiration are touched by the chosen hands, they all ultimately settle upon the all-thrilling tone of the key-note —

salvation through the blood of the Lamb. Isolated and foreign as some parts may at first seem, they all have connection with each other, and exhibit a oneness of interior substance and unity of design, which, as it could not have been the result of accident, and cannot be explained on the ground of concert between the writers, must needs be referred to the mind of God, moving and controlling them all.

The duties of the high-priest, as stated by the apostle, and exhibited in this chapter, divide themselves into two general classes. Some of his services related exclusively to himself, and the rest exclusively to the people. Aaron, though a priest, was still a man, with all the wants and infirmities of men. He consequently needed atonement as much as those for whom he was to officiate. And before he was allowed to proceed with his duties for others, he was required to offer sacrifices for himself. On all public occasions, the high-priest was to begin his work by presenting a sin-offering and a burnt-offering for himself. This requirement was a kind of undertone, or sub-current, in the performances of the ancient priesthood, which pointed to the merely provisional character of the Levitical system. It was to remind Aaron, and to remind the people, that he was, after all, not the true and real priest to make effectual reconciliation for the sins of the world — that he was only a sinful man, set up to represent a priest yet to come — that no one was to look to him as able to open the doors of heaven, but through him to another who "needeth not daily to offer up sacrifice for his own sins" — that he was but a figure for the time then present of good things to come by means of "the great Prince which standeth for the children of his people."

Aaron was first of all to offer *a calf* for a sin-offering. And it may be that this was intended to refer back to his great sin in the matter of the "golden calf," which he had been prevailed upon to make for the worship of the people while Moses was in the mount. It is a hard thing to shake off the degrading recollection of any marked deed of wrong. The soil of sin upon the conscience cannot be easily washed out. Though a man repent never so bitterly, and though he should have the assurance of forgiveness, it still lives like an evil fountain in the soul, ejecting now and then its dark and saddening waters into the stream of his joys. I once heard a man say with tears upon his cheeks, that if he owned a world, he would willingly and gladly give it to have certain recollections of crime blotted from his mind. He was a good and pious man — a man who had solemnly consecrated himself to labors for the good of his kind; but the thought of his former deeds of shame haunted him like a demon, and clouded his brightest peace. Aaron had done a great evil in the sight of God, and the dark shadow of its remembrance followed him even into the honors of his high-priesthood, and stood before him every time he came to enter into the tabernacle of the Most High. And if I am now addressing any who are yet in the virgin innocence of their youth, let me exhort you, as you love your peace, to beware of the first sin. It may seem sweet to the taste, but it will be wormwood and gall within you. Though you should even live to have it forgiven, it will be a dark cloud upon your soul to the hour of your death. It will be a source of mortification to you for ever. It will degrade you in your own thoughts. and hang upon you as a depressing weight whenever you attempt to draw near to God. Fly from it, as you would fly from pestilence and death; for it biteth like a serpent, and stingeth like an adder.

The second offering which Aaron was to make for himself was the holocaust, or whole burnt-offering. In addition to his special sin, he was a common sinner with all other men. He needed justification by the blood of Jesus, just as every body else. There is a sense in which all are equally guilty before God, the high and the low, the rich and the poor, the young and the old, the learned and the ignorant, the priest and the people. And the only deliverance from this common guilt, as from all other guilt, is through the one great offering of "The Lamb of God that taketh away the sin of the world." Not a soul can ever become acceptable to the Lord, or enter heaven, but by this. We may think that little children are so innocent, that surely *they* are fit for blessedness; but not even the youngest and loveliest of our babes could ever be saved, if it were not for the great sacrifice of Calvary, in which the whole nature of Christ came under the penetrating blade and consuming fires of offended sovereignty. By that whole burnt-offering alone do they become acceptable to God, and by that alone can even the holiest and highest of this world's population ever come into the presence of the Almighty and live. Even Aaron in his priesthood needs it just as much as the wickedest and vilest of the race.

These preliminary and personal services having been attended to, Aaron proceeded, as God directed, to perform the duties of his office for the people for whom he was ordained. A sin-offering, a burnt-offering, a peace-offering, and a meat-offering had been prescribed, and his functions with reference to these he now proceeded to discharge. Let us, then, contemplate him in the solemn service.

Aaron's first official duties were connected with the altar at the door of the tabernacle, and were all performed in the presence of the people. Here the sacrifices were brought, and slain, and cut into their several parts, and arranged in the order prescribed. What was to be burned, he put upon the altar; what was to be waved before the Lord, he waved; what was to fall to the offerers he delivered over to them; and the blood that was to be poured and sprinkled upon and about the altar, he poured and sprinkled.

Now, in order to understand the typical meaning of all this, it will be necessary to observe that Christ is at once the priest and the sacrifice. It was impossible to unite these two things in the type. They stand in the Levitical ritual as distinct, and they are not at all confounded together in the great mediation of Calvary. But we must bear in mind, that Christ is at the same time the victim, and the High-priest who officiates in offering that victim. When he was led forth to his immolation, he was the lamb without blemish, and also the one who was to lay its body upon the fires, and sprinkle its blood upon the altar. "Therefore," says he, "doth my Father love me, because *I lay down my life*, that I might take it again. *No man taketh it from me, but* I LAY IT DOWN OF MYSELF. *I have power to lay it down, and I have power to take it again.*" It is altogether too low and unworthy a conception of Christ's offering, to regard him as having been compulsively dragged to his execution, or as having been put to death by the mere power of men. *It was his own voluntary act.* What did he say when the armed host came out by night to take him? "I can now pray to my Father, and he shall presently give me more than twelve legions of angels. But how then shall the Scriptures be fulfilled, that thus it must be?" And to show that this was not vain boasting, he stepped forward in the face of his armed enemies, and said, "*I am Jesus of Nazareth whom ye seek!*" and they quailed before him, and shrank back, and fell as dead men at his feet. And surely He, whose voice had withered the fig-tree in its greenness, and hushed the fury of the tempest into peace, and stilled the uplifted waves of the sea, and recalled the putrefying dead from the grave, could easily have blasted all the strength of Jerusalem's officials, and palsied every hand that could have been raised against his life. No, no; he was not slain because he could not help it. His life-blood was not wrung from him, except as he unmurmuringly and voluntarily consented and yielded. As the apostle tells us, "*He offered up himself.*" He is the great High-priest who officiated at his own immolation. It was he himself that presided at the awful ceremony, in which all his joints were relaxed, and all the binding ligaments of his being cut asunder, and all the tender parts of his most interior nature torn out for burning—and his body, soul, and spirit, laid down as a sacrifice for the sins of the world. It was by his own will that the blow was struck; that the blood flowed; that every covering and protection was torn off; and the whole blessed

Christ reduced to a mangled and lifeless mass around and upon the altar of God.

And it is this very fact that so infinitely ennobles, exalts, and dignifies Christ's sacrifice. It was a willing surrender of himself to death. He "*gave himself for us.*" He "*made himself* of no reputation, and took upon him the form of a servant, and was made in the likeness of men; and being found in fashion as a man, HE HUMBLED HIMSELF, *and became obedient unto death, even the death of the cross.*"

> This was compassion, like a God,
> That when the Savior knew
> The price of pardon was his blood,
> His pity ne'er withdrew.

There is a very remarkable expression in the 15th verse, to which I desire to call your particular attention in this connection. You read there, that Aaron "took the sin-offering for the people, and slew it, *and offered it for sin.*" A stricter rendering of the original, as noted by various critics, would be, "*He sinned it,*" or "*He made it to be sin.*" The same diction occurs in chapter 6 : 26. The idea is, that the sin-offering somehow had the sin transferred to it, or laid on it, or was so linked with the sin for which it was to atone, as to become itself the sinful or sinning one, not actually, but imputatively and constructively. The animal had no sin, and was not capable of sinning; but, having been devoted as a sin-offering, and having received upon its head the burden of the guilty one who substituted its life for his own, it came to be viewed and treated as a creature which was nothing but sin.

And this brings us to a feature in the sacrificial

work of Christ at which many have stumbled, but which deserves to be profoundly considered. Jesus died, not only as a martyr to the cause he had espoused, not only as an offering apart from the sins of those for whom he came to atone, but as a victim who had received all those sins upon his own head, and so united them with his own innocent and holy person as to be viewed and treated, in part at least, as if he himself had sinned the sins of all sinners. He so effectually put himself into the room and stead of sinners, and so really assumed their wickedness, that he came to be the only guilty one which the law could see. Personally he was not a sinner, but, "holy, harmless, undefiled, and separate from sinners;" nevertheless, as he surrendered to become the substitute of the guilty, and undertook to answer for all their crimes, he thereby became to the law as if he were a mere mass of sin, upon which the hottest furies of just indignation and wrath were let loose. Though in his own proper self as unsullied as the highest heavens, in his character as our sin-offering, he took a guiltiness upon him, and a volume of iniquity covered him, as intense and terrible as the combined wickedness of all men. Though never the committer, he became the receiver of sin, and stood to the law as a reservoir into which all the streams of human guilt had emptied themselves.

Think not that I am stating this case too strongly. Ask of the inspired apostle, and he will tell you. Ever memorable are the words which he has recorded on this very point. Taking up the exact diction of Moses in the text, he says that God "*hath made him to be sin for us, who knew no sin;* that we might be made the righteousness of God in him." Here it is,

As the sins of Israel were so put upon the sin-offering that it came to be viewed and treated as nothing but sin, so the Lord hath made our great sin-offering to be — not merely *a sinner*, but the very substance and essence of criminality. "*He made him to be* SIN" — a mere mass of guilt, laid bare to the judgments of Divine wrath. How could it have been otherwise, when, as Isaiah tells us, "*The Lord laid on him the iniquity of us all?*" The iniquity of us all, is no small iniquity. A ten thousandth part of the sin that cleaves even to the most virtuous among men, would be enough, if uncancelled, to sink them to eternal death. How then are we to estimate the mightiness of that sum of crime which has been accumulating since the world began? How shall we measure the ocean of guilt which has been gathering from every generation as from a thousand Amazons? Aye, "there are shadows upon the world that we cannot penetrate; masses of sin and misery that overwhelm us with wonder and awe." Not vaster is the five mile thickness of atmosphere around this globe, than the measure of the iniquities of those who have lived upon its surface. Yet every one of them was laid upon Jesus as the great sin-offering of man. When the holy inquisition of heaven was sent forth to deal out just indignation for earth's amazing wickedness, there was not a sin from Adam's fall to last night's theft, or the wandering thoughts of yon inattentive hearer, which was not found lying to the charge of that spotless Lamb who had undertaken to answer for all. And of all the monsters in crime that this world has ever borne, none ever had upon him such an intensity and vastness of guilt as that which the holy Christ assumed and took upon himself in that dark hour when his soul was made an offering for sin. The law could have seen in him nothing but sin — an embodiment of condensed and unspeakable guiltiness—the very purity of heaven so shrouded and buried up in a sea of vileness that the Father, with all his tender love for his only begotten, for a while turned away his face in abhorrence. Hence that awful cry of the dying Savior, "My God! My God! why hast thou forsaken me!" "The Lord laid on him the iniquity of us all." "He made him, who knew no sin, to be sin for us."

Having attended to what was to be done with the sacrifices at the altar, in presence of the people, the next duty of Aaron, as the high-priest, was, to enter into the sanctuary and the most holy place with the blood of the sin-offering, as directed in the 30th of Exodus. But, before entering upon this second grand department of his priesthood, he "lifted up his hands towards the people, and blessed them." It was a very significant act. It was as if he were emptying over them from his bloody hands all the effects and virtues of that blood. And it pointed forward to those gracious transactions of the Lord Jesus subsequent to his offering of himself for us, and prior to his ascension into heaven. How strikingly it reminds us of those impressive scenes in which the risen Savior appeared unto his disciples, and "shewed unto them his hands and his side," and opened his lips with the comforting words, "*Peace be unto you,*" and "breathed on them, saying, *Receive ye the Holy Ghost.*" How it leads our thougts back to the time when our great High-priest, with his people, stood round their altar upon Olivet, lifting up those hands so lately stained with blood, blessing them before he left them, and as he left them still blessing them! It was the pouring out over them, and through them upon all subsequent believers, the hallowing influences of his atoning sacrifice, and the comforting blessings of his great sin-offering. From those open hands, there still flows down a stream of good, filling many a sad heart with joy, and many a disconsolate home with songs of praise. Though many a long and tedious year has passed since that fountain of blessing was opened upon the world, its glad waters are still as pure and plenteous as ever, and shall continue to flow to generations yet unborn.

> Its streams the whole creation reach,
>   So bounteous is the store;
> Enough for all, enough for each,
>   Enough for evermore.

But having thus spread his hands in blessing towards the people, Aaron "went into the tabernacle," and was hidden from the view of the solemn worshippers. How beautiful the connection between type and antitype! Of *our* Aaron it is written, "he lifted up his hands, and blessed them. And it came to pass, while he blessed them, he was parted from them, and carried up into heaven;"—"while they behold, he was taken up; and a cloud received him out of their sight."

Aaron was to enter into the tabernacle with the atoning blood of the victim slain without. "But Christ being come an High-priest of good things, which were to come, entered into a greater and more perfect tabernacle, not made with hands, not by the blood of goats and calves, but with his own blood. . .

For Christ is not entered into the holy places made with hands, which are the figures of the true; but into heaven itself, now to appear in the presence of God for us."

Moses, as the representative of Jehovah in these transactions, accompanied Aaron into the holy places, and delivered over to his care all the vessels of the sanctuary, and put the ordering of all the sacred services into his hands. And thus also hath Jesus "received from God the Father, honor and glory." "God also hath highly exalted him, and given him a name which is above every name; that at the name of Jesus every knee should bow, of things in heaven, and things in earth, and things under the earth; and that every tongue should confess that Jesus Christ is Lord, to the glory of God the Father." "The Father judgeth no man; but hath committed all judgment unto the Son: that all men should honor the Son, even as they honor the Father." Hence, he said, when about to enter upon his heavenly dominion, "All power is given unto me in heaven and in earth." "The Father hath committed all things into his hands."

Corporeally, then, our great High-priest is no longer with us. He has passed out of our sight within the vail of that holy tabernacle, which the Lord pitched, and not man. He has entered into heaven, into the presence of the eternal God. He is there as our Advocate with the Father, with the blood of sacrifice in his hands, ever interceding for us. He is there as our representative and Lord. Our names he wears in blazing jewelry on his shoulders and on his heart. He is there trimming the holy lamps for our enlightenment. He is there offering our prayers perfumed by the sweet incense of his holy intercessions. He is there to stay the breaking forth of wrath upon our sins. He is there, ordering all things, and keeping the charge of the holy services, that he may ultimately present us as a perfect Church, without spot, or wrinkle, or any such thing. Though we see him not, we know that he is there. Our elder brethren saw him enter there; and some of them in holy vision had a glimpse of him since he has entered there. John was one day in the Spirit, and saw him in the midst of the golden candlesticks, clothed with a garment down to the foot, and girt about with a golden girdle. In his hand were the seven stars, and his countenance was as the sun shineth in his strength. And he heard him say, "I am the first and the last; I am he that liveth, and was dead; and behold, I am alive for evermore, Amen; and have the keys of hell and of death. Write the things which thou hast seen." Yes, he still lives: —

> He lives, the great Redeemer lives;
> What joy the blest assurance gives!
> And now, before his Father, God,
> Pleads the full merit of his blood.

But Aaron did not stay in the tabernacle. He went in after the morning sacrifices were made; but before the evening sacrifices, he again "came out, and blessed the people." The soul kindles as we proceed with these ancient types. They portray so beautifully the grand mysteries of Redemption's progress. When I read of Aaron returning from his duties in the holy place, the words of the bright angels that kept guard at the Savior's ascension gather new preciousness. "Ye men of Galilee, why stand ye gazing up into heaven? this same Jesus which is taken up from you into heaven, shall so come in like manner as ye have seen him go into heaven." Our Lord will come again. "A little while," said he, "and ye shall not see me. And again a little while, and ye shall see me." When about to leave this world, he said, "I go to prepare a place for you, *I will come again."* And hardly had he reached the threshold of the heavenly home, until he shouted back, *"Surely I come quickly."* Soon shall the cloud that received him out of human sight, part asunder again to reveal him to his waiting people. Already the Apocalyptic cry has gone forth, *"Behold, he cometh with clouds; and every eye shall see him!"*

When Aaron came out of the holy place, it was to bless the waiting people. And so it is written of our great High-priest in heaven — "Unto them that look for him shall he appear the second time without sin unto salvation." Most people are afraid of the Savior's second coming, and never think of it but with dread. It is because they have not sufficiently considered its nature, and what it is for. It is not to curse, but to bless. It is not to distress, but to heal and save. It is not a thing to be dreaded, but to be prayed for and most earnestly desired. It is the event that is to finish our redemption, and complete our bliss. Everything now is yet imperfect. Our salvation is yet a thing of hope. Whatever be the strength of our faith, or the extent of our joy, we have not yet reached the promised fruition. Our home is yet in a world of diseases, funerals, graves, crimes, and tears. But when our expected Savior comes, creation's groans shall cease, and peace stretch forth its shady wings over the sons of men, and rivers of joy flow through this vale of tears, and the year of everlasting jubilee begin.

When Aaron came out of the holy place, "the glory of the Lord appeared unto all the people." Nor shall it be otherwise when Christ's epiphany shall occur. When the evening of this world's day shall come, "then shall appear the sign of the Son of Man in heaven, and they shall see him coming in the clouds of heaven with power and great glory." "For the Son of Man shall come in the glory of his Father, with his angels." Then shall Jerusalem's light come, and the glory of the Lord arise upon her. Then shall the pure in heart see God, and the righteous behold the King in his beauty, and cherubim to cherubim sing: "HOLY, HOLY, HOLY, IS THE LORD GOD OF HOSTS; THE WHOLE EARTH IS FULL OF HIS GLORY!"

When Aaron came out of the holy place, "there came a fire out from before the Lord, and consumed upon the altar the burnt-offering and the fat." These things had been "*made sin.*" All else was clean. The sins of all the congregation were upon the victim that lay upon the altar. And as soon as Aaron came forth, the fires of Jehovah leaped forth before him, and consumed that mass of sin. It was the exact picture of what is predicted concerning the reappearance of our great High-priest. "The Lord Jesus shall be revealed from heaven with his mighty angels in flaming fire, taking vengeance on them that know not God, and that obey not the Gospel: who shall be punished with everlasting destruction from the presence of the Lord, and from the glory

of his power." "The day cometh, that shall burn
as an oven; and all the proud, yea, all that do
wickedly, shall be stubble; and the day that cometh
shall burn them up, saith the Lord of hosts." "If
we sin wilfully after that we have received the knowledge of the truth, there remaineth no more sacrifice
for sins, but a certain fearful looking for of judgment
and fiery indignation, which shall devour the adver-
saries." "For our God is a consuming fire."

But the fire that darted forth before Aaron, and
burned up what was accounted to be sin in that
congregation, touched not one of the waiting worshippers. They saw it leap out with lightning fierceness, and lick up the guilty mass in a moment, but
it came not near either of them. Not a saint of God
shall be burned by the terrific fires of the great day.
When the wicked are cut off, they shall see it. "The
Lord shall roar out of Zion, and utter his voice from
Jerusalem; and the heavens and the earth shall
shake: but the Lord will be the hope of his people,
and the strength of the children of Israel." "There
shall be signs in the sun, and in the moon, and in
the stars; and upon earth distress of nations, with
perplexity; the sea and the waves roaring; men's
hearts failing them for fear, and for looking after
those things which are coming on the earth: for the
powers of heaven shall be shaken; and they shall
see the Son of Man coming in a cloud, with power
and great glory." But He who upholds the worlds,
yet marks the sparrow's fall, says to his people:
"When these things begin to come to pass, then
look up, and lift up your heads: for your redemption
draweth nigh."

Nay, when the congregation of Israel saw the fires,

"*they shouted*" and adored. They "fell on their faces" for very ecstacy, and holy worshipful admiration. They had expected much, but the thing transcended their most rapturous imaginings. And so, in the day of our Savior's coming, there is a joy, and glory, and holy exultation, and adoring gladness, for the people of God, which eye hath not seen, nor ear heard, nor the heart of man conceived. Then, from the dwellers in the valleys, and caught up by the inhabitants of the hills, and echoed by the islands over all the seas, shall be sung the Apocalyptic chant of Christian exultation — " Unto Him that loved us, and washed us from our sins in his own blood, and hath made us kings and priests unto God and his Father; to Him be glory and dominion for ever and ever; Amen!" Even the four-and-twenty elders which sit before God, shall fall down on their faces, and worship, saying, "We give thee thanks, O Lord God Almighty, which art, and wast, and art to come because thou hast taken to thee thy great power, and hast reigned." And down the long aisles of everlasting ages, shall be "heard, as it were, the voice of a great multitude, and the voice of many waters, and the voice of mighty thunderings, saying, ALLELUIA! FOR THE LORD GOD OMNIPOTENT REIGNETH!"

TENTH LECTURE.

THE FALL OF NADAB AND ABIHU.

LEV. CHAP. X.

This chapter comes in as an episode in the general current of this book. It gives an account of a sort of accident during the institution of this ancient ritual. But it is not therefore without significance or important typical relations.

At our last view of the tabernacle, we beheld it gay and glorious with the manifestations of a reconciled God, and a delighted, adoring people. This chapter shows it overspread with gloom and sadness. The shout of Israel yesterday, becomes a wail to-day. Such is human life—a ceaseless alternation of lights and shades, joys and sorrows, bridals and burials. The same heart pulsates with delight and throbs with grief. The same walls echo the voice of festivity and the lamentations of woe. The morning calm is often but the herald of the evening tempest. War soon succeeds the profoundest peace; judgments follow upon the heels of mercies; the coffin presently comes after the cradle. There is a bitter for every sweet, a night for every day, a death for every birth. From scenes of glory we pass to scenes of gloom and mourning. The sunshine of to-day is lost again in the clouds of to-morrow. "For all flesh is as grass, and all the glory of man as the flower of grass. The grass withereth, and the flower thereof falleth away."

Nadab and Abihu were no inconsiderable personages. They were the sons of Israel's priest, the nephews of Israel's leader, the head of Israel's princely elders. They had been with Moses and Aaron in the hallowed mount; they had looked upon the glorious vision of God as he appeared on Sinai; they had been chosen and consecrated to the priesthood; they had stood by and assisted Aaron in the first operations of the Hebrew ritual; and in all that camp of God's ransomed ones, Moses and Aaron alone had higher dignity than theirs. But, from the mount of vision, they fell into the pit of destruction. They were accepted priests yesterday; they are disgraced victims of God's holy indignation to-day. The world had not made one of its quick revolutions, from the time the people drew near them as the sanctified of the Lord, until they shrank from them in horror as the accursed of God. In the evening they were accepted priests, with prospects of a bright destiny before them; in the morning they were in the hands of death, and all their hopes were quenched.

An event so startling and melancholy, occurring at the very inception of the Mosaic ceremonies, challenges our special attention, and calls for serious thinking. We cannot consider it too solemnly, nor view it intelligently, without important spiritual profit. It is a sort of finger-post, set up at the starting point of a great history, from which generation after generation, in all succeeding ages, might take warning and learn wisdom.

The death of these men was exceedingly awful,

It came upon them with the suddenness of lightning. I do not know that sudden death is always to be deplored. To a good man, sudden death is only sudden deliverance from the infirmities of life, and sudden glory. It saves from many an anxiety and many a pain. But for a thoughtless and impenitent sinner to be cut off and hurried to the judgment without a moment's warning, is exceedingly terrible. Nadab and Abihu were plunged into eternity with a flash, and that right in the midst of their sin. With their censers in their hands, enveloped in a cloud of incense which was but the expression and signal of their guilt, in the very act of their transgression, a bolt of flame darted out over the mercy-seat, and laid them instantaneously with the dead.

A judgment so marked and terrific argues peculiar provocation. It is not always right to infer special guilt from special affliction. Job's calamities did not come upon him because he was a man of sin. Those Galileans whose blood Pilate mingled with their sacrifices, were not sinners above all the Galileans because they suffered such things. Those eighteen upon whom the tower in Siloam fell, were not sinners above all them that dwelt in Jerusalem because they met a fate so sad. The best men are sometimes the greatest sufferers. There are mysteries in the divine administrations, which often make the way to heaven a way of tribulation and tears. But in this case, there was no suffering for righteousness' sake. It was a plain instance of the breaking forth of God's anger. It was a terrific visitation, miraculous, and direct from indignant Deity. And we are compelled to infer peculiar crime and special iniquity as the cause.

Let us inquire, then, *in the first place*, into the nature of the offence which called out this startling visitation upon these unfortunate men. The record is not very specific, and leaves much to be reached by inference; but enough is said to give us an adequate idea of the sin committed. The context shows that it was not one isolated and specific act of disobedience. It was of a complex nature, and involved sundry particulars, each of which contributed its portion to make up the general crime for which judgment came upon the guilty ones.

The special statute recorded in the ninth verse, of which this occurrence seems to have been the occasion, furnishes ground for the inference, that Nadab and Abihu had indulged too freely in stimulating drinks, and thus incapacitated themselves for that circumspection and sacred reverence which belonged to the priestly functions. We cannot say positively that such was the fact, but the whole nature and circumstances of the case point strongly that way. And if this inference be correct, we have here another among the many sad exhibitions of the mischiefs wrought by indulging in a too free use of intoxicating liquors. The history of strong drink, is the history of ruin, of tears, of blood. It is, perhaps, the greatest curse that has ever scourged the earth. It is one of depravity's worst fruits — a giant demon of destruction. Men may talk of earthquakes, storms, floods, conflagrations, famine, pestilence, despotism and war; but intemperance in the use of intoxicating drinks, has sent a volume of misery and woe into the stream of this world's history, more fearful and terrific than either of them. It is the Amazon and Mississippi among the rivers of wretchedness. It is the Alexander and Napoleon among the warriors upon the peace and good of man. It is like the pale horse of the Apocalypse, whose rider is Death, and at whose heels follow hell and destruction. It is an evil which is limited to no age, no continent, no nation, no party, no sex, no period of life. It has taken the poor man at his toil and the rich man at his desk, the senator in the halls of state and the drayman on the street, the young man in his festivities and the old man in his repose, the priest at the altar and the layman in the pew, and plunged them together into a common ruin. It has raged equally in times of war and in times of peace, in periods of depression, and in periods of prosperity, in republics and in monarchies, among the civilized and among the savage. Since the time that Noah came out of the ark, and planted vineyards, and drank of their wines, we read in all histories of its terrible doings, and never once lose sight of its black and bloody tracks. States have recorded enactments against it, ecclesiastical penalties have been imposed upon it, societies have succeeded societies for its extermination; but, like him whose name was Legion, no man has been able to bind it. For these four thousand years, it has been raging over the world, destroying some of virtue's fairest flowers and some of wisdom's richest fruitage. It was this that brought the original curse of servitude upon the descendants of Ham, that has eaten away the strength of empires, wasted the energies of states, blotted out the names of families, and crowded hell with tenants. Egypt, the source of science — Babylon, the wonder and glory of the world — Greece, the home of learning and of liberty — Rome with her Cæsars, the mistress of the earth — each in its turn had its heart lacerated by this dreadful canker-worm, and thus became an easy prey to the destroyer. It has drained tears enough to make a sea, expended treasure enough to exhaust Golconda, shed blood enough to redden the waves of every ocean, and wrung out wailing enough to make a chorus to the lamentations of the under world. Some of the mightiest intellects, some of the most generous natures, some of the happiest homes, some of the noblest specimens of man, it has blighted and crushed, and buried in squalid wretchedness. It has supplied every jail, and penitentiary, and almshouse, and charity hospital in the world with tenants. It has sent forth beggars on every street, and flooded every city with beastiality and crime. And it has, perhaps, done more towards bringing earth and hell together, than any one other form of vice. Could we but dry up this one moral ulcer, and sweep away forever all the results of this one form of sin, we would hardly need such things as prisons, asylums, charity houses, or police. The children of haggard want would sit in the halls of plenty. The tears of orphanage and widowhood, and disappointed hope, would dwindle in a goodly measure. Disease would be robbed of much of its power. The clouds would vanish from ten thousand afflicted homes. And peace breathe its fragrance on the world, almost as if the day of its redemption had come.

Now for any man, in any way, to give his sanction and endorsement to such a dreadful vice, is a sin, and one which is enhanced in proportion to the official or social importance and dignity of him who does it. It is a sin for any man to drink to intoxication, no matter when or where; it is a guilty unmanning of himself; but it is a special and greater sin for one in high station, or much concerned in giving tone to public opinion. And for an intoxicated man to go to God's altar with the fumes and clouds of this crime upon him, is an abomination which cries unto heaven. Nadab and Abihu, it appears, did this, and hence their awful end. Wherever there is sin, God's anger burns; but fiercest of all does it burn about his holy altar, and upon those who venture to pollute his service with unholy breath or unsteady hands.

But, although drunkenness was most likely *the root* of Nadab and Abihu's offending, it was not *the body* of their crime. If the effects of alcoholic stimulation went no further than to cloud the mind and stupefy the natural senses of those who indulge in it, it would not be so bad. The great mischief is, that, as it clouds the moral nature, it kindles all the bad passions into redoubled activity. It not only enfeebles and expels all impulses of good, but it quickens and enthrones every latent evil, and fits a man for the ready performance of any vile and sacrilegious deed. If these men had not been first " set on fire of hell" by excessive indulgence in drink, they would never perhaps have been driven to the daring impiety which cost them their lives. But intoxication let the demon in, and when he was once admitted, the way was open for them to trample upon the holiest institutes of God, and they went headlong to their ruin.

The head and front of the sin of these men, as I understand it, was the presumptuous substitution of a will-worship of their own, in defiance of what God had appointed. There is a constant tendency in our nature, to attempt to improve on what God has arranged for the good of man, and to engraft human inventions upon Divine institutions. Sin is ever sewing together fig-leaves to hide the shame of its nakedness. It was not enough for the Hebrew camp to have the visible symbol of the Divine presence in a pillar of alternate cloud and fire, they must needs have a golden calf in addition. Naaman is offended at the simple direction to go wash in the Jordan, and wants the prophet to come forth and strike his hand over the leprosy. Peter is not satisfied that Christ proposes to wash his feet, he wishes his hands and head included. It is not sufficient for the Pharisee to fast at the appointed times only, he will make the matter much better, and set apart three days every week for abstinence. Puseyism is not satisfied with the simple word of God, it must instal tradition by its side. Popery is not content with the invisible rule of Jesus in the heart, it must set up a lordly hierarchy to give reality to Christ's dominion, and to act as his visible vicar in the government of men. The two sacraments of God are quite too few for human wants, and great councils must be called to fabricate five more. And so these heated sons of Aaron were not content to abide by the ordinances which the Lord appointed, but must needs arrange matters to suit themselves. In three points did they offend—first, in *the time;* second, in *the manner;* and third, in *the matter* of the service which they undertook. It was the prerogative of Moses or Aaron to say when their services were needed; but they went precipitately to work, without waiting for instructions, or asking for directions. It was for the high-priest alone to go in before the Lord and offer incense at the mercy-seat; but they wickedly encroached upon his functions, and went in themselves. Never more than *one* priest was to officiate in burning incense at the same time; but they both *together* entered upon a service which did not belong to either. These things in themselves evince a very high-handed disregard of Divine order. But the great burden of their sin rested in *the matter* of the service. They "*offered strange fire before the Lord, which he commanded them not.*"

All the fire used in the services of the Hebrew ritual was *holy fire*. It came from heaven. It was kindled by the Lord himself. Its origin is given in the last verse of the preceding chapter. "And there came a fire out from before the Lord, and consumed upon the altar the burnt-offering." Special statutes had also been given for its careful preservation. In the sixth chapter, it was said, "The fire upon the altar shall be burning in it, it shall not be put out; and the priest shall burn wood on it every morning. The fire shall ever be burning upon the altar; it shall never go out." When subsequently lost in the wars of Saul and David, it was restored at the dedication of the temple, in the same manner that it had been originally given. It was doubtless from these manifestations of God in fire, that many things found scattered through the heathen world took their rise. It was this Divine and ever-burning fire in the Jewish worship, that led Zoroaster and the Magi to inculcate such holy reverence for fire, which was said to come from heaven and to be the emblem of God. To the same source may we trace the sacred fires of the Greeks, and the vestal lamps of the Romans. Indeed, all the religious rites of heathenism are but relics of a primitive revelation, or the distorted echoes of the voice of Jehovah to the Jews at Mount Sinai. They are just so many collateral proofs of the truth of these records. *Vesta* is a Latin word, derived from, and corresponding to, the Greek *Hestia*, which is evidently from the Hebrew word *Esh*, which means *fire*. And thus, through the vestal temples of Rome, and the sacred hearths of Greece, and the burning altars of Persia, we get back to the true Divine fire, which came out from God at the consecration of Aaron, and burned unceasingly on the altars of Israel. No incense was acceptable to God, but that which arose from coals of this holy fire. Jehovah will honor no devotion but that which he inspires. The censer was first to be filled with "burning coals of fire from off the altar before the Lord." Such was God's requirement. But Nadab and Abihu paid no regard to it. With their minds clouded, stupefied, and rendered reckless by "strong drink," they did not distinguish "between holy and unholy—unclean and clean." It was a wicked presumption in them to go, of their own accord, to offer incense at all; but it was an unpardonable profanation, when they did undertake it, not to be regardful of the appropriate materials. They "offered *strange fire*"—common fire—fire wholly foreign to the fire which God had kindled for such purposes. They thus obtruded what was profane into what was holy, desecrated God's ritual, cast contempt upon his institutions, put their own will-worship above his sacred regulations, and thus called down upon themselves a judgment which made all Israel tremble. They despised the sacred fire, and in return "there went out fire from the Lord, and devoured them, and they died before the Lord."

FALL OF NADAB AND ABIHU. 187

Let us now, *in the second place*, consider some of the implications, surroundings, and foreshadowings of this sad occurrence.

When I read the account of the sin of Aaron's sons at the organization of the old economy, my mind at once passes down to the organization of the Christian system, and to the conduct of some of Christ's sons under the Gospel dispensation. From the history of the old, I descend to the history of the new; and find so complete a correspondence, that I am constrained to take the one as a type of the other. The shadows of the future were linked in with the facts of the past.

Scarcely had Christianity been constituted, until we find a foreign and fitful spirit insinuating itself into the operations of those into whose charge its earthly services had been given. Paul noticed it already in his day. "There shall come a falling away," said he, "and that man of sin be revealed, the son of perdition, who opposeth and exalteth himself above all that is called God, or that is worshipped. For the mystery of iniquity doth already work." John also directed attention to it, saying, "this is that spirit of Antichrist, whereof ye have heard that it should come; and even now already it is in the world." The grass had hardly grown upon the graves of the apostles, until the reckless doings of spiritual intoxication gradually altered the primitive simplicities of the Gospel, usurped the prerogatives of Jesus the High-priest, mingled the inventions of men with the appointments of God, and introduced strange fire into the holy tabernacle of the Lord God Almighty.

Looking back upon the history of the Church, as

it first went forth under its sublime inauguration to evangelize the nations, the first thing that strikes us is the gradual uprising, from the level of a common priesthood, of a lordly power in the hands of bishops, stealthily concentrating upon Metropolitans, then upon Patriarchs, and finally upon one supreme Pontiff, who, surrounded with his conclave of advisers, claims to have the keys of heaven, to open and shut, and go in and out, as to him may seem good. I look upon his magisterial assumptions, trampling God's Bible under his feet, arrogating to himself all earthly power, arraying himself in the attributes and titles of Jesus, instituting sacraments, and ordaining dogmas of belief which God has not commanded, and undertaking with his heathen pomp to mediate between earth and heaven, — I consider the nature of his proceedings, the elements of his assumptions, the spirit that underlies all his doings, — I analyze his whole official conduct, and reduce it to its principles, — and when the whole thing is sifted, I find it to be nothing but a re-enactment of drunken Nadab, supplanting Aaron, taking the high-priesthood upon himself, and offering strange fire in the tabernacle of the Lord.

Along with pontifical power, came in great doctrinal and moral corruption. The one was a part of the other. They were developed together. They were brothers. As the Church grew, some became Judaizers, and made the first move toward the corruption of the simplicities of the Gospel. Heathen men were brought in without a complete abjuration of all their heathen tastes and ideas. Gnosticism was the result, a kind of eclectic philosophico-religious system, weaving together all sorts of speculations, and wrapping itself around the very heart of the Church. Mediæval religion, with its denunciations of natural relations, its abnegations, monkery, priestly orders, saint-worship, superstition, auricular confession, indulgences, false works, and obscurations of the great Gospel doctrine of justification by faith, was the natural fruit of gnosticism. Penances, masses, priestly absolutions, purgatorial expiations, the mediation of clergy and saints, celibacy, and outward ceremony, were obtruded into the place of repentance, faith, charity, and obedience to Christ's own word. Bishops retired from the pulpits to sit as spiritual lords, superior to all the kings of earth; the virgin Mary was installed as the world's mediator; earthly priests assumed the work of intercession, and undertook to forgive and license crime for a price; the Church was driven to the wilderness; the vomit of hell was upon the robes of Christ's affianced Bride; another Abihu in his drunkenness had entered the holy place, and was offering strange fire before the Lord.

And the thing that hath been, is the thing that is. Philosophy still has its additions to make to the word of God. Heathenish pomp still moves to lift itself up in our temples. Human reason is still at work to devise ways to worship and please God which he has not commanded. Men are still found who claim authority to perform offices for the souls of others, which belong only to our great High-priest in heaven. Thousands there are who flatter themselves that they are doing great things in their worship, though the spirit that is in them is not at all the Spirit of Christ. Inflated Nadabs and Abihus are everywhere seizing hold of sacred utensils, and rushing unbidden into the holy place, and offering strange fire in the tabernacle of God.

But, it shall not always be so. There is a price annexed to all these usurpations and irregularities with regard to holy things. God has magnified his word above all his name; and he that adds to, or takes from it, has his reward specified, and his portion reserved for him. Nadab and Abihu were suddenly and miraculously cut off in the midst of their sin; and so shall it be at last with all the confederates in usurpation and wrong, whether secular or ecclesiastical. *Fire from the Lord shall slay them.* "Jesus shall be revealed from heaven with his mighty angels, in flaming fire taking vengeance on them that know not God, and that obey not the Gospel." So it is written, and so it shall be. In whatever the Man of sin may consist, the Lord shall destroy him with the appearance of his own presence. The arrogant beast shall be smitten, and his body given to the burning flame. Great Babylon, that mother of harlotry and den of uncleanness, shall be "remembered before God, to give to her the cup of the wine of the fierceness of his wrath." "In one day shall her plagues come, death, and sorrow, and famine; and she shall be burned with fire." As to the adherents of antichrist, "their flesh shall consume away while they stand upon their feet; and their eyes shall consume away in their sockets; and their tongue shall consume away in their mouth; and great tumult from the Lord shall be among them." And some of these days, when no one is at all expecting it, the red lightnings shall flash out from the opening heavens, and lay every Nadab and Abihu dead from one end of the earth to the other. And the congregation of God's Israel "shall go forth, and look upon the carcasses of the men that have transgressed; for their worm shall not die, neither shall their fire be quenched; and they shall be an abhorring to all flesh."

An important feature connected with the occurrence narrated in the text, is Aaron's relation to it. Nadab and Abihu were his children—his elder sons. We can hardly conceive of anything more trying and painful to a father's heart, than to see his sons come to such an end. Ye that are parents, imagine yourselves in his place, and think of the awfulness of the blow which it would have been to you. Before his eyes, and with unmistakeable certainty, his two boys at once sink for ever under the curse of God. How do you suppose he felt, as he gazed upon their dead bodies, lying at the foot of the incense altar, smote down by an angry Lord, with not one lingering ray of hope left to comfort a father's heart in his bereavement? Yet, it is written, *"Aaron held his peace."* He knew that it was the Lord's doing; that it was done in the just vindication of the Divine holiness and glory; that it was all richly deserved; and though it carried off his two first-born sons to everlasting death, he "held his peace." He felt it, as any father would have felt it; but the honor and glory of God was to him more precious and valuable than child or friend, and he did not dare to complain or lament when Jehovah's holy law took off his boys. One look at God exalted and glorified, was a sufficient cure for all his natural anguish.

Serious people sometimes wonder how it shall be at the last day,—how godly parents shall be able to bear the sight of their Christless children given over to everlasting death; whether the knowledge or sight of near and beloved relatives in perdition will not interrupt and destroy the peace of heaven. But, if such persons would reason upon the subject from a stand-point higher than the mere sympathies of nature, they would have less trouble concerning it. Aaron looking upon his slain sons, is a picture of how it shall be. When God's ultimate judgments shall go into effect, their justice shall be so conspicuous, and the goodness and glory of God in them shall be so luminous and manifest, that it will not be in the power of any ransomed soul to think of demurring, or indulging one tearful regret. When we come to see things in the light of heaven, every enemy of God will appear so essentially an enemy to ourselves and our peace, that, however otherwise related to us, we will be glad to see them shut up in the dreadful prison-house for ever and for ever. God's dealings with the finally impenitent will be so necessary, so just, so essential to his holy government, yea so good, that not one ransomed soul shall dare, for an instant, to wish it otherwise. When he who died to save them shall once mark them out for perdition, and his great loving heart is brought to say, Let them go down to everlasting death, "*Amen,*" shall be the response dictated by every conscience and every heart. We may sometimes feel now that such a state of things would be impossible. The mother looks upon the boy she bore and nourished on her breast, and says, to see that boy go down to hopeless ruin would change all heaven's glories into bitterness for me. The wife thinks of the partner of her life, and supposes she could not exist if she were to see him taken from her and buried in that grave which knows no resurrection. The fond father yearns over the objects of his tender care, and thinks it would render Paradise a place of everlasting tears to know that those loved ones had been shut up with the devil and his angels. But all such imaginings are erroneous exaltations of earthly and fleshly relationships above the principles of eternal justice. What are domestic ties and sympathies in comparison with the glorious will of our blessed Lord? Jesus says, "He that loveth father or mother more than me, is not worthy of me: and he that loveth son or daughter more than me, is not worthy of me." Every saint is fully wrapped up in the righteousness, wisdom, and goodness of his Lord. Everything that God does carries the heart of the ransomed one so completely with it, and so overwhelms and swallows up all other affections, that they are as utter nothing. Nadab and Abihu may die for ever under Aaron's very eyes, and yet God's honor and glory in it leave him not a tear to shed, and not a word of lamentation to utter.

But Aaron was high-priest of Israel, as well as father to the slain. In this view his silent and tearless submission gathers additional interest. As his priestly duties went on unhindered by any regrets and pains over the fall of his sons; so is it with our great High-priest in heaven. With all the defections of some of his children here, and with all the deep infliction which it is calculated to produce in his heart, the mitre is never once lifted from his brow, and not a single break does it ever occasion in the holy services of his priestly office. Many a pious heart has been saddened, and sickened almost unto death, over the calamities that have befallen the camp of the Lord in the shape of apostasies, false doctrine, unholy living, and reckless usurpation. Who among us, that could not tell the story of many a heart-rending fall in the Church of God! More than once have I seen the young man, very zealous for Jehovah, and singled out by his friends as a model of virtue and piety, gradually relax his fervor, and lessen his activity, and discontinue his attentions to duty, until the den of the gambler took the place of the prayer-meeting, the cup of the drunkard the cup of the Lord, and the lewd song of the libertine that of the Psalms of Zion. More than once have I seen the man in affluent prosperity a great patron of the Church, prompt in his place in all the services of the sanctuary, and esteemed as one of Israel's elders; but when reverses and bankruptcy came, I have seen him turn aside to walk in the ways of the ungodly, the forger, the counterfeiter, the robber, and even the ribald blasphemer. Many a time have I seen the poor man in his daily toil, seemingly walking humbly with his God, and attentive to the things that relate to heavenly treasures; but when the tide of fortune came and gave him riches, or advanced him to places of influence and distinction, he forgot his Church and pious associations, and drifted away into pride like Lucifer's, or into covetousness as niggardly as Shylock's. I have seen men of the loudest professions; yea, men ordained to stand as watchmen on Zion's walls, secretly dallying with the demon of vicious appetite, until they became the reeling sport of boys upon the street, the shame of their denomination, and the tenants of ignoble graves. And history tells again and again of men whose heads reached unto the clouds, who in an unguarded hour came down, like some tall pine of the forest which makes the wilderness howl in its fall; of impious hands touched to the holy vessels of God's sanctuary; of false incense burned in the holy place, until the very lamps and stars were hid, and the very house of salvation made a den of robbery and death. But with all these deep wounds inflicted on the Savior's heart, *his intercessions never stop.* The duties of his priesthood go calmly on. He still remains the active friend and helper of the penitent, the ceaseless Advocate of his true people, the meek and attentive Savior of all who come unto him.

One thought more, and I will close this discourse. Though Nadab and Abihu assumed Aaron's place and prerogatives, Aaron was still the only high-priest. Though they usurped his rights, they could not perform his work. No one could receive reconciliation to God through their services. Though the Pope presumes to occupy Christ's place, and assumes to himself Christ's titles and powers, he does not therefore become Christ, or succeed in doing Christ's work. The priest may pronounce the words of absolution, but they are not therefore forgiveness of sins. He may agree to take a soul safe to heaven, but his agreement avails nothing as to the security of that soul. Heretics may put falsehood in the place of God's truth, but it is no less falsehood because it is so sacredly invested. Let who will undertake to fill Christ's offices, he is still the only Savior. Men may confess, and say prayers, and hear masses, and make pilgrimages, and endure fastings, and hire priests, and commit catechisms, and take veils, and make vows; but, unless they come with an humble spirit directly to the Lord Jesus himself, and rest themselves in simple penitence and faith upon him, they take for priests those who are not priests. Popes may carry keys, and say they are the keys of heaven; but when they come to try them, they will not fit Jehovah's locks, or throw open the everlasting doors. Let popes, and priests, and usurping innovators, make what pretence they please; Jesus says: "I HAVE THE KEYS OF HELL AND OF DEATH." *I am "he that openeth, and no man shutteth; and shutteth, and no man openeth."* And if Jesus has the keys, we know that no one else has them. They who think differently, do but dream, as drunken Nadab and Abihu; and all their will-worship shall only call forth the speedier and more awful death. *Jesus is the Priest;* and no priesthood will avail but his. He IS THE PRIEST, in spite of all invasions of his prerogatives and rights. There is no Virgin Mary, no earthly vicar, no decrees of the Church, and no one, however called or constituted, that can ever fill the place of Him whom God hath made "The Apostle and High-priest of our profession."

> None but Jesus
> Can do helpless sinners good.

Would you come to the joys of forgiveness and eternal life, let no devices of men or spirits ever draw your soul away from God's own Anointed.

> Look to Jesus —
> **Mercy flows through Him alone.**

ELEVENTH LECTURE.

THE CLEAN AND UNCLEAN.

LEV. CHAP. XI.

This chapter brings us to the third grand division of this book. We have had the offerings and the priests—the remedy provided for sin. We are now to have an exhibition of sin itself. We have been shown the way of cure; the next step is to open to us the disease, that we may be impelled to apply the means of relief.

This is not the human method. Man would have considered the disease first. But God's ways are not as our ways. To make known to man the dreadfulness of his spiritual condition, except in connection with a way of salvation already provided, would drive only to despair. God, therefore, constitutes the Physician, before giving a full view of the disorder for which he is needed. The feast is first made ready, and then measures are taken to move and bring in the guests. Christ went through all the great facts of his mediatorial work, before the Spirit was sent to convince of sin, righteousness and judgment. Nor is it possible for us to have a right understanding of sin, except in the light which beams forth from Calvary.

Great surprise and wonder have been expressed by some learned men, at the profound acquaintance with the animal kingdom exhibited in this chapter. Our greatest men of modern science have penetrated no deeper into natural history than the author of these laws. Leibnitz, and Buffon, and Cuvier, and Erxleben, and Humboldt, have been unable to make any material advances upon the classifications and distinctions, in the nature, habits, and qualities of animals, here given long before mere human science, in these departments, was born. And those may well wonder, who allow no higher wisdom in these laws than that of mere man. The fact is, that these Mosaic institutes all have upon them such distinct traces of the hand and mind of God, that it becomes the height of folly to refer them to the mere ingenuity of man. And I will here say, what I truly believe, that it requires vastly more credulity to be an infidel, or so-called free-thinker, than to be a devout Christian believer. I am perfectly satisfied, that people act more against the dictates of plain reason and common sense, in referring the profound science of the Pentateuch to the mere skill and attainments of Moses, than we do in tracing them to that Divine Wisdom which made the world, and fashioned the creatures who people it. It is no evidence of a great or investigating mind to discredit the witnesses which God has given of Himself. Admit that these regulations are divine in their source, and the wonder ceases — the miracle is explained; for he who created the beasts, birds, fishes, reptiles and insects which inhabit the earth, knew exactly how to classify them, and to prescribe concerning their nature Where, but from God, Moses got such wisdom, can never be explained.

This division of animated nature into clean and unclean, as all the rest of these Mosaic institutes, is,

THE CLEAN AND UNCLEAN. 199

of course, to be taken typically. It had direct and natural reasons, but those were not the chief. Some of the forbidden creatures are really not unclean or unfit for food, but nearly as good as some which were permitted to be used. This is not generally true, or to any very great extent; but the simple fact that an animal is proscribed in these laws as unclean, does not necessarily imply that it is in its nature unfit to be eaten, or of a detestable character. All that God has made is good, and embodies divine wisdom and thought. The prohibition is ceremonial. It is an arrangement somewhat arbitrary, perhaps, meant to meet national and religious purposes. The leading intent is typical and moral. The grand aim is to imbue the mind with an idea of moral distinctions; whilst the interdiction is conformed as near as may be needful to the nature and habits of the creatures interdicted.

There is, then, a mingling in these laws of several aims or ideas, each of which deserves attention, and to an exhibition of which I propose to devote this discourse.

I. I find in this chapter a system of wholesome dietetics. All the animals here pronounced clean, are the most valuable, nutritious and wholesome of creatures for human food. It does not follow that none among those forbidden are good for food; but I wish to say, that it is certain, all the animals here called "clean" are the best. Science, and the common sense of mankind, have decided, that the grain-eating and ruminative animals, which divide the hoof and chew the cud, are altogether the most healthful and delightful for the table. The hog, which, under this enumeration, is only half clean, is not near so good an article for food, as the sheep, the cow, the deer, and animals of that class. All physicians tell us so, and facts and experience demonstrate their correctness. Swine's flesh is specially unwholesome in warm climates, predisposing its consumers to all sorts of cutaneous, scorbutic, leprous diseases. I have no doubt that many maladies prevalent among us take their type, if not their origin, from a too free use of this sort of food. It is surprising, when we come to think of it, how the flesh or fat of the hog is mixed up with the great mass of the dishes that come upon our tables. It would, perhaps, be better for us, if it were not so. It is said of the Jews, who religiously abstain from swine's flesh, that in time of epidemic plague or pestilence, they never suffer to the same extent with their swine-eating neighbors. I cannot vouch for the truth of the remark; but I find it announced with confidence. This is in the case of but one class of animals. An examination throughout will show, that the nutriment afforded by the flesh of animals interdicted in this old ceremonial law, is less in quantity, inferior in quality, and more favorable to the production of scrofulous and inflammatory complaints, than any included in the list of permitted meats. It was, therefore, a great mercy in God, in those days of inexperience and exposure, so to frame his legislation as to protect his people against the use of what would have been deleterious. This was not the great, but only an incidental, intention of the enactment; showing, however, in what minute details and collateral bearings the hand of God is concerned for the good of those who obey him. This law is no longer binding upon us, as a religious appointment. Christ has entirely superseded it in this respect. But it may still serve as a guide to our science, and is worthy of careful consideration in connection with dietetics and hygiene.

II. A second, and somewhat more direct aim of these arrangements, looked to the keeping of the Hebrews entirely distinct from all other people. They were to be the light and truth-bearing nation among the families of man. They were elected to perpetuate a knowledge of the true God; and, by their peculiar training, to prepare the way for Christ and Christianity. To fulfil this mission, they needed to be strongly fenced in, and barricaded against the subtle inroads of idolatry. And it was, in part, to effect this segregation of the Jewish people, that this system of religious dietetics was instituted. Nothing more effectual could be desired to keep one people distinct from another. It causes the difference between them to be ever present to the mind, touching, as it does, at so many points of social and every-day contact; and it is therefore far more powerful in its results, as a rule of distinction, than any difference in doctrine, worship or morals, which men could entertain. Kitto says, that when in Asia, he had almost daily occasion to be convinced of the incalculable efficacy of such distinctions in keeping men apart from strangers. A Mahomedan, for instance, might be kind, liberal, indulgent; but the recurrence of a meal, or any eating, threw him back upon his own distinctive practices and habits, reminding him that you were an unclean person, and that his own purity was endangered by contact with you. Your own perception of this feeling in him is not to you less painful and discouraging to intercourse, than its existence is to him who entertains it. It is a mutual repulsion continually operating; and its effect may be estimated from the fact, that no nation, in which a distinction of meats was rigidly enforced as a part of a religious system, has ever changed its religion. It was utterly impossible for the Jews to observe the inculcations of this chapter and be at all familiar in their association with surrounding nations. Animals of the ox kind were sacred to the Egyptians, and were never slaughtered for food; whilst they made free use of others here pronounced unclean. The Phœnicians or Canaanites ate swine's flesh, and even dogs, as well as other animals which the Jews were forbidden to touch. The Arabs ate the camel as common food, the hare, the jerboa, all of which are specified or included in the Mosaic prohibitions. This chapter was therefore a wall of exclusion to the Jews, separating between them and all other people, which has withstood all the wastes and changes of more than three thousand years.

III. A still further and more direct intent of these religious dietetics was, to train the understanding to the perception of moral distinctions — to engrave upon the mind an idea of holiness. Indeed, this was one of the leading objects of the entire ceremonial law. We are sometimes tempted to regard these ancient rites as puerile and foolish; but it is because we do not consider the relation they sustain to what we now think so much better and more rational. There are islands in the sea which would not exist, but for the coral reefs upon which they rest; and so there would be no Christianity without these ceremonial regulations, which, by small beginnings, laid in the human mind the foundations upon which all our Christian convictions have been wrought out. Geologists tell us, that the physical world is composed of various layers, one on the other, from a deep granite base up to the fertile mould which furnishes us food while we live, and graves when we are dead. It is much the same in the moral and religious world. It has been brought forth by degrees. As there have been many geologic eras, so there have been various religious dispensations, each one furnishing the basis for the next succeeding. Each of these successive dispensations furnished a distinct stratum upon which the following one was built. The last could not exist without the first. Each one is a part of the grand whole. And had it not been for these Jewish ceremonies, our moral and religious ideas would perhaps be worse and more confused than those of Turks or depraved Hindoos. The broad sunlight cannot be let in upon the tender eyes of infancy at once. It must at first be veiled and shaded until the powers of vision strengthen and develop. It must be let in by degrees, or the infant shall never be able to see at all. And so it has been in the history of God's dealings with man as a race. It was only by the slow and regular, and progressive gradations of types, ordinances, and veiled prophecies, and outward miracles, that the world has come by that spiritual enlightenment and moral understanding which now distinguish the Christian nations.

Connecting this chapter with the laws concerning offerings and priests, we can easily see how the whole would operate in begetting and establishing the idea of purity and holiness. Dividing off all animated nature into clean and unclean, some would be regarded as better and purer than others. Of this pure kind only, could be taken for sacrifices. And even of the better kind, only the purest and most spotless individuals were to be selected. The sacrificial victim would hence appear very widely separated from the common herd of living creatures, and very clean and good. A thoroughly cleansed and consecrated officer was then to take it in charge, and wash both it and himself before it could come upon the altar. And when the presentation was to be made to the Lord in the most holy place, only the pure blood, in a golden and consecrated bowl, could be brought, and even that with great fear and trembling. Thus, from the clean beast, and the cleaner priest, and the still further cleansing of both, and the most holy place which could be approached only by so holy a personage with such sacred circumspection, the worshipper was taught the idea of holiness, the intense purity of his God, and the necessity of holiness in order to come into his favor. Each additional particular was so ordered as to reflect purity and sanctity on all the rest, converging ray upon ray to bring out in luminous prominence the great conception of Holiness. Apart from these ancient services, the world knows not what holiness is. Ask a man, who has even enjoyed the clear light of the Gospel, *What is holiness?* and it will be impossible for him to give any clear view of it without recurring, in some shape, to these ceremonial regulations, by which the idea itself was generated and formed. It is an abstract quality which has no place in the thoughts of man, except as derived from the outward separations, washings, and consecrations of this ritual. It is said, that "there is demonstrative evidence of the fact, that the idea of perfect moral purity, as connected with the idea of God, is now, and always has been, the same which was originated and conveyed to the minds of the Jews by the machinery of the Levitical dispensation." It is certain that the Hebrew word translated *holy*, was used to express the idea of sanctity as presented in the tabernacle service. It is a predicate of physical purity and cleanness. Hence it was used to signify separation, consecration, of higher qualities than the common multitude, the state of devotion to sacred purposes, and ultimately moral purity. The Greek word for holy, when received into the New Testament, took a meaning which was from the Hebrews, and not from the Greeks. Even our Saxon word *holy*, in Christian language, drops for the most part its old signification of *entireness*, and takes mainly the Jewish idea of cleanness and sanctity. Nor do I know of any word, in any language, ancient or modern, to convey the Scriptural conception of holiness, without first borrowing that meaning from the Jews and the old ceremonial system. The fact is, that the religious world has derived its idea of moral purity from the Mosaic rites. It was part of their great office to teach mankind moral distinctions, and to open the human understanding and conscience to the idea of sanctity.

IV. Connected with this, then, was the still further intent of these laws to give a picture of sin. We here have the finger of God, pointing out on the great map of living creation, the natural and material symbols of depravity. The various kinds of unclean animals are just so many living hieroglyphics, setting forth the uncleanness of man.

You have often heard persons, in common discourse, speaking of the *beastliness* of vice. It is an apt comparison; but it is exactly that which God himself has made in these laws. The combined characteristics of the creatures here declared unclean, furnish an exact exhibition of what sin is. They constitute a living mirror in which the sinner may look at himself.

In the first place he is unclean, filthy, disagreeable, noxious. There may be some good qualities, as there were in many of the unclean creatures; but, upon the whole, he is unclean. Impurity is upon him. He is unfit for holy association, or to come acceptably before God. As Eliphaz, the Temanite, once said, "abominable and filthy is man." "They are altogether become filthy," says the Psalmist. And whoever the sinner may be, he is in the eye of God, and the true people of God, an unclean person.

In the next place, he is brutish. His character is typified by the vile and noxious of living things. He was originally made but a little lower than the angels; but he sinned by listening to a brute reptile, and he has been changed into its likeness. What is a brute? A thing without reason or conscience, which lives by mere impulse, and follows no law but its own animal promptings. And what are the effects of sin upon him in whom it reigns? It dethrones intellect and makes it the slave of mere impulse, nullifies the deductions of wisdom, stifles and overrides the conscience, and makes the man the servant of lust, living only for selfish gratification, and following only the dictates of the baser nature. Sin prostitutes everything angelic in man. It enslaves his spirit to the flesh, subordinates his intellect to his desires, and binds down the whole moral constitution, like another Mazeppa, upon the wild horse of passion. Whatever the sinner has in him more than an unclean brute, is led captive by what he has in common with the brute; so that he may well say with Agur, the son of Jakeh, "I am brutish." With all that can be urged in his favor, he is "altogether brutish."

A brute is a thing bent downward. It goes upon its hands. Its face is towards the ground. It never travels erect. And what is a slave of sin, but one whose eyes have been diverted from heaven, and whose absorbing attention is directed to what is earthy? Sin brings man down from contemplating the lofty things of God and eternity. It sets his affections on things below, instead of things above. It takes from his face the angelic look of innocence, and makes him drop his eyes in betrayal of the vile feelings that play in his hidden heart.

A brute is a creature destined to perish. Its spirit goeth downward. Its end is extinction. How like the sinner in his guilt! What hope has he for another world? "The fool and the brutish person *perish*," says the Psalmist. Sin dooms to eternal death. It puts out eventually every light of the sinner's being. It extinguishes all his proper life. It sinks him for ever. His end is symbolized by that of "the brute which perisheth."

But he is not only like what all brutes are in common, but also more or less like what the several kinds of unclean creatures are in particular. Sin is the ugliness and spitefulness of the camel; the burrowing, secretive, wily disposition of the coney, the rabbit, and the fox; the filthy sensuality of the hog; the stupid stubbornness of the ass; the voracious appetency of the dog, the wolf, the jackall, and hyena; the savage ferocity and blood thirstiness of the tiger, the panther, and the lion; the sluggishness of the sloth; the prowling shyness and cruelty of the cat; and the base treachery and mischievousness of multitudes of unclean creatures that roam in darkness. Sin, enthroned in the soul, is the eagle clutching innocence in his talons, and tearing out its heart with his bloody beak. It is the vulture, with his base taste, seeking out what is abominable, and gormandizing upon foul putrescence. It is the owl taking advantage of darkness to surprise its prey, hooting about the abodes of quietness, and shrinking away to hide from approaching light. It is the slimy fish that creeps among the mud, the poisonous snake watching in the grass, and the legged and scaly thing whose numerous tribes crawl on all the land and in all the sea. It is the abominable thing which God hateth.

There are many who make light of sin, and often esteem it very sweet. Let such study God's special symbols of it, and they will be led to view it in a different light. There is nothing in all the living world around us so loathsome, vile, hateful, dangerous, destructive, and abhorrent, but sin exceeds it. It is of all things the most hideous — an uncleanness which cannot be expressed — a filthiness so intense that God cannot look upon it with the least degree of allowance.

But it is just as abundant as it is hateful. The unclean creatures are as numerous and abounding as they are base. The air is full of them; the earth is alive with them; the ocean teems with innumerable kinds of them. They cover every mountain; they crowd every plain. The crevices of the rocks are filled with them; the deserts have them as

numerous as sands. The trees of the forests are
thick with them; every stream and fountain contains
them. They move about every street; they play in
every field. They are upon the most beautiful
flowers, and crawl within the most guarded enclo-
sures. They are in our houses; they come up upon
our tables; they creep into our very beds. They
are present in every climate. They may be seen at
all seasons. They are as wide-spread as the surface
of the world. They continue with all generations.
And as these unclean things abound, so does sin
abound; for they are God's natural types of sin.

And looking at the appointments of this chapter
as a mere remembrancer of sin, it seems to me very
remarkable. How impressive the arrangement! All
living nature, by a few simple words, at once
transmuted into a thousand tongues to remind and
warn of sin and uncleanness! The living monitor
would meet the devout Jew at every point, and call
to him in words of sacred admonition from every
direction. Sitting down to table, a fly alighting upon
the clean linen, would be a remembrancer that
unholiness is at hand, ready to mingle with all his
enjoyments. Opening his closet, the sight of a little
mouse would be the sign to him that evil is likely
to insinuate itself into the very devotions of secresy.
Looking out at his window, the passing of a camel,
or a dog, or a bird of prey, would be a memorial to
him to make a covenant with his eyes, and to guard
the approaches of uncleanness. Sitting down under
his vine or fig-tree, or going forth to gather a few
flowers, the little insects crawling on the leaves,
would be monitors of the presence of evil. Walking
out into the field, the snail in the path, the hare

starting in the thicket, the snake gliding through the grass, the lizard darting down the side of a log, or the coney looking out from among the pile of rocks, either would serve to recall the fact that Jehovah's eye is on him, and that he can have no fellowship with uncleanness. Approaching the silvery stream or the glassy lake, the frog leaping in from under his feet, the turtle jutting his foul head from the surface, the crooked eel making his way through the waters, and slimy things showing their presence in the marshes, each would have a voice, bidding him beware, and proclaiming uncleanness in all earth's purity. Ascending the mountain cliffs, the croak of the raven there, the rattle of the serpent among the leaves, the eagle darting down savagely from the summit, the track of the wolf upon the sand, or the den of the fox beneath his feet, would be a memorial to him, that all the heights of earthly exaltation are full of savageness, poison, filthiness, and deceit. Looking down upon the open plain, the vultures there contending over their foul food, the fish-hawk on hovering wing watching to dart upon his prey in the waters beneath, and the hoopoe flitting hither and thither in search of worms and ugly insects, would be a remembrancer of the base appetites and dispositions which work in fallen man, and against which he should keep guard. Coming homeward in the evening, the heavy hoot of the owl greeting him from the hills, and the vile bat flapping her greasy wings about his face, and the toad hopping in his path at his feet, and a thousand noxious insects buzzing through the air as he breathes, each would be a picture and sermon to him as to how thoroughly and at all times he is beset and enveloped with vileness and sin, endangering his hopes and peace. And even to us at this remote age, the great lesson still comes flashing upon us vivid and strong from this self-same law, that at home or abroad, asleep or awake, on land and on sea, in the heights above and in the depths beneath, everywhere and in every condition upon this earth, sin encompasses us, and swarms around us, and cleaves to us, and works in us.

Some object to such an account of man's moral condition. They would pronounce this picture quite too highly colored. But it is the picture which God himself gives in the hieroglyphics of his ancient ritual, and has announced in plain words in his Gospel. All these dark lines upon the living world of outward nature, have their counterpart in the moral world within. We may think it incredible that humanity should be so disordered and debased, or that uncleanness should so much abound; but that does not alter the facts. God knew what was in man, and what sort of creatures, and how many of them, he declared unclean. He knew exactly what sort of a picture all these living symbols put together would make. And with all, he solemnly said, *Let it be so.* "The heart of man is deceitful above all things, and desperately wicked; who can know it?" Iniquity is a "mystery." It is more than we can understand. It is an ocean which we are not able to fathom — a darkness which no light of this world can thoroughly illume. Look over the histories of war, tyranny, persecution, and butcheries of men, as they have stained the annals of every age; and see whether there is aught in the bloody doings of birds or beasts of prey to exceed it. Examine the records of lewdness, intemperance, and gluttonous debauchery, and say wherein the accounts fall below what we see in the nature or habits of the vilest of brute creatures. Survey the profaneness, the grovelling passions, the fierce enmities, the malicious spites, the base deceits, the carnal pollutions, and the ten thousand forms of vice which breathe like a sirocco over every clime of the populated world, and point out, if you can, in all the rounds of brute passions, anything to equal what has been seen in man.

And yet, what we see, and hear, and read of, bad as it is, is not the whole depth of human uncleanness. Not a thousandth part of the evil that is in the world is ever manifest to the outward beholder. History is mostly made up of recitals of sin, and wrongs, and wars, and feuds, and rebellions, and gigantic crimes; but there is a world upon which historians have not yet looked — a world in which man appears exactly what he is — a world far wider and deeper than the world without—a world in which all history is enacted before it becomes history — I mean *the hidden world of the heart*. Oh, what animosities, and murders, and envies, and jealousies, and adulteries, and uncleannesses, and dark thoughts of blood and death, exist there without ever once being suspected by the outward observer! We are sickened at every day's reports of open, uncontrolled, actual, villainy and crime. What, then, would this life look like, if we could just lift the cover, and see in addition all that is unseen and unheard! I have sometimes thought that when the day shall come for the all-knowing Lord to lay open every work with every secret thing, the histories of man would look like annals of hell and biographies of devils!

I do not say that there is no good in the world. There are clean as well as unclean. There always have been good and piety in the earth, and some virtuous ones among the base. Jehovah, in all ages, has been gathering to himself a people for his name, who shall shine as stars for ever and ever. And this law served the Jew as a remembrance of goodness and holiness, as well as sin and uncleanness. Going forth to his flocks grazing in the quiet pastures, those gentle creatures would speak to his mind of the clean and holy ones whom the Lord keeps as "the people of his pasture and the sheep of his hand." Beholding the wild goat amid solitary rocks, he would feel himself taught of hidden ones whom God keeps in the deep solitudes, and for whose safety he provides as for the wild goat on its precipices. The gazelle, amid the fragrant shrubs, walking at large amid earth's richest scenery, would tell of the beauty of holiness, and of chosen ones who walk in grace amid the thick showered blessings of an approving God. But, with all, there were more vile than clean. With all the good that is in the world, there is an awful pravity upon man in general, and upon unchristian men in particular. What saith the Scripture? "Their throat is an open sepulchre; with their tongues they have used deceit; the poison of asps is under their lips; their mouth is full of cursing and bitterness; their feet are swift to shed blood; destruction and misery are in their ways." (Rom. 3 : 13–16.)

My brethren, we have not escaped this uncleanness which has gone out over all the earth. "If any man say that he hath no sin he deceiveth himself, and the truth is not in him." We are members of a fallen and corrupt race. All God's dealings with us are such as to teach us that we are guilty in his sight But we are not left to despair. Along with the disclosure of our disease is the exhibition of an ample remedy. Sin abounds, but grace does much more abound. Our uncleanness is intense; but mercy holds out to us the means of complete and glorious deliverance. A fountain has been opened; and all we have to do is, to wash and be clean. The great God calls to us from the heavens, saying, "*I am the Lord your God, ye shall therefore sanctify yourselves, and ye shall be holy; for I am holy.*"

Nor can we be at a loss to ascertain what that sanctification or washing is. Ugly passions must be abjured as unclean. Swinish lusts must be crucified. Carnal loves of darkness and filth must be renounced. Those creeping and grovelling propensities which work so powerfully in fallen man, must be abandoned. That animal proneness must be laid aside for an uplifted look which fastens on the skies. That savage selfishness must be cast away as vile. That troop of unclean thoughts which infest the soul must be brushed out with abhorrence. The mere touch of what is defiling must be shrunk from with horror. And so must we compass the altar of Calvary, leaning on the head and trusting in the blood of the Lamb, until the Eternal king shall say, "It is enough; come up higher."

Sinner, wilt thou accept of these conditions, and fly to the refuge thus set before thee? Thy Savior once again knocks at the door of thy heart, saying, "*Wilt thou not be made clean?*" A blessed immortality hangs on the answer thou shalt give. "WILT THOU NOT BE MADE CLEAN?"

TWELFTH LECTURE.

BIRTH-SIN AND ITS DEVELOPMENTS.

LEV. CHAPTERS XII. XIII.

A POPULAR and eloquent living preacher has remarked of the first of these chapters, that "its chief value lies in the light it casts upon the Virgin Mary at the birth of our blessed Redeemer." To this observation I am not prepared to assent. This chapter is interesting to Christians as containing the law for the purifying of mothers, which the mother of Jesus so meekly obeyed when she brought the two doves as an offering in her poverty for a sacrifice unto the Lord; but "its chief value lies" in quite another direction. Its particular descriptions are not such as to allow much freedom of public comment, but they fill an important place in the typical system to which they belong.

The theme of the chapter is the same as that of the one preceding and the one following. The subject is *sin*, portrayed by symbols. In the division of the animals into clean and unclean, we had the nature of sin in its general character and outward manifestations. It is a brutalization of humanity. It has its type in all sorts of savage, noxious, vile, annoying creatures. But this chapter presents another and still more affecting phase of man's corruption.

Surveying those masses of sin and vileness which

hang about our world, touching the path and defiling the doings of every human being, as we saw in our last discourse, the question arises, Whence comes it? How are we to account for it? That some particular periods, nations, families, or individuals should be depraved and vicious, might perhaps be explained in peculiar outward circumstances. Bad education, bad government, bad religion, bad associations, begetting bad habits, might, in a measure account for it. But the records of inspiration and experience assure us that "*all* have sinned and come short," and that "if *any man* say he hath no sin, he deceiveth himself, and the truth is not in him." There is not a corner of the earth, nor a member of the race, which the great contamination has not touched. The soil of sin is upon every conscience, and its uncleanness is more or less in every heart. To what source or cause are we to refer this melancholy fact? It is useless to attribute it to errors in the structure of society; for society itself is the mere aggregate of human life, feelings, opinions, intercourse, agreement and doings. It is man that corrupts society, and not society that corrupts man. The one may react very powerfully upon the other, as we shall see hereafter; but the errors and corruptions in both must have a common seat and source. What is that seat? Where are we to find this prolific fountain? Penetrating to the moral signification of the twelfth chapter of Leviticus, we have the true answer.

Sin is not only a beastliness and grovelling brutality assumed or taken upon a man from without. It is a manifestation which comes from within. It is a corruption which cleaves to the nature, mingles with the very transmissions of life, and taints the vital forces as they descend from parent to child, from generation to generation. We are unclean, not only practically and by contact with a bad world, but we are innately impure. Man is a creature of wrong impulses, not only by education and association, for he would be the same if he were born in heaven. Uncleanness is upon the very seat of life, and attaches to every one of us from our very coming into the world. We were conceived in sin. We were shapen in iniquity. And it is just this that forms the real subject of this chapter. It is the type of the source and seat of human vileness.

The uncleanness here spoken of, is no more a real uncleanness, than that attributed to certain animals, in the preceding chapter. The whole regulation is ceremonial, and not at all binding upon us, (though a relic of it is still found in some of the churches, known by the name of "*The Churching of Women*"). It is an arbitrary law, made only for the time then present, as a figure of spiritual truths. Its great significance lies in its typical nature. And a more vivid and impressive picture can hardly be conceived. I am checked from entering particularly into it; but solemn and sacred allusions are suggested by it. It imposes a special legal disability upon woman, and so connects with the fact, that "the woman being deceived was in the transgression." (1 Tim. 2 : 24.) It is a vivid remembrancer of the occurrences in Eden. It tells us that we all have come of sinful mothers. It exhibits our very birth as involving uncleanness. It portrays defilement as the state in which we receive our being. For "who can bring a clean thing out of an unclean? Not one." (Job, 14 : 4.)

19

I therefore lay down this doctrine, "that all men who are naturally engendered, are conceived and born in sin; that is, they are all, from their mother's womb, full of evil desires and propensities;" and that this "is the fountain-head of all other or actual sins, such as evil thoughts, words, or deeds."

I am acquainted with the cavils which exist with reference to this doctrine. And the way some state it, I would not undertake to defend it. Some call it "*natural* depravity," and say that man is a sinner "*by nature.*" To say the least of this, it is a misapplication of terms. Nature is God's work; and God never made sin. No being ever came from his hands with a corrupt or wicked nature. He never made a devil or a sinner. And concupiscence and guilt, so far from being natural to man, are monstrous perversions and spoliations of nature. It is not *natural;* but, of all things, the most *unnatural.* God made man upright and good. And if people now have upon them a predisposition to sin, it must be traced to some other source than that of natural constitution. I will join with all heartiness in the expressions of abhorrence at the idea that a holy, just, and benevolent God should have created any being with a nature the inherent tendency of which is to sin. How, then, are we to solve the difficulty? If the Creator never constitutes any being with an evil nature, how is it that all men are born in corruption, and inclined to sin from their very birth? Some have tried to explain it by supposing a previous state of probation. But this solution is so far-fetched, and implies a punishment so wholly divorced from all consciousness of the sin that produced it, that it never has commanded serious belief. How, then,

BIRTH-SIN AND ITS DEVELOPMENTS 219

are we to get out of the difficulty? A very few words will clear up the matter to all right philosophy.

What is an individual human being as he now comes into existence? Is he a new creation, separate and distinct in himself? I say he is not. A modern man is not an original product of creative power. He is not now first created. He is only an outgrowth of one primal humanity which was created nearly six thousand years ago. He is an evolution from principles of life which were constituted in the garden of Eden. Humanity is a stream flowing from one original fountain. God never directly made more than one man and one woman; and all other men and women are but effluxes of that original creation. Nobody now is *created*, in any true sense of that word, but *begotten* and *born* of a creation made thousands of years ago. Any conception of humanity which differs from this, is physiologically and scripturally false. The creation of the first pair was a self-perpetuating creation; and therefore the *only* creation, as respects human existence. There is therefore a very important sense in which we were made in Adam. We are but repetitions of the first pair, according to laws which were located in them. We take our whole being, *body and soul*, from and through Adam. And there is no mere humanity but what has grown out of him. The whole race was once included in him. It is easy, therefore, to see, that whatever damage may have befallen human nature when yet in its parent root or fountain, must needs show itself more or less in all the branches and streams issuing from it. "Like begetteth like." As is the seed, so is the tree; and as is the tree, so is the fruit. "A corrupt tree cannot bring forth good fruit."

You may plant a good seed, and surround it with all the conditions necessary to a goodly plant; but it may put forth so eccentrically, or meet with some mishap in the incipient stages of its development, in consequence of which all its subsequent growth will be marred, and all its fruits give evidence of the adversities that befell it in the beginning. You may open a pure fountain, giving forth nothing but pure good water; yet, the issuing stream may touch upon poison, and take up turbid commixtures at its first departure from its source, and so carry and show pollution whithersoever it goes. And so it has been with humanity. It was created pure and good; but by that power of free choice, which necessarily belongs to a moral being, some of its first movements were eccentric and detrimental to its original qualities. It absorbed vileness at its very beginning. It was hurt when it was yet all in its germ. And hence all its subsequent developments have upon them the taint of that first mishap and contagion. It is worse in some lines than in others. The operations of Divine grace in the parent doubtless help to enfeeble it in the child. And if all men could be at once reclaimed to complete holiness, it would no doubt disappear altogether in the course of generations. But, as things are, it to some extent taints every one that is engendered and born of human kind.

Now it is just to this universal taint of human nature, derived from the defection of Adam, that the whole outgrowth of this word's iniquity is to be traced. By virtue of our relation to an infected parentage, we come into the world with more or less affinity for evil. There is an innate inclination to wrong. The presentation of the objects to which this proclivity leans, awakens those biases into activity. This awakening of the power of lust is what we call temptation. And when the force of temptation has once set the heart upon an object of base desire, and gained the consent of the will to it, the man moves toward evil, and actual sin is born. There is an innate taint or bias, the presentation to which of the objects of evil desire involuntarily excites lust; and from this has flown out the flood of evil which has deluged all the earth.

It would be easy to amplify these views by passages of Scripture, and to trace them in the impressive picture contained in the chapter before us; but I will detain you to make but one other remark in reference to the general subject. And that is, that this native taint that is upon humanity is not a mere venial defect, of no serious account in the eye of the divine law, but a thing so evil as to demand purgation by blood. It unfits for heaven just as much as actual sin. No being upon whom it is could ever be saved, except by the mediation of Jesus. It is that "sin of the world" which requires the Lamb of God to take away. The Jewish mother's uncleanness could only be removed by a lamb, or a pair of doves, offered as a burnt-offering; and even then, it continued for seven days — an entire period of time. And so this original inborn deformity and contamination of our nature, shall not be perfectly rooted out until the period of our appointed time has been completed — until our stay in this world has closed.

We pass now to the thirteenth chapter, in which we have something of a medical treatise, on the subject of leprosy. It is the oldest description extant of any disease. But it is not introduced into this ritual for medical purposes. There were other diseases in the Eastern world more painful, more fatal, more contagious, and equally afflictive; but nothing is said about them. This is specially singled out from all the ills of earth, and made the subject of particular regulations. You will observe that it was to be treated by the priest, not by the physician. It had peculiar disabilities connected with it. Its entire surroundings show that something more than ordinary attaches to it. It is dealt with in a way which cannot be accounted for in the nature of the disease itself. It is therefore to be viewed, like all the other provisions of this law, as a type. It is another parable of sin. It stands here as the illustration of the workings, developments, and effects of inborn depravity.

Sin is a corrupting and disorganizing disease, as well as a brutal degradation and hereditary uncleanness. It is a loathsome putrescence of the whole nature. It is a sickness of the whole head, and a faintness of the whole heart. Deliverance from it is called a cure and a healing, as well as a pardon. He who relieves us of it is called a Physician. It is a disturbance, corrosion, disorder, and cancerous fretting in all the composition of the man. And to signify and picture all this, is the real object of this chapter, and of all the laws respecting leprosy. The Jews called this disease "the finger of God"—"the stroke." In it, and the regulations concerning it, God has pointed out the most vivid and impressive exhibition of the nature and consequences of sin that has ever come under the contemplation of mortals. Under this view, then, let us study and apply it.

Notice its beginnings. Leprosy was, for the most part, hereditary. After doing its work in the parent it was very apt to break out in the child. Sin began in Adam, and having wrought nine hundred years in him, he died; but the taint of it was left in all who sprang from him. But leprosy was not always hereditary. Hence the necessity of a special symbol on the subject of innate depravity, such as we have just considered in the preceding chapter. The germ of all human sin is derived from our connection with a fallen parentage.

But leprosy, whether hereditary, or contracted by contagion or otherwise, began far within. Its seat is in the deepest interior of the body. It is often in the system as many as three or a dozen years before it shows itself. How exactly this describes sin! Nero and Caligula were once tender infants, apparently the very personifications of innocence. Who that saw their sweet slumbers upon the bosoms of their mothers, would ever have suspected, that in those gentle forms were latent seeds which finally developed into bloody butchery, and tyranny, and vice, at which the world for ages has stood amazed! Who that beheld Judas Iscariot in the duties of his evangelic mission among the citizens of Judea, would ever have suspected the treachery which lurked in his soul unknown even to himself! Who would have thought, that in the bold and daring Peter, when he volunteered to die for his master, there existed the root of those oaths and lies which broke from his lips in the porch of the high-priest's palace! And little do we know of those depths of deceit which we carry in ourselves, or to what enormities of crime we are liable any day to be driven. "Let

him that thinketh he standeth, take heed lest he fall."
The taint of leprosy is within, and nothing but
watchfulness and grace can keep it from breaking
out in all its corrosive and wasting power.

The first visible signs of leprosy are often very
minute, and inconsiderable, and not easily detected.
A small pustule or rising of the flesh — a little bright
red spot like that made by a puncture from a pin —
a very trifling eruption, indentation, or scaliness of
the skin—or some other very slight symptom, is usually the first sign which it gives of its presence.
And from these small beginnings the whole living
death of the leper is developed. How vivid the picture of the fact, that the worst and darkest iniquities
may grow out of the smallest beginnings! A look
of the eye, a desire of the heart, a thought of the
imagination, a touch of the hand, a single word of
compliance, is often the door of inlet to Satan and
all hell's troops. All the guilt that ever stained the
earth may be traced to *a look*—the admiring look of
Eve upon the forbidden fruit. No man can tell to
what an issue the smallest sins may lead. Take but
a brick from your pavement, and you have opened
the way for the loosening of them all. Bore but an
auger hole through the breast of a dam, or the bank
of a canal, and you have arranged for a breach that
may extend to the foundations, and carry the work
of years to ruin in a day. Start but a little stone
upon the precipice of the mountain, and other and
greater ones will follow it, until the hill smokes and
the valley trembles with the thunder of rolling rocks.
Touch but a spark to the fuse, and it will multiply
itself, until the very earth rends before it. Open but
one small artery in your arm, and you have done

enough to let in speedy death. Utter but one sinful word, and it may bring after it a train of consequences which will give your name to the court, and link your fame with infamy. Just start an ardent youth upon peccadilloes, and it is like starting a loose wagon on an inclined plane; there is no calculating where he will stop, or how awful is the ruin which awaits him. "Behold, how great a matter a little fire kindleth!"

Leprosy is also gradual in its development. It does not break out in its full violence at once. It works for a while unseen. Its first manifestations are so trifling, that one who did not understand it would consider it nothing at all. It is only by degrees, running through the course of years, that it transmutes its victim into a living embodiment of putrefaction and death. How exact the correspondence between type and antitype! No man is an outbreaking and confirmed villain at once. The devil did not become a devil in a day. Character, whether good or bad, is a growth. It will grow faster in some circumstances and in some persons than in others; but there always is gradation and progress from the less to the greater. If we were to trace the histories of delinquency and crime through which our brazen sinners have reached their eminence in guilt, we should be surprised to find in what a small way they began—how very slight were their first divergencies from rectitude—how very timid and restrained were their first experiments in wrong. Sin wrought in them long before it showed itself at all, and its first manifestations were of comparatively small account. But, having started in the way of evil, one easy transgression made it easier for the next; and so, by an ever increasing momentum, never once checked by repentance, they came to be the impersonations of vileness. An affection apparently lawful, excited by an unintentional curiosity, by little and little turns the mind upon some object of sensual desire; and this is the beginning of voluptuousness. Inquietude follows. Vague wishes form in the soul. Base adventures and familiarities ensue. And before the man is aware of it, a restless and fatal passion takes dominion of him, and he hurries on to the deepest infamy and the blackest hell. No man ever started out with the deliberate resolve, or even the remotest suspicion of becoming a drunkard. There is not a victim of rum in all our gangs of debauchees who at first ever dreamed of becoming the degraded object he now is. A little cheery indulgence because it was the fashion, or contributed to convivial enjoyment, or a little tippling for medicinal purposes, or to quicken the wits and raise the spirits on special occasions, is what laid the foundation of his ruin. And from these small beginnings, harmless in themselves, but serving to beget appetite and fixing into habit, there came that insatiable passion, which has made him a blear-eyed, foul-mouthed and disgusting wretch, a disgrace to his name, a pest to his neighborhood, a mill-stone on the neck of his family, and a blot upon the earth.

People are shocked, and hold up their hands in horror, at great and scandalous crimes; but they forget that these are only the necessary and easy sequences of little indulgences and sins of which they take no account. They forget that the bright spot and the little livid pustule are just as much the signs of leprosy as all the languor and putrescence which follow after. They need to be told, that these little scales and tumors are the things of which comes all the abominable corruption at which they show so much feeling of abhorrence. They need to be told, that there is a close interior brotherhood and cohesion between sins, and that he who takes one to his favor is at once beset with all the rest. David, looking where he should not have looked, was already far on the way to his adultery; and out of that, by a sort of necessary consequence, proceeded his murder of Uriah. Pharaoh the king, easily becomes Pharaoh the tyrant; and out of this, by natural consequence, proceeds one more step, and he is Pharaoh the defiant blasphemer. Judas becomes the money-lover, and thence by easy transition becomes his Lord's perfidious betrayer. The Cæsar who mingles in the strifes of petty warfare, will soon find no refuge left, but must also cross the Rubicon. The boy who disobeys his mother, is already far on his way to be the man who tramples his country's laws under his feet. The young man who loves the theatre, and the ball-room, and the conversations of the lewd and profane more than his books and his home, is already started with vigorous headway upon the track of prostitution, crime, and infamy. And the professed member of the Church who visits the beer-house and the gaming-table, and begins to feel religious duty irksome, is even now far down the rapids which make for the cataract of ruin. Any one sin, however small it may seem, is a seed and root for another. And by the same easy steps by which a man commits his first little sins, he may go on to the most gigantic iniquities. Sin is progressive; and if we give ourselves to it at all, there is no telling to what deeds of wickedness we may come.

Again, leprosy is in itself an exceedingly loathsome and offensive disorder — a kind of perpetual small-pox, only more deeply seated, and attended with more inward corruption. Every vein in every limb of a developed leper, runs down with putrid blood. His head is heavy, sick, and painful. His whole countenance is sallow, death-like, and disgusting. His hair hangs dry, lank and sapless on his blistered brow. The very nails on his bony fingers are discolored and tainted. His gait is slow, tottering and feeble. He is an object of abhorrence to every eye. He is a living parable of death! Nor is it otherwise with sin. It is a filthiness of the flesh and of the spirit — a tainted clog to all the currents of life — a degrading deformity and corruption of the whole man. A developed sinner is a being covered and pervaded with putrid uncleanness. As Isaiah describes the case, "From the sole of the foot even unto the head, there is no soundness in it; but wounds, and bruises, and putrefying sores, they have not been closed, neither bound up, neither molified with ointment." Every vital impulse is enfeebled, every sinew of the soul shrunk and corrupted, every spiritual activity palsied. The soul itself has become a fountain bursting out with corruption. The eye is sickly and vacant, reflecting no more the light of smiling heaven. The heart pulsates only with offensive humors. The hue of death is upon the entire nature. There is a sort of life; but it is clothed with all the uncleanness and putrescence of the grave. From such a soul God turns away his face, and cannot allow himself to look upon it. Words cannot tell how offensive it is to his pure eyes.

Some may think all this extravagance; but I have not gone one hair's-breadth beyond the plain statements of God's own word. Sin is a foulness which cannot be told. All the cancers, and leprosies, and consumptions, and scrofulas, and horrible diseases, and ugly deaths, and graveyard putrefactions, in the world, are but the outward effects and shadows of sin — the visible manifestations of the moral corruption that is in man. What then must it be in its principle and interior essence! Could the sinner but have his eyes opened to see, and feel, and know it, as it is known in heaven, he would abhor himself, and cry out in Bartimean earnestness, "Jesus, thou Son of David, have mercy on me!"

Again, leprosy, under this law, carried with it a most melancholy condemnation. A Jewish leper was not only horribly diseased, but also fearfully cursed in consequence of his disease. He was pronounced unclean by the law and by the priest. That alone cut him off from all the holy services, and from free communication with the congregation of his brethren. But it is the intensest of all uncleanness that is upon him, and he is doomed to a special affliction. The law says, "The leper in whom the plague is, his clothes shall be rent, and his head bare, and he shall put a covering on his upper lip, and shall cry, Unclean, unclean. All the days wherein the plague shall be in him he shall be defiled; he is unclean: he shall dwell alone; without the camp shall his habitation be." Had he a home? He must leave it. Had he friends? He must be wholly separated from them. Had he wife and children? they were henceforward to think of him as dead. Had he hopes and prospects of distinction and greatness on earth? all are suddenly and forever cut off. His joys all turn to mourning. His covering of honor is stripped off to give place to desolation. His lips are covered as shut to all friendly intercourse. He was like one cut off from the assembly of living men, lingering about the gates of death, and hanging about its door-posts, impatient for entrance there. Nobody thought of him any more with any love or favor. He had to dwell alone. He might come up and at a distance view the camp, but he could not approach, and not one would ever come near to him. With all the horribleness of his disease, it excited no sympathy, and loaded him with additional woes, themselves almost unbearable. Such is the type, and it is the same with the antitype. Every sinner is condemned as well as diseased; and condemned for the very reason that he is diseased. There is a sentence of uncleanness and exclusion upon him. He has no fellowship with the saints, and no share in the holy services of God's people. He is as one dead to all sacred joy, and all spiritual good. He may distantly gaze upon happy Israel, and their peaceful tents; but he cannot enter them, or partake of the blessings within. He is a spiritual outcast—a moral leper—unclean, and ready for the realms of everlasting banishment and death.

And yet, the picture is not quite complete. It remains to be said, that there was no earthly cure for leprosy. The prophet of God, by his miraculous power, could remove it; but no human power or skill could. It was beyond the reach of physician or priest. And so is it with sin. It is a consumption which cannot be cured — a cancer which cannot be extracted — a leprosy which cannot be cleansed — except by the direct power of divine grace. All the waters of Damascus — all the balm in Gilead — all the penance and suffering in the world, cannot remove it. Once in the system, God must purge it out, or it will remain there to fester and rot into the soul for ever and for ever. And without this cleansing from God, all the corruptions and woes of the present, are but preludes and shadows of a decay that never ceases, and an exile which knows no end.

Much has been said about the condition of the lost. Some tell us with great assurance that there is no future hell — no lake of fire — no outpoured wrath of God on the souls of men in another life. Be it so. The text opens up a picture on this subject more awful than that of an ocean of flame, or any tempest of fire. It is the simple incurableness of the finally impenitent. They are corrupt and sick; and they shall continue corrupt and sick. Their souls are just so many fountains gushing out streams of corrosive and disgusting corruption, which shall never be stayed or dried up. They are without heavenly communion, and they shall never have heavenly communion. They are without friends and tender sympathy, and they shall continue without them. They are as good as dead, unclean, condemned, cut off from the camp of God, and without hope of being ever any better. They are gloomy and putrid wanderers about the regions of death; and they shall wander there for ever. They are miserable lepers on their way to the lazar-house of eternal decay.

Yes, and I have some of these very infected people

listening to me to-day. Though much stupefied to sacred things, they have caught up the words that I have been uttering. They are sitting with their friends in the pews; but spiritually they are as unclean and disordered outcasts, lingering around the outskirts of the camp, and now and then casting in a sad glance. I have a word for them. Ho, ye leprous ones! The great prophet and priest of God is passing through your country. He is healing the sick, cleansing the lepers, and binding up the broken-hearted. The tread of his footsteps is near you now. Come out from your lonely haunts, and ask that his healing hand be laid upon you. He is not afraid of your uncleanness. His invitation is to all, "*Come.*" He sees you sadly looking in through gates which you feel you dare not enter. He has come down through this land, just to save and heal such afflicted ones as you. And he can do it. His simple touch is healing. His mere look is life. But call to him, and he will hear you. Only bring your case before him, and he will undertake it at once. Now is your time. This is the period of your gracious visitation. Look to Jesus now while he is at hand, and he will relieve you. Call upon him while he is near, and he will save you. Delay not in unbelief, for his stay is limited. Your time is short. Your opportunities will soon pass away. The possibility of cure will soon be for ever gone. The shades of evening are gathering around us. The day is rapidly fading away. The night of death is near. Time is growing short. To-morrow may begin eternity. We know not how soon the final words may drop from heaven—"*It is done!*" Haste you then to Jesus.

Fall down upon your knees before him. Let the deep fountains of your spirit be poured out in this one prayer: *"Lord, if thou wilt, thou canst make me clean!"* And where that prayer exists in real soul-earnest, there is also the effective response, "I will be thou clean."

Thanks be unto God for his unspeakable **gift**!

20*

THIRTEENTH LECTURE.

THE LEPROSY OF GARMENTS.

LEV. CHAP. XIII.

WE have not yet quite done with the thirteenth chapter of this remarkable book. We have considered leprosy as respects *persons;* but it also attached to *garments*, and even to *houses*.

What relates to *clothes-leprosy*, is contained in the latter part of the thirteenth chapter, beginning with the 47th verse.

Now, I do not suppose that this leprosy of garments and skins was just the same disease of that name which attacked the human system. It may have been; and one may have sometimes taken it from the other; but we are not required to take this view. It is enough to understand it to be some affection of woven fabrics bearing a general resemblance to a leprous affection of the living body. A *cancer* is an affection of a living body, and yet we sometimes hear of cancers *in trees*. *Rot* is a decomposition of dead substances, and yet we speak of the rot in living sheep. The affections are not the same, although they are known by the same name. They refer to subjects very diverse in their nature. It is by this sort of accommodation, I take it, that God here speaks of leprosy of garments. As the life and comeliness of the leper are fretted away by his disease, so clothes and skins are affected by dampness, mould, or the settling in them of animalculæ, fretting away their strength and substance.

Michaelis, who very thoroughly investigated this whole subject, speaks of *dead-wool*, that is, the wool of sheep which have died by disease, as particularly liable to damage of this sort. His explanation is, that it loses its points and breeds impurity; and that when made into cloth and warmed by the natural heat of the wearer, it soon becomes bare and falls in holes, as if eaten by some invisible vermin. The unsoundness and unhealthiness of fabrics made of such materials were thought so serious by this learned investigator that he strongly urges the interference of legal enactments to prohibit the use of such wool in the manufacture of cloths. It is evidently to some such affections that God refers in these laws concerning the leprosy of garments; not because they were so particularly noxious or dangerous, but for typical purposes. The proper vindication of all these ceremonial regulations is, their lively signification of moral and religious ideas. Apart from this, many of them appear trifling and inexplicable; but this gives them weight and dignity which fully entitles them to the high place which they occupy in the book of revelation.

We have seen that leprosy in the living body represents sin as it lives and works *in* man. Leprosy in clothing must therefore refer to disorder and contagion *around* man. There is disease breeding in everything about us, as well as in us. Jude speaks of "*the garment unspotted by the flesh.*" Christ commends a few names in Sardis because they had "*not defiled their garments.*" The reference in these and like passages plainly is to the matter of external contact with the world, and to the liability of Christians to be tainted by their earthly surroundings. The phraseology, however, is borrowed from these ancient laws. It contemplates the associations of a man as his clothing. Morally speaking, the state of things in which we live, is our garment. It is that which is put upon us when we come into life, which we continually wear while in the world, and which we put off when we die. It includes all the circumstances in which we are placed, the business in which we engage, the social systems under which we act, our comforts and associations in the world, and all the outward every-day occurrences which enter into and shape our external existence.

You will notice that these laws do not prohibit, but rather enjoin, the use of clothing. Christianity is not an exemption of a man from the common duties and associations of life. It does not encourage that moral divesture of one's self which some religionists have so unnaturally practised, by retiring from society and its cares to live in solitudes and secluded retirement. Asceticism, monkery, nunnery, celibacy, withdrawal from the ordinary associations of life, has not the sanction of God. It is a sort of nakedness, which strips life of its comforts and its real design, and goes far to thwart the object for which we have been placed in this world. All natural associations, and all honest pursuits and employments, are for our moral good. All the cares, anxieties, toils and sorrows of this world, are designed to be steps and rounds by which we may ascend to higher excellence and moral greatness. He that cuts himself off from them, cuts himself off from God's natural sacraments of spiritual blessing. They are our proper clothing. They warm us, and protect us, and beautify us, and may be made to us the means of everlasting praise and honor. They are not necessarily degrading. They are all meant to ennoble us, to elevate us, to bless us. They all have a spiritual aim. And they are all regulated by a wise and beneficent hand as means to our highest happiness. Toil is good; and family relations are good; and society in all its complex and varied affairs is good. We cannot sever ourselves from anything which it imposes without interference with God and detriment to ourselves.

But whilst all these natural surroundings are good, they are liable to disease, and may become the sources of infection and evil. They may become tainted, and so help to render us unclean. Society is as capable of corruption as the individual; and with this augmentation of mischief, that it reacts upon the individual, and may contaminate and deprave him still more than he would otherwise be. The fact is, that our social factors have introduced a great deal of *dead wool* into the fabrics which men in this world are compelled to wear. The signs of leprosy and contaminating uncleanness may be traced at many points.

Take the subject of government. Civil rule is ordained of God. It is meant for good. And when framed upon principles of righteousness, earth knows no higher blessing. It is a defence for the weak, a restraint upon outbreaking passion, a handmaid to social dignity, the bulwark of freedom, the grand regulator of the outward world. And yet, how leprous has government often become! What curses has it inflicted upon man! How has humanity been debased and degraded by the diseases which have fretted their way into it! Though meant to defend the feeble against the strong, to exalt right above might, it has been made, in every age, the prolific source of many of earth's worst wrongs and miseries. Its tyrannies have filled the world with wailing. Its powers, corroded by human passion, have weighed like a millstone on the neck of humanity ever since history began. The corruptions to which it has given birth are *legion*. So sore and evil a thing has it often been, that the names of emperor and king have become an abhorrence unto men. It has been breeding leprosy and plague for six thousand years.

And not the least among its dreadful contaminations has been its deleterious effects upon the virtue of mankind. An arbitrary and tyrannical government cripples and stunts morality in its very germ, by divesting goodness of its proper reward, and making justice yield to the bribes of power and gain. It makes outward authority or sordid passion, instead of inward conviction and moral principle, the rule of conduct. It depresses the conscience, blunts the moral sense, and transmutes the masses into machines, sycophants and rogues, and the few into incarnations of the demon lust for power. How is it in Italy, in Spain, in Mexico, in the Ottoman dominions? Though occupying the garden-spots of earth, the lands are cursed with the basest of all populations by reason of the governments under which they have been reared. The garment has become leprous, and all who wear it are more or less defiled. Even in our own government, boastful and proud as we are of our political institutions, the cloth in many places is growing prematurely bare, weak and rotten; and the taint of unholy influences is beginning to be felt upon the cause of righteousness and the moral purity of thousands.

Take the domestic relations. God saw that it was not good for the man to be alone. Male and female hath he created us. He has set mankind in families. He has ordained the home, and made it the seat and centre of the mightiest influences that work in society. It is a blessed arrangement. As it is the oldest, it is the holiest, external sanctuary upon earth. It is the nursery of sentiment, the sacred enclosure of balmy affections, the primary school of every virtue. It is our innermost garment of fine linen, which, of all outward things, lies the closest upon, and unites most vitally with the springs of character. Its purity is the guarantee of a peaceful state and a happy world. It was made to be the temple of love, and hence of all that is right in feeling and just in principle.

> The dearest spot on earth to me,
> Is Home — sweet Home.

It is a fountain flowing with good. It is the foundation on which the best blessings of society chiefly repose. There is no fathoming of its influences. There is no way of computing its silent mightiness. It is not too much to say, that those who rock the cradle rule the world. In the secresy of home, the pale maternal hand moulds the springs which fashion the ages. Earth's greatest powers, have ever taken their bent from the gentle tones of the mother's voice. And when all effects come to be assigned to their true causes, the nursery chair will after all appear the mightiest throne.

It is exceedingly important, therefore, that the home should remain pure. Transmute the domestic ties into bonds of iniquity, and the race is to that extent bound down to death. Taint these potent surroundings, and it is just so much poison cast into the fountains of life. Yet, how often may we find the leprous plague fretting into the warp and woof of the domestic fabric, and forming a moral atmosphere about the plastic souls of infancy and childhood, more awful than upas shades, and more desolating than Lybian siroccos! I tremble when I think of the responsibility of parents. They tread on ground where every footfall echoes through eternity. And I mourn when I consider how often it is an echo of everlasting accusation.

Take business. It is necessary to engage in it. God himself commands it. Virtue, and religion, and even earthly comfort, require it. But how liable to become corrupt, and a mere instrument of death. "The care of the world and the deceitfulness of riches" are notorious for choking the springing germs of spiritual good. The commercial world is a very trying world upon the health of honor and honesty. It has a climate which is very apt to prove injurious to justice and integrity. The code of moral principles which mostly govern there, are usually set down at a heavy discount. I cannot speak from personal knowledge; but it is easy to see how numerous and powerful are the temptations which beset a man in mercantile life. An old book, which some consider inspired of God, has this remarkable sentence: "*As a nail sticketh fast between the joinings of stones, so doth sin stick close between buying and selling*" Leprosy is

THE LEPROSY OF GARMENTS. 241

exceedingly prone to settle there with all its contaminations.

Take education and literature. We must have schools and books. They are an indispensable part of the great machinery of human progress. But they are apt to become leprous, and to impart contagion. Learning is a blessed thing; its tendency is to elevate and improve. But sometimes it becomes the instrument of demons, and the great plague of men. How is it with the hundred thousand infidel and impure books that are at work in society? How is it with the two millions of volumes of novels and tales which are annually issued from the American press alone? How is it with our systems of collegiate instruction, where the student is directed to feed his pride of learning by joining with the drunken poets of the olden time in their celebrations of the sensualities of the gods? How is it where the power of superior knowledge is not kept in balance by virtuous principles and a benevolent heart? How is it with some of our most elaborate systems of philosophy, which, in their hidden falsehood, are bending thousands from the truth? Oh, what a power of mischief has gone out upon the world from schools and books! How has genius descended from the altars of Heaven, to light her torch at the flames below! *Dead wool* is in much of the cloth she wears.

Take even the Church—the very pillar and ground of the truth — the ark of salvation itself. By it redemption is conveyed to men; and outside of it man has no Savior and no hope. And yet it is one of those garments around us which is liable to leprous taint. Instead of serving as a house of prayer, it has sometimes been a mere den of thieves. Instead of a nursery of faith, hope, and charity, it has often been a nest for pestilential superstition, narrow self-righteousness, and intolerant bigotry. Though meant to be a school of preparation for heaven, men have often made it a feeder to hell.

But I need not enter further into specifications of this sort. You can see plainly that nothing around us in this world is so holy or so good, but that it may be perverted to base uses, and rendered the instrument of contamination and exclusion from the camp of God's saints. Civil, domestic, economical, educational, and even religious associations, have at times exerted amazing power in the work of human degradation. Though intended and capacitated to be engines of good, they have often tended to develop, mature, and confirm depravity, in all the walks of life. We are clothed on all sides with what is liable to disease and contaminating disorder. It is in the country and in the city—at home and abroad. It is in our schools and colleges; in the stores of our merchants; in the shops of our artisans; on the farms of our agriculturalists; and even on the ships that float in the silent sea. And whilst we continue upon the earth, not one of us shall ever be able to escape liability to become leprous from the social influences which hang upon and beset us continually.

Having thus looked at the disorder, let us now direct our attention to the prescriptions concerning it.

1. The first thing I notice here, is, that God set every Israelite on the look out for it. This must necessarily have been the direct effect of the announcement of these laws. Every article of clothing was at once thrown under suspicion. Whether made of

THE LEPROSY OF GARMENTS. 243

hairs or skins of animals, or of the fibres of vegetables; whether woollen, or linen; whether firs, or naked skins, or skins softened into leather; every sort of cloth or manufacture, intended for purposes of clothing, was declared liable at any time to be seized with the plague, and to become unclean and contaminating. Every serious Hebrew would therefore be impelled to keep the strictest watch for any symptoms of disorder, and to look with great suspicion upon whatever bore the least resemblance to it.

Now there is a kind of suspiciousness — a quality or state of mind, keeping back from confidence — which I would not for anything encourage. There is an affection arising from a bad conscience or a bad heart—a feeling closely akin to ugly jealousy, which mistrusts everything and everybody. It is just the contrary of that charity which "believeth all things, hopeth all things." It springs from no generous impulse. It is not based upon any dignified admiration for virtue. It proceeds upon no just zeal for the glory of God, or the good of man. It is a sort of surly selfishness and misanthropy, which is base in itself, and always mischievous in its effects. And the farther any one can keep himself from it the better for his own comfort, and for the good of those around him. But there is a suspiciousness which is virtuous and good. It mingles with the deepest piety and goes along with the greatest usefulness. But it is a suspicion of self, rather than a suspicion of others. It is a jealousy for one's own purity—a holy fear of doing wrong or of being led into evil. It springs from the very heart of charity, and contemplates nothing but good. It is a diligent watchfulness over self — a careful guarding against the contaminations of evil. It is a suspiciousness based upon the clear evidence that everything is liable to corruption, and that there is continual danger of falling into condemnation. It is a sacred dread of sin—the desire of a pure heart to "keep unspotted from the world." It sets a man upon the look out for dangers in all his earthly surroundings. It does not lead him to repudiate government, but to be on his guard that he may not be betrayed by it into disloyalty to his God. It does not prompt him to abjure domestic ties and cares, but to watch them lest they should wean his affections from heaven. It does not render business mean in his eyes, but causes him to be cautious lest it should crowd out a proper care for his soul. It begets in him no disregard for learning, but impels him above all things towards that which maketh wise unto salvation. It does not lessen his affection for the Church, but moves him to watch his heart against exclusiveness and bigotry. It does not in the least alienate him from the proper associations and pursuits of life, but encourages him to use this world, yet with jealous concern that he may not abuse it.

It is easy to see how essential all this is to moral purity in our relation to earthly surroundings. Let him that heareth, therefore, be wise, and learn to keep his garments.

2. A second particular in this law, to which I will call your attention, is, that whenever any symptoms appeared which might perhaps be leprous, the case was always to be immediately submitted to the judgment of the priest. The record says, "It shall be

showed unto the priest; and the priest shall look upon the plague;" that is, with a view to decide whether it is leprosy or not, and to give his directions concerning it. The priest typified Christ; and his office, the office of Christ. And a great Christian lesson here comes to our view.

Human judgment is weak. The wisest of men has said, "He that trusteth to his own heart is a fool." We need light from heaven. Conscience itself is not unerring except it be illuminated by revealed truth. A man may sincerely think he is in the right, when he is in most dangerous error. He may suppose himself pursuing a virtuous course, when he is becoming more and more contaminated every hour. The way of common justice he may easily understand. Reason decides readily against flagrant breaches of morality. But no mere human penetration can find out all the secret lurkings of sin. Jesus is the only reliable arbiter. There are many instances in which nothing can guide us safely but his own decisive word. And this law pointed forward to the fact, that Christ is our teacher and judge—that he is to be our authoritative instructor — and that by his decision we are to know what is not pure. "I am the light of the world," says he; "if I had not come and spoken unto them, they had not had sin; but now they have no cloak for their sin." His word is the great "discerner." "This is my beloved Son," saith the Almighty; "*hear ye him*." True, Jesus is now in heaven, and we cannot hear his personal voice. But his word remains with us. We have only to come to his holy oracles, and we may know the truth

"The Law of the Lord is perfect.
The testimony of the Lord is sure.
The statutes of the Lord are right.
The commandment of the Lord is pure.
The fear of the Lord is clean.
The judgments of the Lord are true, and righteous altogether."

Heathen philosophy is a foggy marsh, through which the soul never can find its way to saving truth. Tradition is a wilderness of conflicting records, confounding the inquirer at every step. But the word of the Lord is pure sunshine from the open heavens, making the way of life so clear, that a wayfaring man, though a fool, need not err therein. And if at any time we have occasion to suspect disease and danger to our souls, our duty is to come at once to consult these oracles of Jesus, and have the matter settled by his own infallible authority.

3. A third particular in these laws relates to the treatment which a garment declared to be leprous was to receive. This varied somewhat with the nature of the symptoms. If the affection was active and rapid in its progress, the article was at once to be burned, "whether warp or woof, in woollen or in linen, or anything of skin." It mattered not how valuable the article was, or how great the inconvenience of its loss, it was to be destroyed by fire. We are bound, as Christians, at once to cut loose for ever from everything infected. Though our renunciation of sin should be to us like cutting off the right hand, or plucking out the right eye, or giving ourselves to complete nakedness, we must give it over to the burning. It is a grand mistake for any one to suppose that sin is in any way essential to him. People plead for leniency in our judgment of the tricks of

trade, the corruptions of politics, and the questionable customs of society. They want to know how they are to get along without them. They tell us that these are common things, and have become necessary to success, etiquette, and respectability, and must be yielded to. But what if they are? What if a man cannot prosper in business without equivocation and deceit? What if a man cannot get into office but by meanness? What if we cannot stand fair with the world without introducing into our homes practices at which conscience rebels. That does not alter right and duty. If the High-priest has said it is leprous, it is our business to burn the last robe we have. Better live beggars all our days — better be accounted the very offscourings of the earth — better die in garrets, and be buried in potter's field, and carried with Lazarus into Abraham's bosom — than to flourish a few years in sin, and then go down with Dives to unquenchable flames. If we cannot drink of Esek and Sitnah without strife; we are to relinquish them forever. If we cannot keep out of Nebuchadnezzar's furnace without bowing down to his image on the plains of Dura, we must promptly bid farewell to earth, and welcome the hottest, whitest flames. If we cannot enjoy Egypt's honors without being tainted with Egypt's idolatry, we must abdicate for ever, and choose rather to suffer affliction with the people of God, than enjoy the pleasures of sin for a season. Though it cost us the fiercest martyrdom, we must not deny our Lord. "For what shall it profit a man, though he shall gain the whole world, and lose his own soul?"

If the affection, however, was not active and fretting, remedial measures were to be adopted, if possible, to cleanse and save the garment. "If the priest shall look, and the plague (after seven days) be not spread in the garment, either in the warp, or in the woof, or in anything of skin; then the priest shall command that they wash the thing wherein the plague is." The natural remedy for defilement was to be applied. And here comes in the whole subject of *reform*. This is the natural remedy for all manageable social disorders. I say all *manageable* ones; for as some garments were so badly affected as to be doomed at once to burning, so there are some infections in the surroundings of man in this world which never can be healed. They are beyond remedy, and we must make up our minds to abandon them to their fate, and to have no connection any more with them. Take, for instance, some of our popular amusements. That they are leprous none will deny. What hope is there of reforming them? Theirs is "a fret inward," and there is no help for them. No washing can get them clean. And the only alternative for Christians is, to separate themselves from them entirely. They do not form a subject for their endeavors at reform. They are doomed to come to an end.

Take that church apostasy known in Scripture as "The Man of Sin." What use is there to try to reform such an establishment as that? No possible process could separate between it and the leprous plague that is in it. God himself has abandoned all hope of its recovery. Strong delusion is there, because there is no love of the truth; and that delusion is sent of God to seal its damnation. Here and there a sound thread may be pulled out and saved; but

THE LEPROSY OF GARMENTS. 249

the garment is profoundly leprous. The great Highpriest has said it shall be burned with fire.

And the same is true of many governments, especially those now occupying the territory of the old Roman Empire. They are leprous to the deepest interior. It is useless to think of reforming them. They are past hope. They cannot be reclaimed. Prophecy sustains this declaration concerning them. God hath said they are unclean. As Christians we must surrender them to their doom. They shall be utterly consumed.

These, and such like infected articles, are past cleansing. But there are others in which the taint is less malignant and less defiling. The leprosy in them is not so deep but that careful washing may perhaps remove it. These are the legitimate subjects of Christian reform. There are many abuses in society which may be corrected. There are many sources of mischief which may be dried up. There are many affections of Church and State which may be cleansed off. To this end, therefore, are our energies to be directed. Every Christian is a *reformer*—not an empty vociferous demagogue, crying down everything, with nothing to put in the place—not a Jacobin revolutionist, who would unhinge society, and overturn, overturn, without restraint, limit, compunction, or fear of God or man—but a genuine *reformer*, whose heart and hand and influence are fully set against what is wrong and corrupting; who would not destroy society, but build it up and establish it upon those strong foundations which God himself has laid for it; and who, in place of putting the child against the parent, the subject against the ruler, and man against his God, bends all his influence to have each one happy in his place by a true harmony with heaven.

But there is one very important peculiarity to be observed in all Christian reforms. The washing of the infected garment was to be done by direction of the priest. "*The priest shall command that they wash the thing wherein the plague is.*" Christ's word is to be our guide for getting rid of social disorders, as well as for the detection of them. He is our Priest, and we must conduct our cleansing efforts upon the basis of his Gospel. The world is full of pretended reformers. Society is sick, and the doctors swarm around the patient, and every one has a prescription to offer. The conflict of opinion abroad over the earth, is like the winds that strove together upon the dark bosom of original chaos. The human mind is becoming completely bewildered and confounded. God is cutting the world loose from its old and false connections, and everywhere we hear the shrieks and behold the struggles which result therefrom. There is accordingly a casting about on all sides, such as never has been witnessed in the earth before. And the great danger is of basing our reformative efforts upon vague notions of philosophy, mistaken impulses, or wild schemes of human perfectibility, which can only delude and disappoint. Our eyes must therefore be ever turned to our Priest, who understands the whole case, and move only as his word directs. The Gospel is the chart by which to direct our way on the heaving ocean. Christ has been ordained to be the centre of the world. Around him everything must be made to revolve. From him all goodness radiates. And without coming under the laws of pulsation and attraction, which proceed from his great heart, even the best meaning men shall become mere wandering stars, whirling headlong through eternal emptiness, to whom is reserved the blackness of darkness for ever. *The Gospel alone is the great regenerator of the world.*

Finally, along with the washing of a leprous garment, it was to be shut up seven days, after which the priest was to examine it again; and if the bad symptoms had disappeared, it was to be washed again, and it was clean; but if the symptoms had not disappeared, it was then to be finally torn or burned. A vivid picture, this, of God's plans with the social fabrics of this world. Some, in which the disorder was great, have already been quite destroyed. Others, in which the affection is less malignant, are undergoing the efforts of purification. They are shut up now until time shall complete its period. The great High-priest and Judge shall then come forth to give them the last inspection. And as things then are, so shall their eternal portion be. The tyrannies and corruptions then found upon the earth shall be adjudged to immediate destruction. And every plant which the heavenly Father hath **not** planted shall be rooted out.

May God give us grace against that day!

FOURTEENTH LECTURE.

THE LEPER CLEANSED.

LEV. CHAP. XIV.

I HAVE stated the fact, that leprosy was not curable by human remedies. It did not always, however, continue for life. It was often sent as a special judgment, as in the cases of Miriam, Azariah, and Gehazi. The Jews generally looked upon it in this light. Its very name denotes *a stroke of the Lord.* This, of itself, rather implies that it may cease with the repentance and forgiveness of the smitten offender. Miriam was healed in the course of a week. And learned men tell us, that it sometimes runs its course in the system, and then dries up as of its own accord. At any rate, we know of many lepers being healed, both in the Savior's time and before, not by human skill, but by divine power and grace.

It was the anticipation of the healing, of at least some persons leprously affected, that formed the basis of the provisions here laid down. They constitute "the law of the leper in the day of his cleansing;" and if there was no possibility of cure, there was no use of this law.

You will observe, however, that these regulations were not for *the cure* of the leper, but for his ceremonial cleansing *after* the cure. The priest was first

THE LEPER CLEANSED.

to examine "if the plague of leprosy had been healed in the leper;" and it was only in case he found the plague healed, that these laws were to go into effect. You recollect the case in the Gospel history, of "a man full of leprosy, who, seeing Jesus, fell on his face, and besought him, saying, "Lord, if thou wilt, thou canst make me clean. And he put forth his hand, and touched him, saying, I will: be thou clean. And immediately the leprosy departed from him." The man was cured. Everything of his disease was quite gone. But still he was not yet restored to his social and religious privileges as a Jew. It yet remained for him to comply with this "law of the leper." Hence the Savior said to him, "Go, and show thyself to the priest, and offer for thy cleansing, according as Moses commanded." We thus have the authority of Christ for it, that this law was for the ceremonial cleansing of lepers after they were cured, and not for their cure. The disease had first to be stayed, and then began this process of cleansing off all its lingering effects and disabilities.

I therefore take the deepest intention of these rites to be, to illustrate the nature of sanctification. Justification is also implied, but only as connected with sanctification. Of course there can be no sanctification without forgiveness and acquittal first. Condemnation must be removed before there can be any advances in holiness. Hence, these cleansing ceremonies were to begin by the priest's inspection of the recovered leper, and the pronunciation of him healed of his disease. Let us look a little at these preliminaries, and we will be the better prepared to appreciate what was to follow.

1. In the first place it is presupposed that the

leper's disease had been stayed. And this healing again points to some putting forth of divine power and grace quite different from anything here brought to view, and far anterior to the commencement of these services. The first motion of our salvation is from God. It begins while we are yet in the very depths of our defilement and guilt. "While we were yet sinners, Christ died for us." The grounds of our justification are all provided for us in the mercy of God, without any sort of co-operation on our part. The first that we know of our spiritual estate, is the Gospel sounding in our ears, telling us that we have been dead in sin, and that God hath found a ransom by which, if we believe and act on his word, "there is now no more condemnation." Our healing is begun in Christ Jesus before we are conscious of it. The very first that we hear on the subject is, the glad tidings that our leprosy is stayed, and that all we have now to do is to go forward with what is prescribed for our cleansing. We need no longer sit brooding in despondency over our leprous condition. All that is as good as cured in Christ Jesus. A full and free forgiveness of all our sins is provided. And the only remaining requirement is, to "go show thyself to the priest, and offer for thy cleansing, according as Moses commanded."

2. The leper, finding his leprosy stayed, was to go to the judge in the case, and claim exemption from the sentence that was upon him. And to render this the more easy for him, the priest had to "go forth out of the camp" to meet him. The very moment the sinner believes in the healing proclaimed to him in the Gospel, and sets himself to move for his cleansing, Christ meets him. The father runs to em-

brace the returning prodigal while yet a great way off. We have only to say to him, "See, I have been a filthy leper. My whole nature has been corrupt and unclean. But here in this Gospel and its provisions is a complete cure. This pure white righteousness of my Savior and surety is enough to exempt me from being any longer excluded from the society of my friends. Examine it, and see whether the disease is not healed. In the power of this holy word I am no longer to be numbered with the outcast and condemned. Deliver me then from this terrible exclusion."

3. And when the healed leper thus presented himself to the priest, there was no alternative left. He had to be pronounced cured. And so Christ hath bound himself to acquit and absolve every sinner who thus comes to him in the strength of the Gospel message. There is no further hindrance in the way. The man is justified. The sentence that was against him is exscinded and taken away. All that concerns our forgiveness or justification then lies in this,—Do we believe the Gospel message? Do we take it to be true that Christ has wrought out for us a sufficient righteousness? Do we rest upon his sacrifice as our propitiation? Do we receive to our hearts and repose upon the announcement of pardon through his mediation? If we do, we are forgiven. Our sins are remembered against us no more. We are absolved. We are justified. The process of our sanctification has begun.

But, the mere absolution of the priest did not fully restore the leper. Though his disease was stayed, there was a taint of it remaining to be purged off before he could join the camp or the holy services.

And so our whole salvation must miscarry, if it does not also take in an active holiness, purifying our hearts and lives, and transforming us into the image of our Redeemer. How this sanctification is effected is what we are now to consider.

I. To cleanse the recovered leper, the first thing to be done was the procurement of two clean birds, the one of which was to be slain, and the other to be dipped in its fellow's blood and set at liberty. These two doves, the gentlest of all God's creatures, at once carry our thoughts back to Christ, and his wonderful history. Like them he was meek and pure— the "gentle Jesus." Like them he was taken from his peaceful home, and made captive to the law. The fate of the one shows us how he was mangled for human guilt, crushed to death for the sins of others, and brought down to the depths of the earth. The other, coming up out of the earthen vessel, out of the blood of its fellow, shows us how Jesus rose again from the rocky sepulchre, and ascended up out of the hand of his captor on strong and joyous pinions far into the high abodes of heaven, scattering as he went the gracious drops of cleansing and salvation.

The introduction of these birds, in this connection, presents a great theological fact. As they typify Christ, they show, that our sanctification, as well as our justification, proceeds from his cross and resurrection. True, it is the Spirit that sanctifies, through the truth; but had not Christ died and risen again, "the truth" would have been disrobed of its power, and the Holy Ghost would not have come. His teachings are indeed sublime and perfect; but they would be dead as man's philosophies, without their proper seal of dying love, and the living energies which flow through them from their Author's triumph over death, and his gifts of power shed from the heavens whither he ascended.

When Themistocles was a young man, and the battle scenes of Marathon were stirring the blood of heroes, for a time he could not rest day nor night. All his common affections seemed to be suddenly stricken dead. Being asked as to the cause, he said, "*The trophies of Miltiades will not suffer me to sleep.*" And so there are certain stirring, melting, transforming potencies, proceeding from Gethsemane and Calvary and Olivet, which

> —— seize upon the mind,—arrest, and search,
> And shake it, — bend the tall soul as by wind, —
> Rush over it like rivers over reeds,
> Which quiver in the current, — turn us cold,
> And pale, and voiceless, —

tearing the sinner from his guilty peace, and thrilling him with thoughts, and fears, and aspirations, which reach throughout eternity. I will not now attempt to explain how it is; but there is a mightiness in the blood-doctrine of the cross, which works upon the human heart, and changes and renews it, as nothing else has ever done, or can do. Let man once fairly see and believe it, and sin that moment loses its supremacy in his soul, and withers and fades. Can I look on a Savior's love, unaided and alone interposing for my rescue, and see my condemnation dying in his death, and the guilt of my past offences buried in his grave, and the decree of perfect absolution issuing from his resurrection, and the invitations to immortality opened to me in his ascension, and not feel a grateful impulse of compliance in my soul which snaps the cords of sin asunder, and covers base passion with infinite contempt? Can I behold so dear-bought and great a salvation brought to my very door and offered freely to my acceptance, and feel no check of selfishness that I may live for ever? Can I believe that all the dreadful weight of my guilt was laid upon that meek Lamb, and expiated in his blood, entitling me to step up and be a companion of angels in the habitation of God, and not feel inwardly impelled to deny my heart its short-lived sinful pleasures that I may have eternal blessedness? Ho, child of folly! Only

> Cast up thy tearful eyes
> To where thy Lord and Love was crucified;
> So shall the world, and all its vanities,
> Appear like dross; — ambition, lust, and pride,
> Shall far, far off their baleful powers remove,
> And in the pure, unspotted mind
> Nothing remain
> But adoration, ecstacy, and love.

Let men reason as they please, it is after all the Savior's blood and resurrection which sanctifies.

> Talk they of morals? O thou bleeding Lamb!
> The best morality is love to Thee.

II. The next thing to be done for the cleansing of the recovered leper, was the arrangement and use of means to apply the cleansing blood. Three different articles were to be combined into one instrument for this purpose — a stem of cedar wood, a bunch of scarlet wool, and a parcel of twigs of hyssop. I will not undertake to say what was the detail of typical signification in these several articles. The cedar wood here spoken of is remarkable for its durability, fragrance, and healthful-looking redness of heart. The scarlet color of the wool, which was much esteemed by the orientals, may have some allusion to the blood of the leper returning again to its natural color, and signify healthiness. Hyssop is a small bushy plant, aromatic, and warming in its medicinal properties. The stick of cedar formed a sort of handle or stem on which the wool and hyssop were fastened, so as to make a convenient instrument for taking of the blood to sprinkle it upon the body of him who was to be cleansed. The whole thing taken together presents us with the fact, that our sanctification by the blood of the crucified and risen Savior is not direct, but through the use of instrumentalities or means. There is always something coming between the purifying blood and ourselves, by which the efficacy of that blood is applied to our souls. Christ has appointed certain instruments and agencies to convey to us the purifying elements. First of all is the cedar stem of his word, durable, fragrant, and instinct with celestial power and life, speaking through all the visible creation, but much more distinctly and powerfully in the written Scriptures. Along with this, and fastened to it, is the scarlet wool of the holy sacraments, absorbing, as it were, the whole substance of Christ crucified, and performing an important part in the impartation of the same to our souls. And along with this scarlet wool, and bound to the same stem, are the many little aromatic stems of prayer, with the sanctifying blood running out and hanging in drops on every point, ready to flow upon and cleanse the humble worshipper. Whether any other means are included in these symbols, I do not know; but these certainly are; and by these, above everything else, is the purifying blood of Jesus brought in contact with our hearts, and made effectual to our purification. These are the glorious channels of saving health to unclean souls. Let a man exercise himself well in the Divine word; let him make his heart familiar with what is there given for his learning; let him know and believe the truth as it is in Jesus, and it will be in him a fountain of purity springing up into everlasting life. Let him attend devoutly to the appointed sacraments, and he will find that word mellowing into still greater adaptation to his wants, and drawing to him in more vivid closeness and power. And let him be diligent and earnest in his prayers, and be found at his wonted times bowed at the feet of his great High-priest in heaven; and there will be all necessary connection and communion with that blood which cleanseth from all sin. To these comes the mystic Spirit of God, viewless as the wind, silent as the grave, but mighty as omnipotence, breathing through all, working in all, making all alive with celestial vigor, reviving, cheering, sanctifying, blessing, and bringing back the lost to life, and home, and heaven. How simple, and yet how beautiful! How easy, and yet how effective! Conceive, if you can, of a polar winter — cold that locks up the sea — darkness that is perpetual — on everything the white shroud and silence of death It is the picture of the moral estate of him who has never been reached by these sanctifying appliances. Conceive, now, of the breaking up of that forbidding scene. The snows melt on their hills; the ice breaks from the seas; the sun forgets to set; the buried earth rises out of its cold shroud; the sea ebbs and flows in joyous freedom; life springs up in the valleys; the wild winds change their savage roar for balmy melody; and the harsh north lays by its fierceness and lies down as a gentle lamb in the continuous sunshine. It is the picture of the sinner passed from death to life. And what has done it? Nothing but one aspect of that law which causes this book to rest upon my hand — the turning of a little wheel in the clock-work of material things. The north turned away from its sovereign in the heavens; and there was cold, darkness, and death. It turned back again; and there was genial warmth, and light, and life, and blessedness. And so, only let the sinner reverse his course, retrace his steps, and turn himself Godward in these simple means; and a hallowing peace and light shall arise upon him, at which his inmost soul will sing, and angels themselves rejoice.

III. A third requirement for the leper's cleansing was, that he should "wash his clothes, and shave off all his hair, and wash himself in water." This was his own work. It was to be done by the leper himself. Its spiritual significance is easily understood. It refers to the sinner's repentance and reformation. He must cleanse himself from all his old and base surroundings. He must separate between himself and everything suspicious. Though the leper was cured, his disease might still adhere to his clothes; he had therefore to wash them. Though clean of his leprosy in every other part, it might still have some hidden symptoms under the hair; he had therefore to shave it all off, even his very eyebrows. There was to be a perfect separation made between himself and the uncleanness which was formerly upon him. To be truly sanctified, we must cut ourselves off from all unholy associations and suspicious honors. We must break up all our old sinful habits, and relinquish all false ways. As the prophet expresses it, we must "cease to do evil, and learn to do well." He that sinned, must sin no more. There must be a complete reform.

A man from another church remarked to me some time ago, that he thought there was one great deficiency in many of the pulpits of modern times; that the preachers make too much of *faith*, and not enough of *repentance;* that our professed Christians are too forward to trust in Christ without a sufficient surrender of themselves to obey Christ; and that the way to heaven is often held forth as so simple and easy, that people are not impressed as they should be with the necessity of a change in the whole manner of life. I will not say how far he was correct. But this I will say, If our religion is not powerful enough to work a complete revolution in our lives, leading us to obey and follow Christ as well as to expect salvation through him, it will avail us nothing before God.

> Mistaken souls, that dream of heaven,
>   And make their empty boast
> Of inward joys and sins forgiven,
>   While they are slaves to lust!
>
> Vain are our fancies, airy flights,
>   If faith be cold and dead;
> None but a living power unites
>   To Christ, the living Head.
>
> A faith that changes all the heart;
>   A faith that works by love;
> That bids all sinful joys depart,
>   And lifts the thoughts above.

THE LEPER CLEANSED.

> Faith must obey our Father's will,
> As well as trust his grace;
> A pardoning God is jealous still
> For his own holiness.

"Not every one that saith, Lord, Lord, shall enter into the kingdom of heaven; but he that doeth the will of the Father which is in heaven." "Whoso looketh into the perfect law of liberty and continueth therein, he being not a forgetful hearer, *but a doer of the work*, this man shall be blessed in his deed." Religion is not mere sentiment.

> 'Tis not to cry, God mercy, or to sit
> And droop, or to confess that thou hast failed
> 'Tis to bewail the sins thou didst commit,
> And not commit those sins thou hast bewailed.
> He that bewails, and not forsakes them too,
> Confesses rather what he means to do.

The command is, "*Wash you, make you clean; put away the evil of your doings from before mine eyes.*" "*Work out your own salvation with fear and trembling.*"

IV. But there is another particular entering into this ritual cleansing. After everything else had been done, sacrifices were to be offered. I need not enter into the details of this part of the service, as they were very fully before us in the first chapters. The general signification of them, in this connection, is, that our sanctification, from beginning to end, depends upon "the blood of the Lamb." We must wash, and repent, and reform; but it avails nought without blood. Water, the purest that ever dropped from mossy rock, or gushed from the mountain spring, is not able to cleanse a man for heaven. Tears of repentance, though pure as those which trickled down the Savior's cheeks, cannot wash out the stains of sin, except they be mingled with the blood that dripped from his wounds. And no moral improvements can entitle us to eternity's honors, if they are not connected with the suretyship and sacrifice of Jesus. The source of all sanctification is in his death and resurrection. All the glories of eternal life, still refer us back to Calvary. Grace in Christ Jesus commenced the work, and grace in Christ Jesus must complete it.

> Grace all the work shall crown,
> Through everlasting days;
> It lays in heaven the topmost stone,
> And well deserves the praise.

The only peculiarity which I notice here, is, that some of the blood and oil was to be touched to the cleansed leper, the same as in the consecration of the priests. The record says, "The priest shall take some of the blood of the trespass-offering, and put it upon the right ear of him that is to be cleansed, and upon the thumb of his right hand, and upon the great toe of his right foot;" and the same with regard to the oil. This completed his cleansing, and joined him to the chosen people in all their privileges and obligations. It points to the very culmination and crown of Christian sanctity. The blood of the trespass offering stands for the blood of Christ, and the holy oil for the Holy Spirit. These are the two great consecrating elements of Christianity. With these our High-priest approaches us through the Gospel to complete our cleansing and ordain us to the dignities and duties of our spiritual calling. With this blood and chrism applied to us, we are clean, and set apart as "a chosen generation, a royal priesthood, an holy nation, a peculiar people," to "show forth the praises of him who hath called us out of darkness to his marvellous light." And this blood and unction are thus applied, when we have fully submitted ourselves to Jesus, and given up to be what he desires to make us.

The grand peculiarity of a Christian, and that which sums up everything else respecting him, is, that he no longer looks upon himself as his own, but as bought with a price, and marked by redeeming blood, and gifts of anointing, to be the Lord's. His head and ears are consecrated. His hands and his feet are consecrated. His whole being is set apart to a holy calling, no longer to be given to selfishness or sin. In the entire bent and purpose of his mind, by force of the blood that was shed for him, and the Spirit that is poured upon him, he is brought clean out of the region and shadow of death, made a part of the congregation of saints, and divorced from all alliances foreign to the theocratic kingdom and the commonwealth of Israel. Expatriated from the realms of darkness, he has become a child of light, whose citizenship is in heaven. He is joined to the camp of God, united to the general assembly — the Church of the first-born, made up to share its fate. His whole interest is embarked with the cause of righteousness. Like the trusting Moabitess of the olden time, his vow is, "Whither thou goest, I will go; and where thou lodgest, I will lodge; thy people shall be my people, and thy God my God." Jesus has laid his hand upon him, and said — "Thou art mine; therefore thou shalt observe to do whatsoever I have commanded, and verily thou shall have thy reward." "*Be it so*," is the deep and firm response of his soul; "*be it unto me according to thy word.*" It is enough. With this all the hopes, and joys, and dignities of the saints are his. He is clean. Like the scape-dove in the text, once a captive and in danger of death, he now is free. His soul may spread its wings, and rise above the common world, and soar away to salvation's sunny hills, and make its nest in the everlasting mountains, "bearing about with it the dying of the Lord Jesus." And when we contemplate the portion of such a soul bounding away, like that liberated bird, to everlasting life, how fitting comes in the Psalmist's wish—"*O that I had wings like a dove! for then would I fly away, and be at rest.*"

V. There is one point more in these ceremonies to which I will call your attention. I refer to the time which they required. A leper could by no possibility get through with his cleansing under seven days. One day was enough to admit him into the camp; but seven full days were requisite to admit him to his home. There was therefore a complete period of time necessary to the entireness of his cleansing. This arrangement was not accidental. It has its full typical significance. It refers to the fact, that no one is completely sanctified in the present life; and that a complete period of time must ensue before we reach the rest to which our cleansing entitles us. Christians now are only in course of cleansing. Recovery has commenced. Leprosy has been stayed. The priest has declared the disease conquered. Its offensive humors have all disappeared. We are absolved and justified. The blood of purification has been sprinkled upon us. We have washed our clothes by repentance and reform. We have been admitted

THE LEPER CLEANSED. 267

to the camp. We are numbered with the people of God. Our names are written in heaven. We have made great advances on what we were whilst rotting in our leprosy. We have attained unto very high honors. We have secured very exalted privileges. But everything has not yet been done, and all our disabilities are not yet removed. Great services yet remain to take place when the seven days have elapsed. And until then we must patiently wait. The influences of sin still linger about the old tenement, and we must suffer the consequences of it until the term of this present dispensation ends. Then shall our High-priest come forth again, and "change our vile bodies, and fashion them like unto his own glorious body." The last lurking places of defilement shall then be cut off. The last act of the leper's cleansing was to shave off his hair. When that was done, he entered upon all the high services of the Tabernacle, and went to his home a saved man.

Some look upon death as the end of man. They think that there is no more of him after he has been consigned to the tomb. A grain of seed dies, and shoots forth a new body and a new harvest; the caterpillar dies, and gives being to the butterfly from the elements of his decay; the day dies, and breaks forth into a new dawn; the year dies, and nature lies dead in her white winding sheet, and then bursts into fresh vigor from her wintry grave; and yet, when man dies, they say it is an eternal sleep — a complete extinction! It is not so. Death is our only proper birth. Then first we are to enter upon the true realities of life. Nature knows no such thing as an eternal sleep. Sleep always implies a future awakening. And if death is a sleep at all, it cannot be eternal. It is but the repose of the night that is soon to issue in eternal day. Death in itself has nothing pleasant in it. It was not an agreeable thing for the leper to have all his hair shaved off from his entire body. It was in itself a great humiliation and dishonor. But in that he received the completion of his liberty. It is sad to see the cheek of a friend grow pale and sunken, and his smile give place to the signs of anguish, and his strong limbs become powerless, and the sick look creep over his flashing eye, and his tongue grow heavy in his mouth, and the work of death going on in his manly form, and his whole visible being turning to offensive corruption. It makes us shudder and weep. It is a melancholy humiliation of the glory of man. But in that very waste and decay he is being born to everlasting vigor. It is his birth to immortality. It is the last of his disabilities. From that sad scene he passes to his home. There is, after all, something bright and joyous connected with the gloom of death. It comes to break the chains of the prisoner; to bring the exile home; to cleanse away the last remains of sin; to lead the ransomed spirit to its rest; to house us with the loving and beloved in the bright mansions of the Father's house.

> Death is the crown of life.
> Were death denied, poor man would live in vain.
> Were death denied, to live would not be life.

All hail, then, to the Gospel which sheds such light upon the mystery of death! All hail to the hopes which bloom upon a Christian's grave! These dark and gloomy doors lead to the land of bliss. These little hillocks, under which our babes and fathers sleep, are but the mountain peaks of another and better world. The king of terrors is a messenger of peace. And connecting death with the resurrection which is to follow it, earth knows of no sublimer transition.

Brethren, we must die. The seven days of life are fast passing away. Very soon we shall sleep our last sleep. It may sadden us and make us shudder to think of it. It requires grace to look calmly on the tomb. But, along with this is another thought — a thrilling thought — that some of these times we shall sleep, and when we open our eyes, we shall say — "What pearly gates are these? What jasper walls, what golden streets, what splendid palaces, are these? What immortal trees, what crystal streams, what amaranthine bowers, are these? Lo! the white-robed hosts that sing redemption's songs! Lo! the King in his beauty, with his everlasting thrones! O! the beatific vision! What a blessed place! Is not this heaven? Can it be a dream? Verily, this is heaven! Heaven — heaven — heaven! HALLELUIA FOR EVER! I AM AT HOME IN HEAVEN!"

FIFTEENTH LECTURE.

THE POOR — HOUSE LEPROSY — SECRET UNCLEANNESS.

LEV. CHAP. XIV. XV.

I HAVE commented upon the fourteenth chapter as far as the twenty-first verse. At this point commence certain modifications of the law for the cleansing of lepers, to adapt it to the peculiar circumstances of the poor. In all ordinary cases, the man to be cleansed was to present three lambs, and three tenth-deals of flour. But God here says, "*If he be poor*, and cannot get so much, then he shall take *one* lamb for a trespass-offering to be waved, to make an atonement for him, and *one* tenth-deal of fine flour, and two turtle-doves or young pigeons, such as he is able to get." Similar exceptions were made in favor of the poor, in the first, second, and fifth chapters.

The poor man is often overlooked. There is always a strong tendency in the more favored classes to pass him by, and to forget, if not to despise him. But God does not forget him. The directions for his particular case are just as special and authoritative as any contained in this ritual. The Lord would thus assure him of his care — that he feels for him the same deep interest as for others, and brings atonement equally within his reach. There is a common level in the divine administrations, upon which "the rich and poor meet together, and the

Lord is the Maker of them all." The poor are his children, as well as the rich. He anointed his Son Jesus, to preach the Gospel to them. And the most neglected and down-trodden child of want has just as good a right to cleansing and heaven, and may count as much upon the sympathy and grace of God as his wealthy neighbor. If he cannot get three lambs, he is just as welcome and acceptable with one lamb and two doves. The poor widow's mite cast into the treasury of the Lord, receives a higher commendation than all the costly donations of the wealthy. Mary, with her two young pigeons, is just as completely cleansed, as she who could add thereto a lamb of a year old.

But, although the law favored the leper who was poor, it did not exempt him. It accommodated the burden to his strength, but it did not remove it. If he could not bring three lambs, he was still bound to bring one lamb and two doves. If he could not get three deals of flour, one deal had to be forthcoming. There are some people who make poverty a virtue, and claim exemption from everything because they are poor. But God's commands are upon the poor, as well as upon those more favored in earthly possessions. He does not excuse them because they are indigent. They are sinners as well as other men, and must be cleansed by the same processes. There is no more merit in being poor than in being rich. Poverty cannot save a man. Beggars may go down to eternal death as well as millionaires. There is often as much crime in rags, as in purple and fine linen. All classes are infected; and all classes must have recourse to the blood of the Lamb, and receive upon them the same " blood of sprinkling," and the same consecrating oil of the Spirit. Without this, no one can be cleansed, be he rich as Solomon, or indigent as Lazarus. "God commandeth all men everywhere to repent." All *can* come to Christ, and all *must* come to Christ. There is no other way of salvation. And no matter what may be an individual's earthly estate, there is no hope but in that High-priest whom God hath set over his house, to whom we must "draw near with a true heart, in full assurance of faith, having our hearts sprinkled from an evil conscience, and our bodies washed with pure water."

A larger expression, however, is required from the rich than from the poor. In God's account, three lambs, and three tenth-deals of flour, are necessary on the part of the man of means, to equal the one lamb, and the one tenth-deal, on the part of the poor man. Religion levies upon every man, but those levies are always graduated according to our several ability. If we are able to give much, God holds us bound to give much, and we are unfaithful to our obligations if we do not give much; and if we are not able to give much, we must still give something, and the little that we are able to give, if we give it with a believing heart, is the same in the eye of God as if we had given as much as the richest. If we have received freely, we must give freely. "Unto whomsoever much is given, of him shall be much required." God has inserted this in his law and in his Gospel; and no man is at liberty to disregard it.

With these remarks, I will now proceed to another subject, beginning with the thirty-third verse, and occupying the remainder of the chapter. Here we have the leprosy as it affected dwellings.

The particular nature of this affection I cannot very certainly determine. Michaelis thinks it was a sort of mural efflorescence, which often appears in damp situations, cellars, and ground-floors, and so corrodes walls and plastering as to affect and damage everything near it, and sometimes quite destroying the entire building. Calmet thinks it was a disorder caused by animalculæ which eroded the walls, and finally destroyed them, if left undisturbed. But perhaps we cannot do better than to agree with the Rabbins and early Christian Fathers, who believed that this leprosy was not natural, but sent of God as an extraordinary judgment, to compel men to the public acknowledgment and expiation of some undetected negligence or crime. It was the stone crying out of the wall against the sinner, and the beam out of the timber answering it. (Hab. 2:11.) It came like a great domestic affliction, saying, "This is not your rest, because it is polluted." It was the hand of God upon the forgetters of his law. It was "the curse of the Lord, in the house of the wicked."

Its typical significance will at once suggest itself. It plainly points to the fact, that, not only man, and his surroundings in life, but his very dwelling-place — the earth itself — is infected. There is disorder attaching to the very rocks and ground on which we tread. Going back to God's reckoning with Adam, we there find it written, "Cursed is the ground for thy sake; in sorrow shalt thou eat of it all the days of thy life; thorns also and thistles shall it bring forth to thee." From that moment a cloud settled upon the glory in which the world was made. Nature itself is a sufferer for the sin of man. "The creature was made subject to vanity." "The whole creation groaneth, and travaileth in pain together until now." A blur has come upon the beauty of the world, and a corroding leprosy into all its elements, and discord into its pristine harmony. Tempests, floods, and fires; volcanoes, earthquakes, siroccos, and deserts; inclement seasons, pestilential malaria, dangerous exhalations, and a thousand things of disharmony, pain and death, combine to form the sad echoes of the sentence pronounced in Eden. The whole surface and framework of the world bespeaks infection, disobedience, and disorder. We must tear it with instruments of iron, and mix its mould with tears and sweat, before it will yield us bread. Walls and houses must be built to shelter us from its angry blasts. And with all that we can do, the sea will now and then engulph the proudest navies, and the hailstones blast the budding harvests, and famine and pestilence cut down the strength of empires, and earthquakes bury up great cities in a common tomb, and the sun and the moon flash down death in their rays, and the very winds come laden with destruction.

And even in a moral aspect, the material world, though meant for spiritual as well as other good, has often been to man a source of defilement. Creation is a standing miracle to show us Eternal Power and Godhead. Every ray of light is an electric cord, let down from the unknown heavens to lift our hearts into communion with "the Father of light." Every night puts us into the midst of a sublime temple in which the tapers burn around the everlasting altar, and through which rolls the vesper anthem of the heavenly spheres, to inspire us with adoration. And the innumerable changes that pass before our eyes, are but so many letters to spell out to us the name of the Unknown God, in whom we live and have our being. But, how often have these very things tended to establish men in unbelief, and tempted them from the ways of piety and peace? How often have persons looked up into the starry sky, and reasoned, until they were led to say, the Gospel is a forgery?—or dug into the earth, and insisted that Moses was mistaken in its age?—or cut among the arteries and tissues of organic life, and denied man's immortality?—or watched the uniformity of God's common laws, and pronounced a miracle impossible?—or dipped a little into physical science, and controverted the very existence of a Deity? How often have earth's products proven to be mere baits and lures to unguarded souls to lead them down to death? How have its wines tempted men to intemperance, and its beautiful groves to the licentiousness of the idolater? How frequently the very gold or silver of its rocks have taken the place of God himself, and fastened everlasting condemnation on the worshipper? And what scene of beauty contained in this world, but has served to draw the heart of some one from the Lord? Aye, "the earth is defiled under the inhabitants thereof. Because they have transgressed the laws, changed the ordinances, broken the everlasting covenant; therefore hath the curse devoured the earth."

Nature now is a crippled thing. She no longer does her work, for body or for soul, with the efficiency which was originally intended. She is leprous. Everywhere, there are signs of some corroding ailment. "When I stand all alone at night in open nature," says Goethe, "I feel as though it were a spirit, and begged redemption of me. Often have I had the feeling as if nature, in wailing sadness, entreated something of me, so that not to understand what she longed for cut through my very heart." What the sentimentalist thus saw and felt, the book of God explains. Yea, "the earth mourneth" — "the world languisheth" — "the whole creation groaneth" — the stroke of the Lord is in our house.

But it shall not always be so. The leprosy in our dwelling-place may pass away as well as leprosy in our persons, or in our clothing. God has appointed rites for its cleansing. The time is coming when "*there shall be no more curse.*" But it is to be the last thing cleansed. Regeneration begins first in the spirit. From the spirit it extends to the outward life, then to the redemption of the body. And after that comes the grand deliverance, when "the creature (or creation) itself shall be delivered from the bondage of corruption, into the glorious liberty of the children of God." Not only our personal nature is to be renewed, but the very world in which we live. For "we, according to his promise, look for new heavens and a new earth, wherein dwelleth righteousness." "Instead of the thorn shall come up the fir-tree, and instead of the briar shall come up the myrtle-tree; and it shall be to the Lord for a name, for an everlasting sign that shall not be cut off." Christ took earth's thorns upon his head, and he will yet bear them quite away. He has mingled his tears and blood with its very dust, and its final sanctification is certain. He has knelt upon its mountains, walked on its seas, and gone down into the heart of its rocks and set it apart to be his—the theatre of his **mediatorial** triumphs, and the home of his saints. And it is only upon the theory of the ultimate and complete recovery of the world from all damage of sin, that the prescriptions now before us can be explained.

The first thing to be done to a house found to be leprous, was, to have the affected stones removed, the walls scraped, and the plastering renewed. This done, all parties were to wait to see what the effect would be upon the disorder. This evidently recalls the flood, and God's dealings with the earth at that time. It was then that he broke up the old and tainted foundations, swept away the scum of its surface, and overcast it with a new order of things. It is impossible to say how great were the changes made in the structure and investiture of the earth by the deluge; but we may suppose that they were very great. The occurrence is spoken of in the book of Job as a breaking down and overturning of the earth. What was uppermost, went down; and what was at the bottom of the sea was lifted into mountains. Rocks fresh from their deep quarries were put into the places of the old. A new arrangement of rivers and hills appeared. The old crust was broken and scraped off, and a fresh coating was put upon the face of the world. God did to it as he here orders for a leprous house, and said, "I will not again curse the ground any more for man's sake; neither will I again smite any more every living thing as I have done." All is therefore in waiting now, till our great High-priest and Judge shall come forth again to inspect the earth.

After the lapse of an appropriate time of trial, which is left indefinite in the record, the priest was again to examine the house that had been thus dealt with; and if the plague had broken out again, and had spread in the house, he was to break it down, "the stones of it, and the timber thereof, and all the mortar of the house, and carry them forth out of the city into an unclean place." If the leprous symptoms were not stayed, it was to be completely and forever demolished. There was no further hope for it. It perished in its uncleanness. Bonar, in his commentary on this book, considers this as a picture of the fate of this world. He thinks that the present earth is to be quite undone — "dissolved" — "burnt up" — and that out of its rubbish is to come the new earth wherein dwelleth righteousness. This does great violence to the type. A house thus demolished was never to be rebuilt. It was unclean and undone for ever. No new fabric ever came out of it. It was only when a dwelling was past hope of cure that this end awaited it. The earth is not past hope. It is to be reclaimed. It is to be cleansed. It is not to perish for ever. I therefore take this direction as a type, not of what is to befall the world, but of *what would have befallen it without the redemption that has come in to stay its corruption and save it from ruin*. To take this demolition of the incurable house as a type of what this world is to come to, is to say that the curse has broken out afresh since the flood, and spread more thoroughly through the earth than at first; which is not the fact. It is no more an infected place now than in the days of the antedeluvians. We may say the plague is stayed. The effects of it are still present. It needs the cleansing ceremonies that are to restore it to its pristime purity and sweetness. But the plague is stayed. There is no spreading of

THE LEPROSY IN DWELLINGS. 279

it — no sign of a new outbreak. It has grown no worse since the time of Noah. Like the recovered but still uncleansed leper, the earth may be regarded as lingering on the outskirts of the camp, calling for the Priest, and uttering its mournful prayers for his forthcoming. "The earnest expectation of the creature waiteth for the manifestation of the sons of God." It is subjected to the same in hope. It is therefore the proper subject of those cleansing rites which yet remain to be considered.

How, then, was a leprous house to be cleansed? We have seen what was to be done to it upon the first appearance of the plague. We accordingly read, that, after the lapse of a suitable time to test whether the infection was stayed, "the priest shall come in and look upon it, and behold if the plague hath not spread in the house after it was plastered, then he shall take to cleanse the house two birds, and cedar wood, and scarlet, and hyssop; and he shall kill one of the birds in an earthen vessel over running water; and he shall take the cedar wood, and the hyssop, and the scarlet, and the living bird, and dip them in the blood of the slain bird, and in the running water, and sprinkle the house seven times; but he shall let go the living bird out of the city into the open fields, and make an atonement for the house, and it shall be clean." All this refers us back to the blood-shedding, death, and resurrection of Jesus Christ, and holds forth the great fact that the world is made clean to us now, and will be entirely cleansed hereafter, by virtue of the redemptive work of our great High-priest. It is "the blood of sprinkling," and "the washing of regeneration" in Christ Jesus, that does the business. It is part of Christ's pur

chase on Calvary, and a part of the efficacy of hi
resurrection and ascension, to cleanse the infected
dwelling-place of man. He took the whole curse of
earth upon him, and by his stripes everything is
healed. The blood and water that fell from his cross
upon the earth shall bless it. It has blessed it already.
It speaketh better things than the blood of Abel.
All its utterances are full of hope. Its words are
promises. It says to every believer, "Thou shalt
kı ow that thy tabernacle shall be in peace; and thou
shalt visit thy habitation and shalt not sin." It is
God's seal to the assurance that "the righteous shall
inherit the land, and dwell therein forever." Because
Jesus was slain, and has redeemed us to God by his
blood, the saints may take it as their song, "*We shall
reign on the earth.*"

Some suppose that this dwelling-place of man is
some day to fall to pieces, and pass away, and be no
more. Had Christ not died, or having died, not
risen again, it might be so; but now a light of glory
rises upon its futurity. It shall not die, but live.
Great changes may yet pass upon it, but it shall
survive unharmed. The theatre of the Savior's
mighty deeds of love shall not be blotted out. The
rocks on which he knelt, the dust he wore upon him
self, the waters that he consecrated, shall never
become trophies of hell, or the prey of destruction.
This wide world shall yet become an Eden, where
none shall shiver amid arctic frosts, or wither under
tropic heat, or lie down and perish with disease.
These fields of snow and arid sands shall all blossom
yet with roses. And whatever may be the pangs of
that new birth, when he that sitteth on the throne
shall make all things new, these very hills shall clap

their hands, and these valleys lift up their voices, and this whole down-trodden earth rejoice in a finished redemption, when "the wolf shall dwell with the lamb, and the leopard lie down with the kid, and the calf, and the young lion, and the fatling together, and a little child shall lead them." This world was heaven's gift to man. It was his patrimonial estate. It was his sin that blighted it. And just so far as he is redeemed, he shall get his own again, and hold it by a charter written in his Savior's blood. *"Blessed are the meek, for they shall inherit the earth."*

We pass now to the fifteenth chapter. It is not necessary that I should read it. It is a collection of types of the secret flow of sin. All the uncleannesses here enumerated, are such as were, for the most part, unknown except to the individual alone. They must therefore refer to sins of solitude and secresy. The lesson is here taught, that we may be great sinners without anybody else knowing anything about it. There may be no word spoken, no act done, no voluntary motion put forth, and we still be unclean by a silent and unintentional oozing out of a carnal heart. There may be a very correct exterior life, and yet a secret cherishing of pride, and lust, and unbelief, and a secret painting of the walls with imagery, as much unfitting us for the society of the pure and good, as any open and outbreaking wickedness. "The lively imagination of a gay poetic mind is not less sinful when it scatters forth its luscious images, than the dull brutal feelings of the stupid, ignorant boor." "As he thinketh in his heart, so is he." Even the quiet and involuntary exudations of natural feeling are often to be numbered with the uncleanest things.

It is amazing how deep-seated the contaminations of sin are. A man may be truly penitent. He may be a true believer. He may be set to be a good servant of God. The empire of sin may be dethroned in his heart. And yet, every now and then, he will find the disgusting uncleanness of sin quietly and unintentionally escaping from him, contaminating himself and those who come in contact with him, or touch what he has touched. His whole nature is yet so full of remaining corruption, that the least agitation causes it to trickle over. He lies down to sleep, and presently he finds it in his dreams. He puts forth his hand to welcome a friend, and the very touch sometimes awakes wrong echoes in the soul. He is accidentally thrown into the mere neighborhood of sin, and the very atmosphere about him seems at times to be laden with excitations of impurity. His depravity cleaves to him like an old sore. It defiles his solitude with unclean thoughts. It taints his repose with the outflowings of evil. It springs uncleanness upon him in his holiest associations. And even in his looks towards heaven, it interposes suggestions which come like impure birds between him and the sky. In all situations, towards all persons, at all seasons, this remaining filthiness of the secret soul will occasionally obtrude itself. "I find a law," says Paul, "that when I would do good, evil is present with me." There is no escape in this world from the workings of inborn evil. "If a man have an ill neighbor," says the distinguished but quaint Boston, "he may remove; if he have an ill servant, he may put him away at the term; if he have a bad yokefellow, he may sometimes leave the house, and be free of molestation in that way; but should the saint go into a wilderness, or set up his tent in some remote rock in the sea, where never foot of man, beast, nor fowl had touched, there it will be with him. Should he be, with Paul, caught up to the third heavens, it will come back with him. It follows him as the shadow does the body; it makes a blot in the fairest line he can draw. It is like the fig-tree in the wall, which, how nearly soever it was cut, yet still grew till the wall was thrown down." "I know," says Paul, "that in me, that is, in my flesh, dwelleth no good thing. . . . O wretched man that I am! who shall deliver me from the body of this death?"

Nor are these secret and involuntary outflowings of corruption mere trifles, unworthy of notice. They are here set forth under images and types among the most offensive and disgusting. They are too loathsome for public recital — too hideous even for the mind to dwell upon. God intends thus to signify his deep abhorrence of our inherent corruptions. He means to intimate to us that we have reason to be ashamed and confounded at the secret disorder which still works in us. Nay, he yet adds to these defilements a judicial sentence. They were uncleannesses which excluded from the sanctuary, and everything holy. They brought condemnation with them. And some of them were so bad as to need atonement by blood. The unclean thoughts, desires, and imaginations which casually rise unbidden in the heart, even the unholy dreams that flit over us when we sleep, and the blushes of passion which flash upon us in a moment, are things offensive to the pure eye of God, and would ruin us for ever, were it not for the ever efficacious blood of Christ, and the clean flood of grace that comes in ever and anon to wash out after these filthy intruders. We need, therefore, to be on our guard against the beginnings of evil. We have reason to take alarm at the most silent wish, and at the most quiet complacence in the contemplation of sin. These are usually the germs of transgression — the floating seeds which drop into the heart, ready at any moment to strike root and spring up into deadly iniquity. We should regard them as the hiss and rattle of the serpent admonishing us of the presence of danger. Yielding to them in the least, we take a viper to our breasts which may sting us unto death.

It is indeed melancholy, my brethren, that we, as Christians, still have so much impurity cleaving to us — that with all our efforts so much evil still works in us — that with all our penitence, prayers and resolves, there yet is this frequent oozing out of contamination — that with all the doings of God to cleanse us, we still have so much cause to hang our heads in shame, and humble ourselves in dust and ashes — that not one of us but would blush and be mortified almost to death to have all our thoughts and feelings suddenly laid open to the inspection of those around us. But still it is not without its good effects. We need something to keep us humble, to drive us continually to the throne of grace, and to keep us ever mindful of our dependence upon the mercy of God. If we were not troubled with these secret flows of sin, we would be in great danger of growing spiritually proud, negligent, and over-confident. But this keeps us down at the foot of the cross, and ever prompts to more earnest prayer, and keeps the soul from stagnation. It makes us feel the presence and power of the foe, that we may be stirred up to ever-renewed zeal, and be strengthened the more by our trying encounters with the enemy. It helps to soften us towards the failings of others, and to make us charitable in our judgments of offenders. Though it is painful, and keeps us in constant peril of making shipwreck of our faith, I do not know whether I would have it otherwise if I could. I fear that we should be too much at rest and satisfied in this present world, if we were not thus made to feel the inconvenience of living in the flesh. It helps greatly to reconcile us to the idea of dying. It contributes to make our dying day, a blessed day; because it will put an everlasting end to these vexations. Then we shall be delivered "from the body of this death."

> Sweet is the scene where Christians die,
> Where holy souls retire to rest;

and all the more sweet, because it ends the strife with corruption, and lands the soul beyond the reach of earth's temptations. Farewell then to the languor that now comes in to load our hearts with miry clay, and to the unstable thoughts that wander off when we bow the knee before our Maker. Farewell then to those base imaginings which come in in spite of us to mar our devotions and disturb our peace, and to all those hidden flows of sin whose uncleanness comes upon us when we sleep and when we wake. We may not be clean till evening comes; but with its balmy shades and starry glories, the yoke shall drop from our necks, and we shall lie down under the eyes of watchful angels, and be for ever at rest. Egypt may pursue us to the sea, and its men of war go with us into the waves, but there shall the oppressor cease. From that flood he shal. never rise again. He shall never reach the other shore, or set foot in heaven. God shall there take off his chariot-wheels, and he shall pursue and oppress us no more. Oh, happy, happy day! that thus lays all our tormentors for ever with the dead.

And then, again, this constant consciousness of sin assists in endearing to us the cross and righteousness of Jesus. Though evil ever works within us, we have a remedy. We have an Advocate in heaven ever interceding for us. Though uncleanness clings to us, life and purity flows down through him to cover our unrighteousness and to help our infirmities. With all our weaknesses, in him we are strong. Let faith but touch the hem of his garment, and healing is at hand. Let the poor sinner but press to him, and all these disgusting issues shall be as though they were not. Blessed Physician, that God hath sent to us from the heavens! How precious the virtue that goeth out from him! He healeth all our diseases. His blood cleanseth from all sin.

Allow me, then, my dear friends, to commend this Savior to you. He is what you need; and he is ready to become everything to you that is necessary to complete your peace. You may find yourself full of sin; but he is able to cleanse you. You may be poor and friendless; but he sympathizes with you, and proposes to you eternal riches. In more than angelic meekness, he spreads out his hands to you, and says, "Come unto me, all ye that labor and are heavy laden, and I will give you rest." Only accept that call, and you shall be blessed forever.

SIXTEENTH LECTURE.

THE DAY OF ATONEMENT.

LEV. CHAP. XVI.

Some have thought, that the proper place for this chapter is immediately after the tenth, instead of after the fifteenth. It has been supposed, that the delivery of it was thus delayed, by accident—in consequence of the sin and fall of Nadab and Abihu. To me, its proper place seems to be exactly where God has put it. It is a sort of synopsis and condensed recapitulation of all that has preceded it. It sums up in one grand and solemn national service all that had previously been given in minute detail. And just so far as it would be incongruous and illogical to recapitulate before going through with the principal discourse, it would have been improper to introduce this chapter at an earlier stage in the delivery of these laws. Thus far, three principal subjects have been considered: *Offerings*, *Priests*, and *Sin*, for which they were intended to be the remedy. We now come to survey them all under one single view.

There is often much gained by frequent repetition. It is by going over his lessons again and again, that the school-boy masters his tasks, and becomes so much wiser than he was before. It is by the oft hearing of a thought, that it becomes rooted in our hearts, and welds itself to our souls as a part of our mental life. The success of the pulpit, and the benefit of our weekly attentions upon the sanctuary, depend much more upon the continuous reiteration of the same great truths of the Gospel, than upon any power of invention in the preacher. It is not so much the presentation of new thoughts and brilliant originalities that converts men and builds them up in holiness, as the clear and constant exhibition of the plain doctrines of grace. When Dr. Chalmers was asked to what he attributed his success in the ministry, he answered, "Under God, to one thing; repetition, repetition, repetition." And so God, in his law, reiterates and repeats in details and in summaries, line upon line, and precept upon precept, to ground his people well in all the great facts of his will and purposes.

The chapter before us prescribes the most solemn and interesting round of ceremonies contained in the Hebrew ritual. It presents God's law for the great Day of Atonement—the most impressive day in the Jewish calender—a day to which all classes looked with peculiar anxiety—a day when they were to lay aside every secular employment and afflict their souls—the day when the high-priest was to go into the Holy of holies, and to make an atonement for all the sins, irreverences, and pollutions of Israel, from himself down to the lowest of the people, for the entire year—a day of solemnities connecting directly with Calvary and the whole redemption work of Christ Jesus. In this light, then, let us consider it, and endeavor to have our minds filled, and our hearts warmed by the glorious truths which it was meant to foreshadow.

By referring to the 29th verse, you will find that

THE DAY OF ATONEMENT. 289

this day of atonement was appointed for "*the seventh month.*" Seven, as you remember, is a symbol of completeness. This location of these solemnities in the seventh month, would therefore seem to refer to the fact noted by the apostle, that it was only "when the fulness of the time was come, God sent forth his Son to redeem them that were under the law." There is wisdom and order in all God's arrangements. Had Christ come earlier than he did, though the intrinsic virtue of his mediatorial work would have been the same, yet, the absence of due preparation to appreciate, receive and spread it, would have rendered it much less influential upon mankind. His coming was accordingly delayed until that Augustan age, when his cross would necessarily stand in the centre of history and in sight of all the nations of the earth. He lived when the world was sufficiently at peace to give him a hearing — when the human mind was maturely developed, and competent to investigate his claims — when the ways were sufficiently open for the immediate universal promulgation of his Gospel — and when the experience of four thousand years was before men to prove to them how much they needed such a teacher and priest as he. His appearance, therefore, to take away our sins, was in "*the fulness of time*" — in the Tisri or September of the world — when everything was mature and ripe. He put the day of atonement in "the seventh month."

You will also notice that this great expiation service occurred but once in a complete revolution of time — "*once a year.*" A year is a full and complete period. There is no time which does not fall within the year. And the occurrence of the day of atonement but once in the entire year plainly pointed to another great fact noted by the apostle, that "*Christ was once offered to bear the sins of many.*" There is no repetition in his sacrificial work. In the whole year of time there is but one atonement day. The common sacrifices were repeated every morning and evening, to show that men are constantly in need of atoning services; but the great transaction in which that atonement was really effected was performed but once in a complete period. When our High-priest made his great expiation in the seventh month, it referred back to all the past months of the world's age, and forward to all months to come. There is a mighty sublimity in this thought. It throws a grandeur around the cross of Calvary which renders it awful to contemplate, even apart from any other considerations. It was there the ages met. There are no days for man which were not represented in that one atonement day. It is the keystone of the arch which spans from eternity to eternity. The events of that day have no parallel in history. They constitute the one, great, and only transaction of the sort in all the revolutions of time. To gaze upon the scenes of that occasion is to behold what the world for four thousand years was waiting for — what has absorbed the profound attention of the good in all ages — and what shall be the chief theme of the songs and celebrations of everlasting life. "Christ was once offered;" and in that one offering of himself, all the eras of human existence were condensed and included. It was *the event* of this world's year.

It is also to be observed, that the atoning services of this remarkable day had respect to the whole nation at once. They were "to make an atonement for the priests, and for all the people of the congregation." Most of the other offerings were personal, having respect to particular individuals, and to special cases of sin, uncleanness, or anxiety. But, on this day, the offerings were general, and the atonement had respect to the entire people. This recalls another great evangelic truth, namely, that Christ "*died for all*"—"*gave himself a ransom for all*"—"by the grace of God *tasted death for every man*"—and "*is the propitiation for the sins of the whole world.*" There are theologians who talk of "a limited atonement." But, if they mean by this that the expiatory sufferings of Christ were not meant for all men, I must reject such theology as unscriptural. Jesus commands that his Gospel be preached "to every creature;" and if it was not meant for "every creature," I cannot see how to justify the command. The angel who announced the Savior's advent, said, "Behold, I bring you good tidings of great joy, *which shall be to all people.*" But these good tidings are no good tidings to those for whom they were not intended. To offer people redemption and eternal life which never was meant for them, would be, not to bring them good tidings, but to mock them. And as the Gospel is to be good news to all, it must needs be available to all. The apostle says, in so many words, that "the offering of the body of Jesus Christ" was made "ONCE FOR ALL." (Heb. 10 : 10.) Not all are benefitted to the same extent—not all are reconciled and saved—but the reason is that some despise, spurn or neglect a salvation brought to their very doors, and by unbelief make themselves guilty of the blood of Him who laid down His life for them as well as for others. It is no fault of the atoning regulations, and owing to no lameness or arbitrary limitations in the remedy for sin. Redemption is free. The day of atonement was meant to provide forgiveness for the whole people.

Let us then look a little more particularly into the transactions of this important day. I propose to consider them *first*, as regarded the high-priest, upon whom all the services of the occasion devolved; *second*, as regards the atonement itself; and *third*, as regarded the people to be benefitted. Having surveyed these particulars, we may form a correct conception of the great day of atonement.

1. It was to the high-priest a day which imposed numerous inconveniencies, anxieties and humiliations. Seven days before it came, it severed him from his family and home, and confined him to the work of preparation for what was coming. The humbler duties, which at other times devolved upon the ordinary priests, all were on that day to be performed by him. He was put upon slender diet, and, on the atonement day, was required to fast entirely until evening. In order to enter upon the atonement services, he had to divest himself of all his high-priestly habiliments and put on the simple linen dress of one of the common priests. And to all this was added fear and trembling lest he should die as he went into the holy of holies. And so was it with our great High-priest when he undertook to expiate the guilt of man. "Being in the form of God, and thinking it not robbery to be equal with God, he made himself of no reputation, and took upon him the form of a servant, and humbled himself, and became obedient unto death." Separated from his

heavenly home he became a suffering, laborious, self-denying servant. No gold glittered upon his brow, or tinkled with his steps, or mingled its glory with royal colors to adorn his robe. No jewelry sparkled on his shoulders or on his breast. No chariots of grandeur bore him to the place of his mighty deeds of love. He did have on a robe of purple; but it was a robe of mockery. He did wear a crown; but a crown of thorns, pressed on his brow by malicious enemies. He had in his hand a sceptre; but it was "a reed," placed there in contempt to deepen his abasement. "Though he was rich, yet for your sakes he became poor, that ye through his poverty might be made rich." Though he had glory with the Father before the world was, he laid it all aside, and went forth with "neither form nor comeliness, nor beauty that we should desire him." And thus amid privations, humiliations, and anxieties which made him sorrowful even unto death, did he go through with the services of the great day of the world's expiation.

2. It was to the high-priest a day which imposed all its services upon him alone. He was neither to be accompanied nor assisted by any one. Everything to be done was to be done by himself, with his own hands. The law said, "There shall be no man in the tabernacle of the congregation when he goeth in to make an atonement in the holy place, until he come out, and have made an atonement for himself, and for his household, and for all the congregation of Israel." Even the ordinary services on this particular day, the trimming of the lamps, the reviving of the fires, the daily sacrifices, the slaying of the animals, the carrying and sprinkling of the blood,

the burning of the sacrifices and incense, *everything* had to be done by himself alone. Thus, when Jesus undertook the expiation of the world's guilt, "of the people, there was none with him." No one shared in the labor. Isaiah says, "I looked, and there was none to help." His "own arm brought salvation." He "his own self bore our sins in his own body on the tree." When his soul was made an offering for sin, it was he alone that officiated. On that solemn day, all helpers were withdrawn. Lover and friend were put far from him. All alone he wrestled in the garden. All alone he hung upon the cross. Even his heavenly Father seemed to retire from him. All the hopes of the world trembled in that one breaking heart, isolated and unhelped. If he faltered, or his strength failed, salvation was lost for ever. The cup was given him to drink, and there was silence in heaven whilst he shuddered over it. The immortality of millions hung upon his drinking of it. And amid "sweat, as it were great drops of blood falling down to the ground," he said, "*O my Father, if this cup may not pass away from me, except I drink it*, THY WILL BE DONE;" and he drained it with all its bitter dregs, *alone*. Ask him now, "Wherefore art thou red in thine apparel, and thy garments like him that treadeth the wine-fat?" and the response is, "*I have trodden the wine-press* ALONE; *and of the people there was none with me*."

3. The day of atonement was to the high-priest also a very oppressive and exhausting day. His duties, in his complete isolation, were really crushing. The mere responsibility that was upon him that day was a weight that not every man could bear. In addition to that, he had all the duties concerning the holy

ordinances and the sanctuary to perform, including the slaying and offering of some fifteen or seventeen animals. So laborious and trying was his work, that, after it was over, the people gathered round him with sympathy and congratulation that he was brought through it in safety. But it was only a picture of that still more crushing load which was laid upon our great High-priest when making atonement for the sins of the world. None among all the sons of the mighty could ever have performed the work which he performed, and lived. All his life through, there was a weight upon him so heavy, and ever pressing so mightily upon his soul, that there is no account that he ever smiled. Groans and tears and deep oppression accompanied him at almost every step. And when we come to view him in his agonizing watchings and prayers in the garden, and under the burdens of insult and wrong which were heaped upon him in the halls of judgment, and struggling with his load along that *dolorous way* until the muscles of his frame yielded, and he fell faint upon the ground, and oppressed upon the cross until his inmost soul uttered itself in cries which startled the heavens and shook the world, we have an exhibition of labor, exhaustion, and distress, at which we may well sit down and gaze, and wonder, and weep, in mere sympathy with a sorrow and bitterness beyond all other sorrow.

> Tell me, ye who hear him groaning,
> *Was there ever grief like his?*

II. We come now to look at the atonement itself. Here we find that several kinds of offerings were to be made. The object was to make the picture complete by bringing out in different offerings what could not all be expressed by one. They were only different phases of the same unity, pointing to the one offering of Jesus "Christ, who through the Eternal Spirit offered himself without spot to God.' There was a ram for a burnt-offering, and a kid for a sin-offering, not to signify that Christ was offered more than once, or that there was another offering beside his; but to set forth the fact, that Christ's one offering was for all kinds of sin; as it is written, "The blood of Jesus Christ cleanseth from all sin." There is a multiplication of victims, that we may see the amplitude and varied applications of the one great atonement effected by Christ Jesus.

The most vital, essential, and remarkable of these atoning services was that relating to the two goats, as provided for in the seventh, eighth, ninth, tenth, fifteenth, sixteenth, seventeenth, twenty-first and twenty-second verses. One of these goats was to be slain as a sin-offering, and the other was to have the sins of Israel laid upon its head, and then to be taken away alive and left in the wilderness. The one typified the atonement of Christ *in its means and essence;* the other, the same atonement *in its effects.*

It may at first seem a little repulsive to us, to have the blessed Savior typified by a goat. The animal familiar to us by this name, and our tastes respecting it, are by no means favorable to such an association of ideas. But the Syrian goat is a graceful, dignified and clean animal. It was often used as the symbol of leadership and royalty. It was very highly appreciated by the Jews, and was one of the most valuable of their domestic animals. It had none of those bad associations which attach to our goats. The laws of Moses contemplate it with great favor. To an ancient Israelite, it was a pure, elevated, vigorous, useful and noble creature. Contemplating Christ through it, they would have conceived of him as a great leader, strong, virtuous and exalted.

The goats to be used on the day of atonement were these Syrian goats — kids of the first year, without blemish — pictures of our Propitiation, spotless, perfect, and elected to bleed on God's altar in the freshness, prime and vigor of his manhood. They were to be furnished by the congregation of Israel, procured at the expense of the public treasury, and brought forward by the people. So there was a price paid by the Jewish officials for the apprehension of Jesus. At thirty pieces of silver they procured him. And the people brought him forward to the altar, saying, "*Crucify him, crucify him!*" The sacred lot was to decide which one should die. So, after all, it was God who made the selection. It was the Eternal Father who set apart Christ to bleed for man. The Jews acted out their own malicious counsel when they brought him to the slaughter; but he was, at the same time, "delivered by the determinate counsel and foreknowledge of God." (Acts 2 : 23.)

The lot having designated the victim, it was to be slain. "Without the shedding of blood is no remission." Israel's sins demanded an offering, and the sacrificial blade soon left that spotless lamb quivering in the agonies of death. The law said to Aaron, "Kill the goat of the sin-offering;" "and he did as the Lord commanded." And thus was the blessed Savior brought as a lamb to the slaughter. The guilt of ages was crying out for blood; and the holy law pointed to him, and said, "*Awake, O sword, against the man!*" Heaven looked on in breathless wonder. Bound hand and foot to the stake with rugged irons, the clammy sweat gathered on his brow, the languor of receding life settled in his eyes, the exclamations of an unmeasured inward anguish quivered on his parched and sorrowful lips, a convulsive struggle thrilled through his mangled frame, at which a tremor ran down all nature's nerves, and the Lamb of God hung dead in the face of heavens, which shut their day-beams up and staggered at the awful spectacle! He was taken, and with wicked hands was crucified and slain — *slain as the sacrifice for the sins of the world!*

I know that there are great and perplexing mysteries surrounding this doctrine, at which the faith of some is staggered. Nor would I expect to find it otherwise with reference to a subject which is at once the centre of all revelation — the treaty ground on which the sublime attributes of Deity embraced each other and united in the wondrous offer of amnesty and reconciliation to a race of rebels under sentence of eternal death — the very foundation of a plan of grace which lay before the great mind of God for unmeasured ages, as the chosen and appointed outlet of glorious immortality to fallen man. The mere signs and manifestations of nature, which attended the death of Jesus, are beyond the grasp of human comprehension; and how much less, then, is it for man to reason out all

> —— the sweet wonders of that cross,
> Where God the Savior loved and died!

But of this I am assured, that "Christ, our passover, was slain for us;" that "for the transgression of my people was he smitten;" that "his soul was made an offering for sin;" that "we were not redeemed with corruptible things . . . but by the precious blood of Christ, as of a lamb without blemish and without spot;" and hence, that in the crucifixion of Jesus of Nazareth, the great foundation was laid which is the stepping stone to glory and eternal life.

But, the mere slaying of the victim was not all. Its blood had to be carried and sprinkled before the Lord in the Holy of holies.

The mere death of Christ was not the atonement. It was the preparation, material, groundwork, for the atonement; but not the atonement itself. He needed to rise from the dead, and ascend into heaven, and "appear in the presence of God for us," before all the requirements of the case were met. Hence, Jesus, made an High-priest for ever, has "for us entered within the veil" — "passed into the heavens" — "not into the holy places made with hands, which are figures of the true, but into heaven itself, now to appear in the presence of God for us;" — "not with the blood of goats and calves, but with his own blood, he entered in once into the holy place," and is "even at the right hand of God making intercession for us." And by these holy services, which are now going on in heaven, it is, that he "obtains eternal redemption for us."

> The Father hears him pray,
>   His dear anointed One;
> He cannot turn away,
>   Cannot refuse his Son;
> The Spirit answers to the blood,
> And tells us we are born of God.

The offering is accepted. The cry of wrath is hushed. The account of sin is cancelled. Believing Israel is cleansed and free!

Now, the more effectually to portray and signify this forgiveness, was the second goat introduced into these services. The law said, Then "Aaron shall lay both his hands upon the head of the live goat, and confess over him all the iniquities of the children of Israel, and all their transgressions in all their sins, putting them upon the head of the goat, and shall send him away into the wilderness; and the goat shall bear upon him all their iniquities unto a land not inhabited; and he shall let go the goat in the wilderness." Interpreters have been at a great loss in disposing of this scape-goat, and have shown great fertility of imagination in explaining what it signifies. Some think it was a prophecy of the subsequent fate of the Jews; some, that it was a type of Christ's temptation in the wilderness; and some, that it represents something devoted to the devil. If any of my hearers can receive opinions so wild and incongruous, they are at liberty to adopt them. The true interpretation seems to me so plain, that I am surprised to find that any one should have missed it. That the scape-goat was meant to represent Christ, in some aspect of his atoning services, I have not a shadow of doubt. Everything on the great day of expiation referred to Christ. It was a condensed pictorial summary of redemption through the Son of God. And I cannot see how this goat can be made to insinuate any other subject. Only give this goat its proper place in the service, and every difficulty vanishes.

You will notice, that the scape-goat is not introduced until after the first goat had been slaughtered, and its blood accepted as an atonement in the holy of holies. It does not therefore refer to anything in the Savior's history by which atonement was made, but to something subsequent — something going out from the atonement — to some *effects or results*. It does not represent Christ in his temptation, dying, rising, ascending, or intercession, but *in the blessed consequences flowing out from these to such as believe*. Christ is the scape-goat, in so far as he bears away our sins where they are seen and heard of no more. Nor can I conceive of a more beautiful or impressive figure. There stood the gentle creature, meekly receiving upon its head "all the iniquities of the children of Israel." In that I see a picture of the patient Savior as "the Lord laid on him the iniquity of us all." The victim is led forth, and passes out of sight. In that I behold the bearing away of the load of sin from all them that believe. The animal is set loose in the wilderness and is seen no more. It is the significant symbol of the penitent sinner's forgiveness. His guilt is borne quite away out of view. It is remembered against him no more. It is clean gone for ever. Christ his scape-goat has borne it to the unknown land from which it shall return no more. With this the atonement of the great day was complete.

III. A word now with regard to the people to be benefitted by the services of this remarkable day.

That the services and offerings of this day were meant for the entire Jewish nation, is very clear and distinct. But, not all were therefore reconciled and forgiven. The efficacy of these services, in any given case, depended upon the individual himself. There was a way prescribed for the people to keep the day; and to fail in that, was, of course, to fail in the benefits of the day of atonement. It was a day on which God's requirement was, "*Ye shall afflict your souls, and do no work at all. It shall be a Sabbath of rest unto you, and ye shall afflict your souls.*" There was a practical and spiritual experience to go along with the priestly services. The blood, and sacrifice, and incense, and solemn entrance into the Holy of holies could do no one any good, and the scape-goat bore no one's sins away to forgetfulness, who did not come to these services with humbled and penitent hearts, and afflicted souls. The atonement day was to be a day of contrition—of weeping—of soul-sorrow for sin—of confession, reformation, and return to God—a day of heart-melting and charity. Without these accompaniments, its oblations were vain, its incense useless, its solemnities but idle ceremonies. And, as it was with the type, so is it with the antitype. Christ's atonement is not for them who know not how to appreciate it, whose hearts are not softened to contrition by his dying love, who feel no compunction for their sins which murdered him, and no fond affection for those whom he has redeemed. In vain do we dream of heaven, if we have not repented of our wickednesses, or think of condemnation gone, if we have not broken with all our evil ways. Useless is it to talk of penances and fasts, of good deeds and charities, if the spirit aches not at the remembrance of Calvary. Naught to our souls is all the pardon-speaking blood of Jesus, if there be no breaking and contrition in our own hearts to accompany the offering of it. Nay, without repentance on our part, his glorious mediation fails to become ours, and is the same, yea worse, to us than if it had not been. "Wash you; make you clean; put away the evil of your doings; cease to do evil; learn to do well; judge the fatherless; plead for the widow; cover the naked; and out of cheerful gratitude to Him who bled for thee, go do his holy bidding;"— such are the commands that are upon us to render us acceptable worshippers. "*It is such a fast that I have chosen, a day for a man to afflict his soul,*" saith the Lord.

Would you then have Christ's atoning day to be a blessing to thy soul, come to it with a moved and melting heart. Come to it with thy spirit bowed for thy many, many sins. Come to it as the humbled prodigal came back to the kind Father he had wronged. Come to it as the poor heart-broken publican came, smiting thy guilty breast and crying, "God be merciful to me a sinner!" Think of Gethsemane, and weep. Think of Calvary, and weep. Think of the Savior's great agonies, and weep. Weep in sympathetic sorrow for his mighty griefs. Weep at the sad wrongs which there came upon celestial innocence for thy good. Weep at the prayers of love and intercession which thy dying Redeemer poured out even for his murderers, among whom thou art, in a sense, to be numbered. Weep at being an inhabitant of a world and a member of a race that could thus abuse and kill the very Son of God. Weep at the nails and spear that pierced him, and the crown of thorns pressed on his bleeding brow, and at the anguish uttered in his expiring cries so meekly borne for thee. Press to his cross and plead to be forgiven. Fall on thy face at his grace, and abhor thyself for the vileness that could be expiated only at such a price. Yea, enter that rocky cavern damp and dark, and lay thy hand upon his cold and bloody forehead, and mourn there at that guilt of thine which murdered him. Afflict thy soul, and weep; weep bitterly; but weep in hope that there is pardon yet through that precious Savior's death; so shall thy light break forth as the morning, and thy peace flow as a river.

It was a beautiful arrangement in this connection, that when the year of jubilee came, it always begun with the evening of this day of atonement. The law says: "Then shalt thou cause the trumpet of the jubilee to sound: in the day of atonement shall ye make the trumpet sound throughout all your land." The day was interesting and beautiful from its earliest commencement. If you would have been in Jerusalem as the atonement day drew on, the night before, you would have seen the city become silent and still, as the sun set. No lingerers in the market; no traders; no voice of business. The watchmen that go about the city, you would have heard humming the penitential psalms, reminding themselves of their own and their city's secret sins, seen through the darkness by an all-seeing God; and the Levites from the temple singing responsively as they walked around the courts. As the sun rose again on the Mount of Olives and brought the hour of morning sacrifice, you would have seen the city pour out its thousands, moving solemnly to the temple — to the heights of Zion's towers or the grassy slopes of Olivet — to witness with contrite hearts the solemn services which were to take away their sins. The priestly duties having been performed — the atonement made — the scape-goat led away and gone — and the hearts of the people bowed in humble thankfulness for the favors God had shown them — it remained only for Aaron to put off his linen garments, put on his attirements of gold, purple, and jewels, and make his appearance once more; and instantly, the silver trumpet sounded, and the shouts of Israel echoed over Olivet, and thrilled through all the land: *"The year of jubilee is come!"* In the morning there was bitterness and tears. In the evening there was triumphant peace. The day of the sinner's soul-sorrow begins the year of his rest.

Such, then, is the great day of atonement, in its type and in its antitype — a wondrous day — a day on which all man's days of peace depend — the birth-day of spiritual joy, hope, and immortality — the day from which salvation springs — the day in which the Christian's heaven has its roots — the day that ushers in the everlasting year of jubilee. And that day to us *is now*. This hour that you have listened to me is one of its hours. Even now the Savior stands before God in the Holy of holies with incense of supplications for us. What then? Shall we shout, or shall we weep? Shall we rejoice or shall we tremble? Some of you, perhaps, have entered upon this solemn day with hearts sportive and gay. While the Lamb of God was being exhibited dying and dead before you, you, perhaps, were laughing. While Jehovah has been saying, *"Afflict your souls,"* some have been reviling or carousing. While the Son of God lay lifeless and murdered for the sinner's sins, those meant to be brought to penitence have been dancing and making merry. While hell's fires were licking up his blood as the only atonement for human guilt, heaven has seen the scowl and heard the words of mockery on the lips of those for whom he died. Meanwhile the day is passing. The shadows of the evening are at hand. And what, oh sinner, if it should close, and leave thee with thy guilt unpardoned, and thy soul uncleansed!

SEVENTEENTH LECTURE.

LAWS FOR HOLY LIVING.

LEV. CHAPTERS XVII. XVIII. XIX. XX.

I have not undertaken the exposition of this book of Leviticus with a view to explain and refine upon everything which it contains. Too much commentary is sometimes worse than none at all. In order, therefore, to prevent this series of discourses from extending to wearisome length, I will collect the remaining chapters into groups, and treat only of their general significance. There is, at any rate, much in them unsuited for public or family reading, and which cannot with propriety be made the subject of particular elucidation.

The text for to-night will accordingly embrace four chapters; the seventeenth, eighteenth, nineteenth, and twentieth; as their various provisions may be very conveniently comprehended in one view. All the laws in these several chapters relate to what is more or less personal and private. We do not again meet with any public services until we come to the twenty-third chapter. From the sixteenth to the twenty-third, everything relates to the duties, qualities, and associations of individuals in private life. This fact, coming as it does right after the great day of atonement, is very suggestive. It indicates that God contemplates much more respecting us than the mere pardon of our sins; that justification is not the whole intent of the Savior's redemptive services; and that there is to be a personal righteousness and purification which rests upon our own exertions. The atonement has been made; reconciliation has been effected; and to every one who has faith to believe it, all past sins are for ever borne away, to be seen and heard of no more. But this does not include everything. It does by no means embrace the whole object which Christ had in view, when he, "through the eternal Spirit, offered himself without spot to God." Having thus purged our consciences from dead works, it is that we may now go on "to serve the living God." Having by his awful bloodshedding procured us hope, it is that every man may purify himself as He is pure. Having "delivered us out of the hands of our enemies," he intends that we should "serve him without fear, in holiness and righteousness before him, all the days of our life." Having bought us with a price, it hence devolves upon us to glorify him in our bodies and our spirits which are his.

There is a sense in which salvation is altogether of God — a matter of free bounty from him. Upon this point the words of the apostle are clear and conclusive. "By grace are ye saved, through faith, and that not of yourselves; it is the gift of God; not of works, lest any man should boast. For we are his workmanship, created in Christ Jesus." I may illustrate this by the case of a vessel at sea, which has by some mismanagement anchored too near the shore, and which the receding tides have left aground in the deep mire. There lies the noble fabric, helpless, useless, and a wreck for ever. All the nautical skill and strength in the world cannot avail to save her. God must interpose and bring back the tides, or she must lie there and rot. This is a picture of the sad estate of man without Divine grace. He is aground in the deep morasses of sin. The tides have gone from him. He is nobly endowed and equipped; but it all avails nothing for his deliverance. God must send out his power, or he will stay there to perish without hope. But, there has been a mighty pulsation in the ocean of Jehovah's love. We have seen the motion of it in the moving scenes of the day of atonement. It has raised a tide of mercy around the helpless sinner. Its majestic swell has lifted him up from the depths to which he had sunk. He is again made to feel the motion of the waters. He is once more erect upon the broad and even surface of the sea. He is saved from the terrible doom which impended over him. Now, to what would you ascribe the salvation of a ship in such circumstances? to the men on board, or to the tides? to the capacities and powers of the mariners, or to that God whose footsteps are in the sea, and his wonders in the great waters? There can be no doubt as to your answer. It was God, in those benevolent laws of his which are everywhere at work. And in this sense, salvation is altogether of God. It is the flood-tide of Almighty grace, gathered around and under the grounded ship, and setting the sinner afloat when there was no other help.

But, there is another sense in which salvation depends upon our own exertions. On this point, the same apostle is equally plain and positive. "*Work out your own salvation*," are his words. There is then something for us to do after all. Another apostle is still more specific. "What doth it profit," says he, "though a man say he hath faith, and have not works? Can faith save him? . . . Faith, if it hath not works, is dead, being alone. . . . By works a man is justified, and not by faith only." The same figure will serve to illustrate this feature of our salvation. After the tides have come in and raised the grounded ship, and freed it from its helpless estate, then comes in the activity of those on board. If they do not weigh anchor, and spread the sails, and take hold of the helm, and exert themselves to get away from the spot, their case will be no better than if the tides had never come. So, as Christ has come and freed us from condemnation, and recovered to us our lost power, and reconciled us to God; it is now for us to bestir ourselves to get away from the ugly spot, and to set sail for a voyage directly for the home-port of everlasting rest. The atonement is God's work; and we become participants of its benefits only by the abundant outflowing of his unsearchable grace; but now that the tide of his mercy has reached us, we are gratefully and obediently to take advantage of it, and go to work ourselves. The day of atonement must be followed with a good life, for which that atonement was meant to prepare us, or we sink again into the same hopeless condition in which we were before atonement came; and with this augmentation of our wretchedness, that "there remaineth no more sacrifice for sin." Saved by grace, and created anew in Christ Jesus, it is "unto good works, which God hath before ordained that we should walk in them."

And when I speak of good works and a holy life, I do not mean a life of melancholy asceticism, or retirement from the common cares, activities, affec tions and duties appertaining to our earthly estate. People are quite too much disposed to frame their ideas of sanctity from the cloister and the convent. Talk of holy men, and they at once begin to think of those who wear cowls, and tell beads, and keep solitary vigils, and devote themselves to an endless routine of prayers and fasts in monastic cells. But if they would ascertain God's idea of holiness, let them come to Jesus and learn of him. The true pattern of a holy life was set in that divine man, who pleased God without making the wilderness his home, or interposing iron grates and massive doors between himself and the common world—who found it no contamination to mingle with publicans and sinners, but served his heavenly Father as he walked the fields of Galilee, and frequented the villages of fishermen by the sea, and kept up communication with those who dwelt in Judah's towns and thronged Jerusalem's busy streets. "In him was life," and his "life is the light of men." Without some degree of conformity to him, our religion is but a shadow and a name. For so it is written, "If any man have not the Spirit of Christ, he is none of his."

Let me invite attention, then, more specifically to the means and elements of a good and holy life, as they are shadowed forth in the chapters before us.

I. The principal, and, perhaps, the only permanent provision contained in the seventeenth chapter, is that which respects the manner of treating blood. No matter how or from what animal it came, it was always to be looked upon with consideration. While the Jews were in the wilderness, they were not permitted to slay an animal even for food, except at the door of the tabernacle, where its blood had to be taken by the priest and sprinkled upon the altar of the Lord. It was by no means to be devoted to heathen gods, or demons, to appease their anger. Neither was it at any time, or in any form, to be eaten. Even the hunter, in the excitement of the chase, if he succeeded in taking an animal, was required to stop and drain out its blood, and then reverently cover up that blood with dust. There is also a reason assigned for all this. God says, "the life of the flesh is in the blood; and I have given it to you upon the altar to make an atonement for your souls: for it is the blood that maketh atonement for the soul. Therefore no soul of you shall eat blood." The use of blood was not forbidden because it was unclean, but because it was sacred. It represents life. It is that by which life was redeemed. It is that, flowing about the altar, that reconciled between them and God. And for this reason they were to be particular about it, and reverence it. The simple fact that they were saved by blood in the sacrifices, was in their eyes to consecrate all blood; so that whenever they saw blood, they were to think how their own lives were forfeited by their transgressions, and how the blood of atonement sheltered them.

Now, it is easy to see how a law of this sort would work to solemnize, restrain and soften the heart of a conscientious Jew. It would keep the solemn atonement before him whithersoever he went. The very huntsman would be met by it in the deep recesses of the forest. And if we desire to learn what constitutes the deepest essence of a good Christian life, we here have it most beautifully typified. We must keep in view the blood of atonement. We must remember Calvary — the sacrifice which there was made for us—the love which there was lavished upon our souls — the condemnation due to our sins which there was met. We must never lose sight of that bleeding Lamb of God which taketh away the sin of the world. All Christian goodness finds its spring and fountain there. It is the lifting up of Christ that draws men from the ways of sin. It is the Savior's love that subdues the rebellious heart to obedience, and constrains it to apostolic devotion and martyr constancy. It is our clear and continual recognition of what Jesus has done for us, that weakens temptation, disposes to duty, and prompts to the deeds of righteousness.

I remember to have met with an affecting little incident in Roman history connected with the death of Manlius Capitolinus, a renowned consul and general, who was once proudly hailed as the savior of Rome. It happened one night when the Gauls threatened to overwhelm the capitol, that he bravely took his stand upon the wall where they came on with their attack, and there fought singly and alone until he had repelled them, and so saved the city from destruction. It so occurred that this distinguished man was afterwards accused of some great public fault, and put upon trial for his life. But just as the judges were about to pass sentence upon him, he looked up at the walls of the capitol, which towered in view, and with tears in his eyes pointed to where he had fought for his accusers, and periled his life for their safety. The people remembered the heroic achievement, and wept. No one had the heart to say aught against him, and the judges were compelled to forbear. Again he was tried, and with the same result. Nor could he be convicted until his trial was removed to some low and distant point, from which the capitol was invisible. And so, while Calvary is in full view, in vain will earth and hell seek to bring the Christian into condemnation. One serious look at the cross, and at the love which there, unaided and alone, when all was dark and lost, interposed for our salvation, is enough to break the power of passion at once, and to strike dead every guilty proceeding. Low must the believer sink, and blotted from his heart must be the recollection of that scene of suffering for him, before he can ever become faithless to his Redeemer, or perfidious to his Savior's cause. There is a power in the bloody monument of redeeming love, which baffles all the allurements and accusations of hell. It is the great propelling motive to a holy life. It is the potent source of Christian loyalty and devotion. And if we would be virtuous and good, the first and grand requisite is, never to lose sight of Christ's atoning blood.

II. Passing to the eighteenth chapter, we find sundry laws, but all bearing upon two general points. The first relates to the customs of the Egyptians, from among whom the Jews came, and of the Canaanites, whose land they were to inherit. God here says to them, "After the doings of the land of Egypt, wherein ye dwelt, shall ye not do: and after the doings of the land of Canaan, whither I bring you, shall ye not do; neither shall ye walk in their ordinances." These were heathen and defiled nations. They are the types of all such people as are living in impenitence and sin. Israel was to be a holy nation, and therefore was not to follow the ways of the unclean. The greatest danger of a purified man, arises from his old habits and associations. It is not easy to turn a stream quite out of the channel in which it has been flowing for ages. It is a mighty work to revolutionize a character which has been forming for years, or to tear quite away from a long-continued routine which includes all our recollections of infancy, and in which our life took its chief attractions. It is like the leopard undertaking to change his spots, or the Ethiopian setting himself to whiten his dark skin. It cannot be done at all without the converting grace of God. And even after the divine finger has dispossest the unclean spirit, and swept and garnished the house, there is great danger of the return of that spirit with seven other spirits worse than himself. There is need that the doors of the soul be carefully watched and strongly barricaded against him. Even after Israel had crossed the sea in triumph, there rose up lusts after the flesh-pots of Egypt. The sow that has been washed, still has strong affections for the mire.

The second grand element of a good Christian life, therefore, is, a complete and thorough reformation with regard to old habits. If we have been in close intimacy with the vile, we must withdraw from their communion, and keep aloof from their wicked ways. If we have been giving way to bad passions, we must cut ourselves off from the occasions of our transgressions, and beware of putting ourselves into circumstances which invite temptation.

It is said of the elephant, that though he may be thoroughly subjugated and domesticated, if, in after years, his owners are so unfortunate as to bring him into the region where he was captured, the wild fire of his eye comes again, and he casts up his trunk in the air as if to throw off all his bonds, and with a shout bounds away to his native wilderness in spite of all the efforts of his keeper to retain him. And just such an elephantine nature do we carry with us, that the mere neighborhood of old vices will sometimes kindle it with ancient passion, so that despite all previous discipline and conviction, away it goes to the miserable haunts of its days of uncleanness. We must guard against old customs, and keep away from associations in which we were once in the habit of transgressing.

III. The other specifications of the eighteenth chapter, all relate to sexual purity. They typically refer to the necessity of a proper government of the affections. We are very much the creatures of feeling. God has endowed our nature with many tender susceptibilities, which impart a zest and warmth to life which it could not otherwise possess. He has also so constituted human society as to furnish abundant room for their healthful and happy play. Nor does it enter at all into religion to deaden, eradicate, or stint our natural affections. The Scriptures constantly class those who are destitute of natural affection, with the basest of mankind. It is only sin that acts as an astringent upon the warm feelings of our nature, and defiles, corrodes, shrivels and destroys them. It is one of the offices of piety to quicken the pulse of love, to soften our ruggedness, to expand the heart, to sweeten the ties of tender regard, and to fill all the arteries of the social system with a bounding stream of warm and zealous interest and fondness. If Christianity had been sent to extinguish social affections, it would be a blight instead of a blessing to the world.

But whilst piety does not seal or freeze up the flow of feeling, it rigidly requires that it be governed, modulated and controlled by principles of purity and righteousness. Like every other impulse or susceptibility, natural affection may be perverted and become the occasion of great sin and degradation. Our hearts must therefore be watched. We may love; but we must love virtuously. We may cherish the most tender regards; but they must not rest upon criminal hopes. Our warmest feelings may be enlisted and indulged; but we must be cautious that they do not betray us into sin and shame. All affections have their proper objects, and to these they must be confined and kept in healthful moderation; otherwise they become fires of ruin. Hence the precept of the apostle, "Mortify your members which are upon the the earth, fornication, uncleanness, inordinate affection, evil concupiscence, and covetousness, which is idolatry; for which things' sake the wrath of God cometh on the children of disobedience." Even the secret thought of unchasteness, the hidden incontinent wish, the impure desire, the cherished hope of unclean gratifications, must be spurned and crucified as criminal before God, and crushed as an enemy to the peace and good of society. The heart must be kept with all diligence; for out of it are the issues of life. It is God who saith, "Defile not yourselves in any of these things."

IV. We come now to the nineteenth chapter. Here we have quite a list of moral precepts setting forth an extensive code of Christian righteousness. The provisions of the preceding chapter were negative; these are mostly positive. In the one God shows us how we are to "cease to do evil;" in the other he instructs us how to "do well." I have not time to comment upon all these precepts at length. Indeed it is hardly necessary to do more than state them in a general review of the sort now in hand. We have seen that we as Christians are to keep in view the atonement of Christ, to guard against old habits and associations, and to purge and purify our affections. We here have another general direction. And that is, to submit ourselves obediently to the moral law, of which this chapter is a sort of special and authoritative exposition.

We must be deferential to parents and authorities. God says, "Ye shall fear every man his mother and his father;" and of course all such as occupy corresponding relations to us. Disobedience in the family, is at the same time treason to the state, and rebellion against the sovereignty of heaven. Parental authority is part of God's grand scheme of government, and it is sin to disregard it.

We must attend to the ordinances of worship. God says, "Ye shall every man keep my Sabbaths." As Paul expresses it, we are to be considerate, "not forsaking the assembling of ourselves together, as the manner of some is; but exhorting one another." To neglect God's rites of worship, is to neglect our souls, and to despise the most potent means of our sanctification.

We must worship God according to the simplicities of his own appointments. His word is, "Turn not," or rather, "*look not* unto idols (*vanities*), to make to yourselves molten gods." The idea is, that we are not to be captivated with the vain pomps or attractive elegances of heathen worship, to engraft them upon our worship of Jehovah. We must keep to what he has prescribed, and present and eat our peace-offerings as he has directed.

We are to be kind to the poor, and appropriate of our abundance for their benefit. We are only the stewards of God in what we possess. Our harvests and our income are from his gracious hand. And he claims a portion of them for "the poor and stranger."

We must be rigidly honest in our transactions with our fellow-men. God says, "Ye shall not steal, neither deal falsely, neither lie one to another; neither swear falsely by my name, nor profane the name of God. Thou shalt not defraud thy neighbor, neither rob him. The wages of him that is hired shall not abide with thee all night until morning." Without obedience to these precepts there can be no social confidence; and without mutual confidence this world would be worse than a Bedouin desert, and all its population Ishmaelites. Unless man can trust in his fellow-man, business stagnates, the machinery of the world stops, and social peace is at an end.

We must pity the infirmities of the unfortunate, and not mock at or take advantage of their weaknesses. God says, "Thou shalt not curse the deaf, nor put a stumbling-block before the blind." "Who hath made man's mouth? or who maketh the dumb, or deaf, or the seeing, or the blind? have not I the Lord?" To make sport with those who suffer thus, is therefore to mock at God, and to revile his holy administrations. He hath put such afflicted ones in our world to teach us sympathy and gratitude, and it is wicked to amuse ourselves with their privations.

We must be just in our decisions, without predisposing affection for the poor, or desire to secure the fawning flattery of the rich and great. The ancient heathen pictured the goddess of justice as blind, that she might not see what parties were awaiting her decisions. And so Jehovah says, "Thou shalt not respect the persons of the poor, nor honor the persons of the mighty; but in righteousness shalt thou judge thy neighbor."

We must put a bridle upon our tongues. God says, "Thou shalt not go up and down as a talebearer among thy people." It is the devil who is the accuser of the brethren. And I know of nothing more diabolical than the slander-monger. There are people

> Whose hearts are gall — whose tongues are fire —
> With souls too base for generous ire —
> With swords too keen for noble use —
> Whose shield and buckler are abuse.

And many who are not habitually malicious, and do not mean to do mischief, yet are so fond of retailing ill news of their neighbor that one can seldom hear them talk without trembling for the reputation of his friends. There are some souls like certain birds which seem to live only on what is vile. It was such, I suppose, that James had in view, when he said, "The tongue is a fire, a world of iniquity; it setteth on fire the course of nature. . . It is an unruly evil, full of deadly poison." It needs taming beyond every other member.

We must be charitable. God says, "Thou shalt not stand against the blood of thy neighbor. Thou shalt not hate thy brother in thine heart."

And yet, we must not connive at sin. "Thou shalt in any wise rebuke thy neighbor, and not suffer sin upon him." It is a charity to admonish him of his faults, that he may repent and be saved. But it must not be done in spite or malice. "Thou shalt not avenge, nor bear any grudge against the children of thy people, but thou shalt love thy neighbor as thyself." He is thy brother; and one God is the judge of us all.

We must refrain from any attempt to join together incongruous things, or what God has put asunder We cannot serve God and Mammon. Heathen lewdness and worldly folly must not be permitted to mingle with Christian profession. There is a distinctness in holiness which must be preserved against all commixtures.

We must not use power and station for sensual gratifications. It is high trespass against Almighty God.

We must put a check upon appetite, and accustom ourselves to self-denial. Israel was not permitted to eat fruit from any tree until the fourth year after it began to bear.

We must not trust to signs and omens, or resort to auguries and fortune-telling. "Thou shalt not use enchantment," saith the Lord. Jehovah, he is God; and on his good providence must we rely.

We must be moderate in our griefs when bereavement comes. God says, "Ye shall not make any cuttings in your flesh for the dead, nor print any marks upon you." Tears may flow; for Jesus wept; but we must not sorrow as those who have no hope. God reigneth.

Nor are we to seek communication with the dead, or fellowship with those who pretend to bring us messages from the departed. God says, "Regard not them that have familiar spirits, neither seek after wizards, to be defiled by them." There always have been people who profess to communicate at will with beings of another world — to be inspired by demons — and to do wonders by compact with the devil or his angels. Nor am I prepared to say that their pretence is false. But whether false or true, God's people are to have nothing to do with them. They can only defile. Jehovah says, "The soul that turneth after such as have familiar spirits, and after wizards, I will even set my face against that soul, and will cut him off from among his people."

In addition to all this, we must be respectful to age, kind to strangers, honest in our weights and measures, and obedient to all God's statutes and judgments. So shall we be holy and good. And the Lord Jehovah shall be our God, and we shall be his people.

A remark or two, now, upon the twentieth chapter, and I will close this discourse.

We have been contemplating the laws of holy living. In this chapter we have God's threatenings against those who violate them. It is a chapter of penalties. God is not only our adviser, but our Lord and Judge. His commands are not only gracious counsels, but authoritative *laws*. They are not without penal sanctions. A law, from its very nature, must have penalties attached to it. God's commandments are laws, and hence, he who will not obey them, but sets at naught the authority by which they are given, must meet a doom commensurate with his crime. Sinai still thunders and smokes against those who live in unrighteousness, notwithstanding the atonement-work of Christ. The axe is laid at the root of the tree, and if it bringeth not forth good fruit, it shall be hewn down, and given to the flames. The Gospel is indeeed *glad tidings* — glad tidings of great joy. It is a call of mercy from the heavens to the suffering and the lost. But, it is a call to holiness. And whilst it is a glorious savor of life unto life to them that yield to it, and walk in its light, it is a fearful savor of death unto death to those who despise or disobey it. I know of no responsibility so awful as that which the Gospel itself imposes. The Holy Ghost tells us, that we had better never known the way of righteousness, than after we have known it, to turn from the holy commandment delivered unto us. It opens to us a sublime heaven, and a safe and easy way of entering into it; but at a cost so great, that the deepest hell is for him who despises and disobeys. The very grace that has brought salvation to man, must needs become a curse to deepen the perdition of those who refuse to accept and obey it. As to the disobedient Jew, God says, "I will set my face against that man, and will cut him off from among his people — he shall be put to death — his blood shall be upon him — he shall be burnt with fire." Did Jehovah mean what he said? Literally were these penalties meant for the faithless son of Abraham; and typically are they meant for us. And if they seem terrific as they applied anciently to this world, still more terrific are they as a type of what is to come upon the faithless and impenitent hearer of the Gospel. What saith the Scripture? "Indignation and wrath, tribulation and anguish, upon every soul of man that doeth evil, of the Jew first, and also of the Gentile."

Brethren, God is merciful. His grace is unspeakable. But he also is just, and must support the honor of his throne. Let men disguise it as they may, the day of atonement does not supersede the day of retribution. There is one question on this subject, put by the Spirit of God, that is enough to make the soul shudder. "He that despised Moses' aw, died without mercy under two or three witnesses: of how much soever punishment, suppose ye, shall he be thought worthy, who hath trodden under foot the Son of God, and hath counted the blood of the covenant, wherewith he was sanctified, an unholy thing, and hath done despite to the Spirit of grace?"

Brethren, there is terror enough predicted in this Bible to make one's hair lift. When David looked in upon the portion of the wicked, he was appalled beyond measure, and cried, "Horror — horror hath taken hold upon me!" When that dauntless man of Tarsus, "who shook his chain in the face of kings —whose spirit no sufferings could subdue or dangers disconcert—who stood as unmoved amid a thousand perils as ever rock amid a thousand billows," surveyed the doom of the faithless, his hand trembled, and the big tears dropped from his manly cheeks, as he wrote down their end. Jeremiah seems overcome with emotion when thinking of the portion of the wicked. "O that my head were waters," said he, "and mine eyes a fountain of tears, that I might weep day and night for the slain!" Ah, that lake— that lake! Explain it as you please, it is awful to think of. That worm that never dies — those fires that are never quenched—that blackness of darkness for ever—refine upon the words as you will, there is something there which makes my heart ache, and my soul tremble.

LAWS FOR HOLY LIVING.

Brethren, the gates of salvation stand open to us to-day. The arms of gracious heaven are stretched out to embrace us. The mansions of eternity are ready to receive us to them. The prayers of the great Intercessor have joined with his blood to secure for us a home in the New Jerusalem. The fruits of immortality are waving for us on the everlasting branches of the tree of life. But, between us and them lies a path of good deeds and consecration to God. Jesus says, "If thou wilt enter into life, keep the commandments." And if we are not willing to obey, we must let go our hope. There is no other alternative. God be our helper! Amen.

EIGHTEENTH LECTURE.

PERSONAL REQUIREMENTS OF THE PRIESTS.

LEV. CHAPTERS XXI. XXII.

In the chapters last under consideration, we had the laws for holy living, as they applied to the people generally. We now enter upon a list of corresponding requirements relating specifically to the priests. God holds all public officers to a special accountability. He looks with a jealous eye upon all who exercise authority, and particularly upon those who are called to minister at his altars. When he puts men in office, and entrusts them with administrations over their fellow-men, he lays his solemn demands upon them, and holds them with a tighter rein. Office and high station are mighty things. It is by them that the masses are moved and moulded. They are the fountains of social influence, the springs of public sentiment, the hands which fashion the destiny of society. They therefore impose awful responsibilities upon those who occupy them.

The Jewish priest was an exalted officer. The high-priest especially held the highest position of any man upon earth. He occupied relations to God and man above all others. He was the centre of the whole Mosaic system. He was the grand impersonation of the Hebrew religion. It was through him the people came to God, and through him and his ministrations that God let forth his favors to the people. He was to be the interpreter of the divine will to the tribes of Israel, and to bear their offerings of gratitude and penitence to Jehovah. The whole religion of the nation leaned upon him. He was not a king; yet he was more than a king. He was not a prophet; but he was more than a prophet. He was Priest of the Most High God; and in this, respect he occupied an elevation above all his fellows. So conspicuous a personage, and so deeply identified with everything sacred, needed to be a man of special excellence, or religion itself would suffer from the deficiency. Neither could he typify Christ without the utmost personal perfection and social purity. God has therefore laid down the most rigid laws upon this subject. The Jewish priest was required to be in all respects a complete man, symmetrical in all his members, perfect in his humanity, not crooked, not maimed, not diseased. He that had any bodily blemish was not allowed to enter this office, or to touch anything relating to its functions. He had also to be entirely free from any suspicious social alliances. Even his wife had to be a particular kind of a woman, and also his daughter. Nothing about him, that could in any way be made a subject of reproach, was at all allowable. And even then, his office was to rise paramount to all social ties and sympathies. Under the severest domestic afflictions, he was always to remember that he was a priest, and not permit himself to be unfitted for the priest's duties by giving way to the promptings of grief. God said of all these things: "He shall not defile himself, being a chief among his people." He had to be blameless, a model man, a consecrated officer, who was to know nothing but his calling.

Some have reasoned from this to the Christian ministry, and apply to the preacher what was laid down for the priest. If this were allowable in a literal sense, there could be no legitimate minister of Christ who is not of the tribe of Levi, and of the house of Aaron. No man could be a priest under these rules but a Jew of this particular stock. And to say that no one has a right to preach the Gospel but a Levite of the flesh, is more than Christians generally would undertake to do. And if one of these laws is inapplicable to the Gospel ministry, of course the others are also, except so far as founded upon other principles than the mere regulation of the Jewish priesthood.

There is a sense, however, in which these ancient laws become suggestive of what is very important to a proper and successful ministry of the Gospel. Paul's portraiture of a bishop takes in many of the requirements which rested upon the old priesthood. "A bishop must be blameless, the husband of one wife, vigilant, sober, of good behavior, given to hospitality, apt to teach; not given to wine, no striker, not greedy of filthy lucre; but patient; not a brawler; not covetous; one that ruleth well his own house, having his children in subjection with all gravity; not a novice, lest being lifted up with pride he fall into the condemnation of the devil. Moreover, he must have a good report of them which are without." (1 Tim. 3 : 2–7.)

It is a truth, my brethren, which ought ever to be before the minds of those who minister in holy things, and deeply graven upon their hearts, that righteousness of life, and consistency in private conduct, is the most vital element of a preacher's power.

Let his ordination, his talents, his attainments, his eloquence, be what they may, without a life corresponding to his teachings, he is only "as sounding brass, or a tinkling cymbal." Actions speak louder than words. Character is more eloquent than rhetoric. What a man *is*, always has more weight than what he says. And to preach Christ, and act antichrist; or to give people good instruction, coupled with a bad example, is but beckoning to them with the head to show them the way to heaven, while we take them by the hand to lead them in the way to hell. If a man's character contradicts his teaching, people may admire his learning and his fluency, but he will have no power over their consciences and hearts. His badness by no means exempts them from receiving and obeying the truth; but they will ever be finding apology in his inconsistencies for despising his pious counsels. Human nature is at any rate disinclined to be schooled. Self-love is wounded at the idea of submitting to receive instruction and warning as if from one wiser and better than ourselves. And when one comes to us in this high office, and reproves our wickedness, we are tempted to avenge ourselves by carping, either at the doctrine or the teacher. He at once becomes an object of our unamiable scrutiny. We want to know who made him a judge over us, and what better he is than those whom he has undertaken to rebuke and correct. And if so fair a mark for censure be himself in darkness while undertaking to guide the blind, there is something in us which grows indignant, and turns upon him with a resentment against which all his learning and eloquence are powerless. "Physician, heal thyself;" is the sentiment that rises in our hearts, and breaks the force of all his good words. An unholy, unprincipled preacher, must ever be an object of unmitigated contempt. He will be hissed and reprobated to his very grave. And it is right that he should be. God has made it the first business of him who is a leader in holy things, to see to it that he himself has submitted to the Gospel which he asks others to obey. Not only the lynx eyes and argus eyes of unconverted men are upon him, to search and sift him, to magnify his deficiencies, drag forward his defects, and thus break his influence; but the all-seeing eye of Jehovah is upon him, and the hand of a heavenly Master holds him over to the solemn judgment, to act according to what he preaches. Like the high-priest, he is "chief man among his people," and all their interests, as well as his own, demand that he should "walk as becometh the Gospel." And if withal he is inconsistent, dishonest, trifling, and faithless, it is but just that the condemnation of heaven and earth should be upon him. "A bishop must be blameless."

And in the same proportion that an unholy life weakens a minister's influence, does uprightness, fidelity, and consistency, enhance it. A truly honest and good man, whatever his sphere, will always have weight. However people may revile his profession, they always feel rebuked in his presence, and pay homage to him in their secret souls. There is might in virtue. It tells upon a man in spite of him. It strikes at once into the heart and conscience. It is more powerful than eloquence. It is the most effective armor that man can wear. And when a minister has a pure and spotless life to sustain his

PRIESTLY REQUIREMENTS. 331

profession, he becomes a host in strength. His silence is a sermon, and his words are sharp in the hearts of his enemies. We have an illustration of this in the case of Jesus. Whatever elements of character and wisdom concurred to give weight to his teachings, there was nothing more effectual than his immaculate goodness and fidelity to the truth. The very men who were sent to seize him, when they heard him, fell back in terror, saying, "Never man spake like this man." The highest authorities of Judea stood in awe of that meek and guileless Nazarene. A saintly preacher is an awful being. The stoutest hearts bend before him. He carries an influence which none else can wield. At his voice, the conqueror has been known to stay his steps, the monarch to hide his paled face, the judge to tremble on his seat. And if all Christ's ministers were examples of the religion they preach, there is nothing in this world that could withstand them. The potencies of hell would melt out of the earth like snow before the sun. Above all things, therefore, does it become a minister to be a pattern of his teachings, and a living record of the Gospel which he utters. Jehovah says of his priests, "They shall be holy unto their God, and not profane the name of their God." "He that ruleth among men must be just, ruling in the fear of the Lord."

But, the law prescribes for the domestic relations and social surroundings of the priest, as well as for his personal perfections. Upon this point also it becomes a minister to be particular. It would seem like scandal for me to speak freely of the miserable and disabling fetters into which many ministers of God have inconsiderately put themselves in these respects. Alas, how has the cause of the blessed

Jesus suffered from the unfortunate alliances of those who have been solemnly ordained to go forth as the preachers of his Gospel! How has Satan hedged up the way and crippled the energies and usefulness of good men, by the entanglements which he has thrown around them in life! How many eloquent tongues has he thus put to silence! What noble ministerial gifts has he thus rendered of no account! What glorious achievements for God and for his Christ has he thus prevented! How many a prince among the virtuous and good has he thus induced to curse God and die! Who shall write the secret history of the clogs which he has thus succeeded in fastening to the wheels of the chariot of salvation! "Tell it not in Gath; publish it not in the streets of Askelon; lest the Philistines rejoice, and the daughters of the uncircumscribed triumph." Though the angels have wept over it, let it be for eternity to reveal. With all its sadness, the history of the celibate is worse. There is a good side as well as a bad.

But these laws concerning the priests were not given to show us what Christian ministers are to be. The Christian Church has suffered not a little by what has been imported into it from Levi and Aaron. It was a sad day for Christianity when the tiara of the Jewish priest was transferred to the brow of a Christian bishop. Aaron was meant to be a type of Christ himself. What was required of him was most of all intended to shadow forth the qualities, and character, and office of that great High-priest that has passed into the heavens, and through whose sublime mediation alone any man can come unto God. In this aspect then let us consider it.

I. The ancient priest was required to be physically

PRIESTLY REQUIREMENTS.

perfect. Otherwise he could not be a fit representative of that perfect humanity which was found in our Savior. Upon this point Bonar has expressed the truth with much force and beauty. If the priest were "blind," then the people would be led to misapprehend the type; he could not represent Him whose "eyes are as a flame of fire." If the priest were "lame," he could not represent Him whose "legs are as pillars of marble." If "mutilated in the nose," he could not be the type of Him whose "countenance is as Lebanon, excellent as the cedars." If "superfluous in any limb," shorter in one than in the other, he could not set forth Him who "cometh leaping on the mountains as a roe and young hart." If "broken-footed," he was unlike Him whose feet are as "sockets of fine gold," bearing "pillars of marble." If he were "broken-handed," he could not be a picture of Him whose "hands are as gold rings set with beryl," and of whom it is written, "not a bone of him shall be broken." If the priest were "crookbacked," then would he have represented the Highpriest of the Church as inferior to the Church herself, "whose stature is like the palm-tree." If "a dwarf," he would ill suit as a type of Him who is "the chiefest among ten thousand." If in his eye were any "blemish," no one could have seen in him the picture of the Beloved whose "eyes are as doves by the rivers of waters, washed with milk and fitly set." If "diseased in his skin," he could not be a type of Him "who is all fair," having "no spot or wrinkle." And if deficient in any particular of masculine perfection, he could not be the representative of Him whose Church, made like to himself, is "all glorious." He was therefore required to be without bodily blemish, that Israel might know what sort of a Priest Messiah to expect. Their eyes were to be directed to Jesus as one "altogether lovely."

II. The ancient priest was required to be properly and purely mated. As a type of Christ in all other respects, so was he also in his espousals. The Lamb is not alone He has his affianced Bride — his holy Church. He hath chosen her as a chaste virgin — as one whom "the daughters saw and blessed." Not a divorced woman — not a vile offender — not an unclean thing — is the Church of Jesus. What saith the glorious Bridegroom concerning his Spouse? "Now when I passed by thee, and looked upon thee, behold, thy time was the time of love; and I spread my skirt over thee, and covered thy nakedness; yea, I sware unto thee, and entered into covenant with thee, and thou becamest mine. Then washed I thee with water; yea, I thoroughly washed away thy blood from thee, and I anointed thee with oil. I clothed thee also with broidered work, and shod thee with badger's skin, and I girded thee about with fine linen, and I covered thee with silk. I decked thee also with ornaments, and I put bracelets upon thine hands, and a chain on thy neck. And I put a jewel on thy forehead, and ear-rings in thine ears, and a beautiful crown upon thine head. Thus wast thou decked with gold and silver; and thy raiment was fine linen, and silk, and broidered work; thou didst eat fine flour, and honey, and oil; thou wast exceeding beautiful, and thou didst prosper into a kingdom. And thy renown went forth among the heathen for thy beauty: for it was perfect through my comeliness, which I had put upon thee." Thus "Christ loved the Church, and gave himself for it; that he might sanctify and cleanse it with the washing of water by the word, that he might present it to himself a glorious Church, not having spot or wrinkle, or any such thing; but that it should be holy and without blemish." And the priest's wife had to be pure to typify these pure espousals of the Lamb, and the excellencies of that Church which he has chosen for his everlasting Bride.

III. It was required of the ancient priest that his children should be pure. The transgression of his daughter degraded him from his place. It is one of the demands laid upon Christian pastors to have "faithful children that are not accused of riot, nor unruly." The reason is obvious. A minister's family, as well as himself, is made conspicuous by the very nature of his office. Their misdeeds are specially noticed by the world, and readily laid to his charge. Any unholiness in them operates as a profanation of his name. It is so much taken from his power. The Holy Ghost therefore calls upon him to "rule well his own house, having his children in subjection." But the law was typical. It relates to Christ and his Church. It points to the fact, that everything proceeding from his union with his people is good and pure. The Savior's marriage with the congregation of believers, is a fountain of virgin excellencies. From this proceeds the highest virtue, peace on earth, and fitness for heaven. From this have come the sublimest adornments of human society, the loveliest graces, the sweetest affections, the noblest impulses, the sunniest enjoyments, the chastest moral attractions, that have ever appeared in our world. No grapes of Sodom, no bitter clusters grow upon this vine. No lures to ruin are found within its bosom

But everything which originates there is like the priest's daughter, pure, lovely, of good report, and full of praise.

There is often much in the character and conduct of professing Christian people, which is neither lovely nor commendable. There is much that pretends to come from fidelity to Jesus, which we can neither approve nor admire. But it is not the product of true Christianity. It is the fruit of man's own depravity and narrowness. It has not come from Christ. No man can convict the Gospel of fostering or countenancing anything wrong, or subversive of the peace, good, and excellence of society. It is a spring of unmingled blessing. All who partake of its life are necessarily chaste virgins to the Lord.

IV. There are other requirements which were made of the ancient priests, both in the twenty-first and twenty-second chapters, which I will sum up under the general name of *holiness*. They were not to defile themselves with the dead, or by eating improper food, or by contact with the unclean, or by irreverence towards the holy things. They were to be very particular about all the laws, and to devote themselves to their office as men anointed of God. In one word, they were to be *holy;* that is, *whole*, entire, complete, fully separated from all forbidden, and fully consecrated to what was commanded. This was necessary for personal and official reasons; but especially for the high-priest as a type of Christ. It was a requirement to shadow forth the character of Jesus, and the sublime wholeness and consecration which were in him.

It is remarkable how much there is in this ritual pointing to this very particular. Next to the fact of atonement, it is perhaps the most prominent subject in the whole system. It is brought forward in nearly every chapter, and reappears in nearly every provision. The reason is obvious. Nothing in the whole mediatorship of Christ enters so largely into it as his personal holiness. He had to be perfectly pure, in order to be acceptable to God; and the same unexampled excellence was necessary to attract the attention and command the confidence of men. Much is therefore said bearing upon this particular. And just as the ancient types foreshadowed, and as the nature of the case demanded, Christ was a being of transcendant holiness. All the qualities of goodness and magnanimous righteousness were combined in him. The moral significance of his life is one of the most impressive of themes. The wisest and best men have been searching and expounding it for the last eighteen hundred years, and yet it remains unexplored. Ages of study and eloquence have not brought to light all the truth, good, and beauty hidden in that man of Nazareth. There are depths there which no man has fathomed, and glories of goodness to which no human mind can discover the limits. Contemplate him in any aspect in any of the trying scenes of his life, and he still comes before us the same miraculous being, "holy, harmless, undefiled, separate from sinners, made higher than the heavens."

We are not generally moved by the character of Christ, as we ought to be. We are so familiar with its exterior facts, that we pass it without due attention, and without understanding it. Familiarity and much handling of truths sometimes soils them to our perceptions. What is before us every day is apt to lose its meaning and its charms. A glorious creation is this by which we are surrounded, but it is so continually before us that we think but little of it, and are more moved by a show of fire-works than by the blaze of the all-enlightening sun rolling his golden chariot through the immense of heaven. We need to have some poetic thrill, some special prompter, to enable us to see in what a world of beauty and magnificence we live. And so it is with regard to the character of our Savior. We have a vague impression of its general goodness, but we do not intelligently realize it. As a distinguished divine has remarked, "Men become used to it, until they imagine that there is something more admirable in a great man of their own day, a statesman or a conqueror, than in Him, the latchet of whose shoes statesmen and conquerors are not worthy to unloose."

But, blinded to the truth, as many may be, the character of Jesus for holiness and sublime consecration, stands alone upon the records of time. It has no analogy in nature, no archetype in history. There is nothing like it. It has no parallel in heaven above, or in the earth beneath. It is the sublimest of all the miracles of God, the most wonderful of all his displays to man. All other miracles have been reviled, but this cannot be. Men have despised and desecrated the sanctity of everything else related to religion; but when they came to the character of Jesus, their hands grew powerless, their hearts failed, their utterance choked, and they turned aside in reverent awe of a goodness and majesty which could not be gainsayed. Infidelity itself has freely and eloquently confessed to his matchless excellence. Paine disavows "the most distant disre-

PRIESTLY REQUIREMENTS. 339

spect to the moral character of Jesus Christ." The French atheist Leguinia agrees that "He who called himself the Son of God, always displayed virtue — always spoke according to the dictates of reason — always preached up wisdom — sincerely loved all men, wishing good even to his persecutors—developed all the principles of moral equality and the purest patriotism—met danger undismayed — described the hard-heartedness of the rich — attacked the pride of kings — dared to resist even in the face of tyrants — despised pomp and fortune—was sober—solaced the indigent — taught the unfortunate how to suffer — sustained weakness — fortified decay — consoled misfortune—shed tears with those who wept—and taught men to subjugate their passions, to think, to reflect, to love one another, and live in peace." Rousseau is struck with admiration at his excellency. "What sweetness, what purity in his manner! What an affecting gracefulness in his delivery! What sublimity in his maxims! What profound wisdom in his discourses! What presence of mind, what subtlety, what truth in his replies! How great the command of his passions! Where is the man, where the philosopher, who could so live, and so die, without weakness and without ostentation? . . . Yea, if Socrates lived and died like a sage, Jesus lived and died like a God." These are the testimonies of men who refused to receive him as their Savior. Nor is there anything in all the records of unbelief, ancient or modern, Jewish or heathen, to affix the least stain upon his spotless life. Those who knew him best, testify with one voice to his unexampled excellence. Peter says he did no sin, that guile was never found in his mouth, that he was without spot, and that his life was spent in doing good. John says, "in him was no sin." The timid judge who gave him up to be crucified solemnly washed his hands before the crowd, saying, "I find no fault in this man." Judas who betrayed him confessed himself guilty of innocent blood. The heathen captain who presided at his crucifixion, said, "surely this was the Son of God." The truth is, the world has never contained another instance of piety so sincere, of philanthropy so pure, of liberality so magnanimous, of love so true, of candor so unfaltering, of sympathy so tender, of teachings so faithful, of mercy so condescending, of endurance so patient, of power so gracious, of prudence so wise, of devotion so self-sacrificing, of integrity so perfect, of wronged innocence so meek, of zeal so free from bigotry, of such mighty goodness without one single taint. Yes, those little Gospel incidents which we are so prone to pass over as insipid, are the sublimest records of earth. They tell us more than is to be found in all the histories of the greatest or best of other men. Jesus taking little children in his arms, is a more wonderful picture than Alexander's conquest of the world. The Son of God stopping the funeral procession at Nain, or halting to answer the cries of Bartimeus at Jericho, or standing in tears at the grave of Lazarus, is a mightier fact than the discovery of a new continent. His one prayer on the cross, "*Father, forgive them,*" is worth more to the human family than have been all the kings, from Nimrod until now. These humble records of Matthew, Mark, Luke and John, outweigh in value all other books that ever were written. Worlds could not compensate for the loss of them. Strike them out, and you tear from the earth its sublimest history, and rob humanity of the sublimest displays of majesty and goodness that were ever made in mortal flesh. Earth knows not another character so precious or so indispensable as that which they present in the case of that humble man of Nazareth.

Brethren, what would man be without Christ—without his holy life? In him, and in him alone, earth rises into communion with heaven, and light shines in upon our benighted humanity. "In him was life." Life in him received its true expression, and its real explanation. In him human existence rose up to its true nobility and proper achievements. Everything appertaining to a right use and the right meaning of life, was summed up and set forth in him. "In him was life, and *the* life (that is, his specific life) was *the light* of men." There mankind must learn, if they ever learn, the secret life of life. Man must either be reduced to a perishing thing of dust, and his soul be trampled beneath the material senses, and his existence and condition remain a riddle for ever, or Jesus must be hailed as the head of the race—the door of opening between light and darkness—the bond of connection between us and God. We need him. We need his life. We need him in all his attributes of goodness and offices of love. We need him as the exponent of God, and we need him as much as the exponent of man. We need his instructions; but still more his personal exemplifications of them. We need him as a great Prophet sent from God; but still more as a companion, such as this world cannot furnish, to rebuke our sins, to encourage our faith, to quicken our virtue, to alleviate our sorrows, to smooth our dying pillows, and to pilot us to the haven of everlasting rest. And the sublimest of all his wonderful adaptations to our wants the apostle finds in this, that he was "holy, harmless, undefiled, and separate from sinners." "Such a High-priest," says he, "became us."

V. There is yet one particular in the requirements concerning the ancient priests, to which I will refer. It is said of the high-priest, "he shall not uncover his head, nor rend his clothes, nor go in to any dead body, nor defile himself for his father, or for his mother; neither shall he go out of the sanctuary (in consequence of domestic bereavements); for the crown of the anointing oil of his God is upon him." That is to say, he was not to allow any natural sympathies to interfere with the pure and proper discharge of the duties of his high office. Some have regarded this as a coldness and harshness thrown around the old priesthood, which has nothing to correspond to it in the Christian system. I do not so understand it. The very reverse is the truth. The high-priest was a great religious officer for the entire Jewish nation. He belonged more to the nation than to his family or himself. It would therefore have been a most heartless thing to allow a little natural domestic sympathy and affection to set aside all the great interests of the Hebrew people. So far from throwing a chilliness around the high-priesthood, it gave to it a warmth and zeal of devotion, and showed an outbreathing of heart upon the spiritual wants of the congregation, superior to the love of father or mother. And it was meant to shadow forth a precious truth; viz. that Christ, as our High-priest, concentrated all his highest, warmest and fullest sympathies in his office. He loved father and mother, and was properly obedient to them; but when it came to the great duties of his mission, the interests of a perishing world were resting upon his doings, and he could not stop to gratify domestic sympathies. Rising then above the narrow circle of carnal relationships, "he stretched forth his hand toward his disciples, and said, Behold my mother and my brethren!" His sympathies are those of the spirit, and not of the flesh. His parents may be in great anxiety about him; but his sublime response is, "I must be about my Father's business." His mother may attempt to control his movements; but he declines compliance, saying, "Woman, mine hour is not yet come." Everywhere did he subordinate mere natural affections to those higher sympathies for a world perishing in sin, for which he gave himself, and died, and now intercedes in heaven. Dearer to him are the souls of men, than the bodies of earthly relatives. He is not without sympathy and the fondest tenderness, but it follows the leadings of a higher, wider, sublimer relationship than that of mere flesh and blood. He has a warm and brotherly heart; but it is most of all for them that seek to imitate him, and obey God. "Whosoever shall do the will of my Father which is in heaven," says he, "the same is my brother, and sister, and mother." On such his heart is set. To them his affections flow deep and mighty as the infinitude of his nature. "We have not an High-priest which cannot be touched with the feeling of our infirmities." He hath given himself to us He knows our wants. His great spirit yearns for us. As a father pitieth his children, so he pitieth them that fear him. A mother may forget, but he will not

> His heart is made of tenderness
> His soul o'erflows with love!

NINETEENTH LECTURE.

THE HOLY FESTIVALS.

LEV. CHAP. XXIII.

This chapter treats of times and seasons—of sacred days, festivals, and solemn convocations — such as the Sabbath, the Passover, the feast of Pentecost, the feast of Trumpets, the Day of Atonement, and the feast of Tabernacles. These solemnities were not all now first instituted, but are here brought together under one view, that their relations to each other, and their general significance, might be the more clearly perceived.

There are three general aspects in which these remarkable festivals may be considered. They had important relations to the peace and prosperity of the Jews as a nation; they embodied a great religious idea; and they presented a chronological prefiguration of the great facts of our redemption. Without undertaking at all to exhaust the subject, I have something to say of it in each of these relations. May the Lord direct us in our meditations!

I. Commentators generally, on this part of Hebrew Law, have remarked upon the social, political, and commercial benefits resulting to the Jewish people from these national festivals and convocations.

They served to unite the nation, cemented them together as one people, and prevented the tendency to the formation of separate cliques and conflicting clans or states. Three times a-year did these feasts bring vast multitudes together from all sections of the country to meet each other on a common religious ground, requiring of them the acknowledgment of descent from a common father, of consecration to the same God, of heirship to the same promises, and of subjection to the same theocratic system. Persons of different tribes and distant localities thus met on terms of brotherhood and fellowship, fostering old and creating ever new relationships, and familiarizing all with each other. They were thus strengthened in unity of faith and interest against internal ruptures, division, and idolatry.

If hostility had sprung up between any of the tribes, the occurrence of these holy assemblies required of them to lay down their arms, and come together as brethren around the same altar of their common God, to offer the same sacrifices, sing the same grand songs, and bow down with each other before the same almighty Jehovah. It was impossible for a people to obey such regulations and become disunited. The actual split of the ten tribes from Judah, under Rehoboam and Jeroboam, could and did not become very serious until they set aside that part of the law relating to these national festivals.

These convocations also had great effect upon the internal commerce of the Hebrew people. They furnished facilities for mutual exchanges, and opened the ways of trade and business between the various sections. Such festivals have always been attended with this effect. The famous old fair near Hebron, arose from the congregating of pilgrims to the terebinth tree of Abraham. The yearly fairs of the Germans are said to have had a similar origin. And so the annual pilgrimage of the Mohammedans to Mecca, in spite of many adverse circumstances, has given birth to one of the greatest markets in the eastern world. And thus, perhaps, more of the wealth of the Jews, and of the greatness and glory of Jerusalem, is to be traced to the simple laws of this one chapter, than to all the wisdom and power of either or all their kings.

We can thus perceive a wisdom and sagacity in these laws, even apart from their religious and typical significance, which every thoughtful man must be surprised to find among a race of semi-barbarous people, nomadic in their habits, and the immediate descendants of slaves. Such political foresight, under such circumstances, can, with no show of reason, be referred to the mere ingenuity of man. Such masterly arrangements, so many-sided, and on all so complete and admirable, originating with such a people, must have come from a wisdom higher than earth — from a hand more skilful than the hand of mortal. These laws everywhere bear the impress of a divine original; and he who disputes it, calls upon us to exercise a credulity much greater than is agreeable to sober reason. Skepticism may vaunt and boast as it pleases, but it embraces more absurdities than it has ever imputed to the faith of believers. And before the infidel undertakes, on that score, to extract the mote from the Christian's eye, it would be well for him first to remove the beam from his own. *"Physician, heal thyself,"* is about answer enough to all the arguments and ridicule of unbelief and atheism.

II. But there was also a direct religious value and forethought in the appointment of these festivals.

They prescribed public consociation in worship. Man is a worshipping being. It is not only his duty, but his nature and native instinct to worship. His very position in the universe, as a creature, dependent, needy, and the recipient of so much good, calls for it. Hence, the best and the great majority of men, in all ages, have given their sanction and example to it. Even before

> man learned
> To hew the shaft, or lay the architrave,
> And spread the roof above them — ere he framed
> The lofty vault, to gather and roll back
> The sound of anthems; in the darkling wood,
> Amidst the cool and silence, he knelt down,
> And offered to the Mightiest solemn thanks
> And supplications.

But mere isolated worship, without association in common set services, soon dwindles, flags, degenerates, and corrupts. Neither does it ever reach that majesty and intense inspiration which comes from open congregation in the same great acts of devotion. "As iron sharpeneth iron, so a man sharpeneth the countenance of his friend." And just as the multitude of these mutual sharpeners is increased, will their common devotion be deepened and augmented. There is sublimity in numbers. There is something in a great congregation to impress, move, and invigorate. And when it pulsates with one thought, one feeling, one aim, and that in the direction of the infinite and divine, the impulse is like that of the gathered strength of the waves of the sea, profound, majestic, overwhelming. I know of nothing earthly that is more beautiful, more impressive, more soothing to the inmost soul, and more kindly in its effects.

than a devout assembly, convened for the worship of their common God and Father. The mere congregation of such a number of precious souls, filled with holy reverence, their differences all forgotten, the hearts of all classes mingled into one, and all their diversities of station and office melted away before the majesty of the Maker of them all, causes a heavenly awe to steal upon the spirit, and a kindliness to distil upon the soul, which far exceeds all that such services ever cost. It is like a great home gathering of children to receive the benedictions of a gracious Father. It is a drawing together by holy ties to a board where Deity ministers most perceptibly to man. The Spirit of the Almighty One is there. He who died on Calvary walks unseen among the waiting ones, and lays his hand upon the heads of the contrite, and whispers quiet consolation to them that mourn. Loving angels move there with hearts full of sympathy for their young brethren in the flesh. Burning thoughts and holy aspirations take wings there, and soar in poetic numbers and blending sounds of linked sweetness to mingle with the songs of seraphim. Truth there sends forth its rays right from its everlasting Source to warm, and melt, and cheer, and animate, and bless. Earth there rises into neighborhood and fellowship with heaven. And in the deep, still intervals of those solemn transactions, the mellowed soul may feel the soft and gentle beatings of the pulse of immortality. Even the silent atmosphere seems to whisper — "God is here." And who, indeed, has ever seen or felt anything of the hallowing inspirations of these sacred assemblies, but is ready to exclaim with Israel's royal bard — "*How amiable are thy tabernacles, O Lord of hosts!*" The highest hopes of the world linger about our sanctuaries. Heaven looks to them as its grammar schools. They are the inlets of grace and salvation to the soul. Yea, to close them, would well nigh "shut the gates of mercy on mankind."

For the sake of religion, therefore, as well as for politics and commerce, it was a wise and benignant arrangement which called the tribes of Israel together three times a year in sublime congregation, to acknowledge their common Lord, to wait before him in the services of his temple, and to adore, praise and worship him who made them. From those festivals there went forth a religious life, which was felt to the utmost extremities of the land, and which made the great Lord love the gates of Zion more than all the dwellings of Jacob.

III. But I propose to speak more particularly of the typical relations of these holy feasts and seasons. They have an interest and value far above that of their immediate uses and effects. They were prophecies and portraitures of good things to come. We have in them a system of types, chronologically arranged, to set forth the true *Course of Time* — to prefigure the whole history of redemption, in its leading outlines, from the commencement to the close. In this light, then, let us briefly review them.

The first in the list of these holy convocations was *the Passover*. This was a sacramental observance, first instituted in Egypt, and first kept on that dreadful night when the destroying angel went through the land slaying the first-born of every house which had not been sprinkled with the blood of the slain lamb. It was a sort of perpetual commemoration of their deliverance from the oppressor and from death — a standing testimonial that their salvation was by the blood of the Lamb. It was the key-note of the Christian system sounding in the dim depths of remote antiquity. That bondage in Egypt referred to a still deeper and more degrading slavery of the spirit. That redemption was the foreshadow of a far greater deliverance. And that slain lamb and its sprinkled blood, pointed to a meeker, purer, and higher victim, whose body was broken and blood shed for us and for many for the remission of sins. It was only another form of setting forth "Christ and him crucified." It was the clear prefiguration of "Christ our passover sacrificed for us." As God found Israel in bondage, so he finds all men in the slavery and degradation of sin. As he begun Israel's redemption by holding up to them the slaughtered lamb, so the spirit and essence of all his gracious communications to our fallen race has been, to point out "the Lamb of God which taketh away the sin of the world." The sprinkled blood of the lamb saved Israel from the dreadful destruction which overwhelmed their enemies; and thus are we "justified through the redemption that is in Christ Jesus, whom God hath set forth to be a propitiation through faith in his blood." The passover feast occurred but once in a complete period of time—once a year—so "Christ was once offered to bear the sins of many." In all time there shall be no repetition of his sacrifice. The passover was a feast for the whole nation, of which all were called to partake; so "Jesus, by the grace of God, tasted death for every man." "He died for all, that we which live might not henceforth live unto ourselves, but unto him that loved us and gave himself for us." The paschal lamb was to be eaten as food by those who kept the feast; so Christ's flesh is meat indeed. He is "the living bread which came down from heaven, of which, if any man eat he shall live for ever." And this Passover was the first of the feasts ordained for Israel. Jesus is "the Lamb slain from the foundation of the world." The first utterance of grace to sinful man held forth this glorious deliverer. The first altar we read of exhibited the slain lamb. The first deed of the new dispensation was the pointing out of "the Lamb of God" and his offering for the sins of the world. The first cry that reaches the sinner's heart is, "*Behold the Lamb!*" His first experiences of real spiritual bliss lie in his partaking of Christ our Passover sacrificed for us. And the first visions of the glory to be revealed in the heavenly sanctuary, disclose the same "Lamb that was slain," loved, adored, ruling, and reigning, with all the inhabitants of bliss looking on with worshipful thankfulness and delight. The Passover is the primary feast.

The next in the list was *the Feast of Unleavened Bread*, which was a sort of continuation of the Passover, and followed right after it on the next day. In both Matthew and Mark, these two festivals are reckoned as one; the Passover being regarded as the first day of the feast of Unleavened Bread. The one refers to what Christ does and is to the believer, and the other refers to what the true believer does in return. The one refers to our redemption by blood and our deliverance from condemnation; the other to our repentance and consecration to a new life of obedience, separated from the leaven of unrighteousness. It is therefore plain why both were thus joined together as one. Redemption is nothing to us if it does not lead us to a purification of ourselves from the filthy ways and associations of the wicked. In vain do we eat of the paschal lamb or sprinkle its blood, if it be not immediately followed with the purging out of the old leaven to keep the feast of unleavened bread. Our salvation only *begins* in Christ's sufferings and death; it then remains to be practically wrought out in a new life of consecration to God. The Passover must be succeeded by the feast of unleavened bread. Christ's sacrifice is to serve to put us in a position, and to furnish us with motives and opportunities to march forth out of the land of bondage to go to the holy land. A redeemed man must needs be a holy man. We can only effectually keep the Gospel feast by purging out the old leaven of malice and wickedness.

Seven days was this feast of unleavened bread to be kept—a full period of time. We are to "serve God in righteousness and holiness all the days of our life." Our work is not done until the week of our stay in this world ends. We must be faithful until death.

Joined with the Passover and the feast of unleavened bread, was the additional service of presenting before God the first sheaf of the barley-harvest. The Jew was not allowed to touch his crop until he had first gathered a sheaf, and presented it, along with the usual burnt and meat-offerings, as a gift to the Lord. "This," says Cumming, "was a beautiful institution, to teach the Israelites that it was not the soil, nor the rain-drops, nor the sunbeams, nor the dews, nor the skill of their agriculturalists, that they had to thank for their bounteous produce; but that they must rise above the sower and reaper, and see

God, the giver of the golden harvest, and make his praise the key-note to their harvest-home." It was all this, but it had also a deeeper and more beautiful meaning. The broad field, sowed with good seed, with its golden ears ripening for the harvest, is Christ's own chosen figure of his kingdom upon earth, and the congregation of his believing children maturing for the garners of eternal life. In that field, the chief sheaf is Jesus Christ himself; for he was in all respects "made like unto his brethren. *He is "the first fruits."* He was gathered first, and received into the treasure-house of heaven. It was the Passover time when he came to perfect ripeness. It was during these solemnities that he was "cut off." And when the Spirit of God lifted him from the sepulchre, and the heavens opened to receive him, then did the waving of the sheaf of first fruits have its truest and highest fulfilment. Until this sheaf was thus offered along with the blood of atonement, there could be no harvest for us. "But now is Christ risen from the dead, and become the first fruits of them that slept." It is as our representative and forerunner that he has been thus lifted up before God. There is, therefore, a harvest for man—a gathering into the garner of heaven. "The field is the world; the good seed are the children of the kingdom; the harvest is the end of the age." And when that "end" arrives, a voice shall come forth from the eternal temple, "Thrust in thy sickle, and reap; for the time is come for thee to reap; for the harvest of the earth is ripe." And then upon every Christian's grave shall be set up a sheaf, glad and glorious, beautiful and full of blessing, to be gathered, amid the shouts of angels, into the everlasting store-house of the Father. But, as yet, we are no further than the waving of the first fruits of barley-harvest — the lifting up of Christ as the pledge and pattern of our own resurrection.

There was another harvest, and another festival service connected with its opening, fifty days later than the barley harvest. This was the wheat harvest, at which was celebrated *the Feast of Weeks*, otherwise called *Pentecost*. The modern Jews make this festival celebrate the giving of the Law from Sinai; though there is nothing in the Mosaic record to give it such a connection. It was properly a harvest festival, at which the Jews were to render their thank-offerings for the bounties of the field, along with the first fruits of the same, previous to the commencement of the general reaping. They were required to baptize all their blessings in the fountain of life before using them, that they might never forget whence they came, and to whose honor they were to be employed. There was a wide difference, however, between the offering of the first fruits of this, and those of the barley harvest. In the one case *the sheaf* was to be presented; in the Feast of Weeks two loaves of bread, prepared with leaven, were to be waved before the Lord. The fact of there being two, and those made up with leaven, *i. e.* more or less mingled with corruption, precludes the typical application of this to Christ in his own proper person, as in the other case. He is *one;* and nothing corrupting ever attached to him. The key to the true explanation, is found in a hint given in the twelfth of John. Christ there likens himself to "*a corn or grain of wheat,*" and his death to the planting of that grain, and the fruits of his death and passion to the products growing from that planted grain. Here then comes in a wheat harvest — the product of Christ's planting in, and rising from the grave — which is redemption let forth to mankind. But the fruit of wheat was to be presented at this feast, not in its natural condition, but in the form of *loaves* made up with leaven. The reference, therefore, is plainly to redeeming grace, *as wrought up into believers*, in which state there is still much corruption mingled with it. The Passover shows us Christ crucified. The *sheaf* of first fruits shows us Christ raised from the dead and lifted up to heaven as our forerunner. And the Pentecostal feast, with its two leavened loaves, shows us Christ in the gracious influences of his Spirit wrought into the hearts and lives of those who constitute his earthly Church.

This spiritual kneading took its highest and most active form on that memorable Pentecost, when the disciples "were all with one accord in one place," and the Holy Spirit came down upon them with gifts of mighty power. Three thousand souls were that day added to the Church. It was a glad and glorious day for Christianity. It was the first fruits of wheat harvest brought with joyous thanksgiving unto God. But it was *only* the first fruits — the earnest of a vast and plenteous harvest of the same kind ripening on the same fields. Thenceforward the world was to be filled with glad reapers gathering in the sheaves, and with laborers kneading the contents of those sheaves into loaves for God. Leaven there needs is in those loaves; but, presented along with the blood of the chief of the flock and herd, they still become acceptable to Him who ordained the service. And this same reaping and kneading is to go on, until God shall say, "It is enough. The mystery is finished. Come, ye priests, and feast upon the labors of your hands."

There was a peculiar requirement connected with these laws for the wheat harvest, well worthy of special attention. The corners of the fields and the gleanings were to be left. God said, "When ye reap the harvest of your land, thou shalt not make clean riddance of the corner of the field when thou reapest, neither shalt thou gather any gleaning of the harvest; thou shalt leave them unto the poor and the stranger." This was a beautiful feature in these arrangements. It presents a good lesson, of which we ought never to lose sight. But it was also a type. Of what, I have not seen satisfactorily explained, though the application seems easy. If the wheat harvest refers to the gathering of men from sin to Christianity, and from subjects of Satan to subjects of grace, then the plain indication of this provision is, that the entire world, under this present dispensation, shall not be completely converted to God. I believe that the time will come, and that it is largely and fully predicted in the Scriptures, when "all shall know the Lord from the least unto the greatest" — when there will not be a single sinner left upon the earth. But, that time will not come until a new dispensation, with new instrumentalities, shall have been introduced. Some are looking for the ingathering of the whole race to Christ and the Gospel, simply by the appliances of grace as we now have them. I find no authority for this in Scripture, or in reason. My learning of this subject is, that, with all that we can do, though the world should continue ten thousand years, there will still be outskirts and corners unreapt, and gleanings left all over the field, which must be gathered, if gathered at all, by other ministers and other hands, under another order of things. For eighteen hundred years has the Gospel now been operating in our world. Fully fifty generations have successively passed under its administrations. Much of the mightiest energy and eloquence on the earth, in every generation, has been expended in its favor. And yet, in all this accumulation of centuries, there never has been a nation, or state, or city, or neighborhood, or village, under heaven, in which every individual of the population was a true member of Christ. There is not a spot on the surface of the world of which it ever could be said, "All the dwellers here are sons of God and heirs of heaven." Even in the hands of inspired apostles, whose very words were miracles, yea, even in the hands of the adorable Savior himself, the Gospel has not converted all to whom it was brought. And "the thing that hath been, is that which shall be." With all the efforts of the Church, there will still be unconverted and unholy people in the world —corners and gleanings which have not been turned to any good account— which strangers to us must gather, and which only another economy shall reach. Even down to the time when the Son of Man cometh, the world will be *"as it was in the days of Noah."*

Some will say that this presents a sad and gloomy prospect. I answer, no; it consoles rather than discourages me. It keeps me from that despondency which would otherwise weigh upon my spirit. I look at the history and doings of the Church. I see

faithful men everywhere laying themselves, body
and soul, as living sacrifices on God's altar. And
yet I find multitudes whom their efforts cannot move
—their own brothers, friends and relatives continuing
in unrighteousness, and dying impenitent. What
am I to think of this upon the supposition that the
Gospel is omnipotently endowed over all antagonism
of resistance and rebellion? Am I not driven to
suspect that there has been some miscalculation of
its power, or that, in part at least, it has been a
failure, and hence not what it professes to be? The
inference seems harsh, bewildering, and vastly depressing to a confiding faith; and yet, I know not
how to escape it upon the common theory. But
when, in God's pictures of futurity, he shows me
corners unreapt and gleanings still ungathered after
the present gatherers have done their work, the perplexity is met, and the depressing doubt is removed.
I see then that the present are not God's ultimate
arrangements — that there is to be another economy
and other agencies — and so I can labor on without
discouragement at the limited success which attends
upon Christian efforts. It is enough that the Gospel,
as it now is, is able to gather up a people for the
Lord, to be the kings and priests of "the world to
come." In this I find motive and glory enough to
work diligently, though there be corners which
cannot be reached, and gleanings which cannot be
gathered.

The next in this list of festivals, was *the Feast of
Trumpets*. This was held on the first day of the seventh month of the ecclesiastical year, which was
the same as the first month of the civil year. It was
therefore a new-year festival, and at the same time

the feast of introduction to the sabbatic month. Its chief peculiarity was, the continual sounding of trumpets from morning till evening. It was the grand type of the preaching of the Gospel. Christ having been sacrificed and raised again, as shown in the Passover and its connected services, and the organization of grace having been completed, as prefigured in the Feast of Weeks, the next great step was, to let the world hear of it, and to call the people to come and rejoice in it. And this call is what the Feast of Trumpets foreshadowed. In one respect, it began a new year; — it introduced a new dispensation. From the day of the Pentecostal outpouring, there went forth a joyful sound — the voice of trumpets — in every direction, over hills and valleys, mountains and seas. It was the glad peal of Gospel tidings, announcing the arrival of the holy month, and proclaiming rest to the weary world. It was not only at this feast that the trumpets were sounded. They were more or less used in every holy convocation. But it was only at this particular feast that they were heard in all their mightiness. Something of the Gospel has been heard in every age. Its first notes were sounded in Eden, and their echo was heard through the centuries before the flood. At every great feast God has provided in the history of time, its sound was more or less mingled with the festivities. But, not until after the glorious season of Pentecost did its combined trumpet tones break forth upon the ears of men. Then first did it utter itself in that fulness which has startled empires, thrilled ages, and still holds millions of immortal minds trilling to its vibrations.

The Feast of Trumpets was, to a great extent, a

preliminary of the great Day of Atonement. We have already considered the peculiarities of this solemn day. Its leading thought is contained in its name — *at-one-ment;* that is, agreement, reconciliation, harmony, and peace with God. The Feast of Trumpets was a call to this *at-one-ment.* The Gospel is an appeal to men to be reconciled to God. One of its great objects is to urge sinners to afflict their souls — to repent of their sins — to accept contritely of the forgiveness found in the blood of Jesus. "Now, then," says Paul, "we are ambassadors for Christ, as though God did beseech you by us: we pray you in Christ's stead, be ye reconciled to God." Every Gospel minister is thus a trumpeter, to call men to the holy services of expiation. And if people will but listen, and be admonished, and come to the solemn feast, and afflict their souls with real penitence, God is at peace with them, their sins are remembered no more, condemnation is gone, and the pledge of eternal life is theirs.

My friends, through the whole day of our lives thus far, the silver trumpets have been sounding in our ears. And still they sound. From the battlements of the heavenly Jerusalem their clarion tidings of salvation ring o'er land and sea, saying, "Hear, O careless sinner; bestir thee; rouse from thy stupor; come to the feast of pardon; afflict thy haughty spirit, and bow down thy pride, and enter in those everlasting gates which now stand open to receive thee!" —"*He that hath ears to hear, let him hear.*"

Immediately succeeding the great solemnity on the fifteenth day of the month, began another remarkable festival, called *the Feast of Tabernacles.* This was the most joyous of the Jewish annual feasts. Its leading peculiarity was, that the people left their dwellings and made themselves tents, or temporary shelters, in which they remained seven days, rejoicing in the great things which God had done for them. It was to commemorate the forty years of tent life which their fathers led in the wilderness, and pointed, the same as that which it commemorated, to that period of the Christian's career which lies between his deliverance from bondage and his entrance into rest,—that is, between his reconciliation to God and his final inheritance of the promises. It celebrates the state of the believer while he yet remains in this present life.

This world is not our dwelling place. We are pilgrims and strangers here, tarrying for a little season in tents and booths, which we must soon vacate and leave to decay. "The earthly house of this tabernacle" must "be dissolved." The places that know us now, shall soon know us no more. "Seven days"— a full period—were the people of Israel to remain in these temporary tabernacles. And thus shall we be at the inconvenience of a tent-life for the full period of our earthly stay. But it was only once in a year that Israel kept the Feast of Tabernacles. And so, when we once leave the flesh, we shall never return to it again. Our future bodies shall be glorified, celestial, spiritual bodies. "When the earthly house of this tabernacle shall be dissolved, we have a building of God, a house not made with hands, eternal in the heavens." "In this tabernacle we do groan, being burdened, earnestly desiring to be clothed upon with our house which is from heaven." Nevertheless, if we be the people of God—if we have listened to the call of the trumpets, and kept the day of atone ment by a godly affliction of soul for our sins,— even our stay in these poor shelters is a joyous and a blessed estate. It is a continuous feast upon forgiveness and blessed hope. Christianity gives wings to the soul by which we may mount up as eagles. It introduces light into the darkest houses, and joy into the frailest and poorest tent. It gives a sacred buoyancy to the elastic steps of youth, and it is a rod and staff to the tottering feebleness of age. It adds a gilding to the saddest lot, and a lining of silver to the blackest clouds. It may turn us all into pilgrims, but pilgrims ransomed from the power of tyranny, and on our way to the land of rest. It may separate us from much that vain men think good and precious, but it joins us to the assembly of those whose peace flows like a river, and whose songs shall never, never cease.

It is also a precious thought connected with this subject, that when the Jews left their tents at the conclusion of the Feast of Tabernacles, *it was the Sabbath morning*. This frail tent-life is after all to be rounded off with the calm quiet of a consecrated day that has no night, and to merge into a rest that is never more to end.

The Sabbath is the most sacred of the days. It is as old as man. It has come down with him from the days of his innocence. It is a part of that moral code delivered on Sinai, and written on the granite rock to last as long as the world. It is a sweet remembrancer of God and his great works of power and goodness. It tells of that joyous time

> When the radiant morn of creation broke,
> And the world in the smile of its God awoke

It carries back our thoughts to the period when the whole earth was sinless, and man in his innocence was blessed. It now celebrates the Savior's triumph over death—the bursting forth from Joseph's tomb of the germ of another creation brighter than the first — the bringing of life and immortality to light. It tells of rest that was, and of rest that is to be. I love this holy day — this solemn pause amid our earthiness — this breathing-space for man —this "halt of toil's exhausted caravan"—this weekly drop of heavenly sweetness in the bitter cup of life. I hail it as the channel and the prophecy of heaven's sublimest gifts to man. God makes this whole round of sacred festivals both begin and end with it. It was the first feast which God appointed for man, and it is to be kept when all other feasts have passed. It was given before sin had touched or soiled our noble nature, and it is to be the crown of that redemption which removes those stains again. It was the inheritance of man in his innocence at the beginning; and when we leave these earthly tabernacles, it shall meet us with a soothing calm on every breeze, and a heavenly sweetness and quiet on every ray, transcending all that ever attached to it before. The Saturday of life's weary week brings after it an everlasting Sabbath in the skies. Whatever, then, may be the sorrows, disabilities, and weaknesses of earth, our consolation is, that "*there remaineth a Sabbath for the people of God.*"

> There is an hour of peaceful rest,
> To mourning wand'rers giv'n;
> There is a joy for souls distressed,
> A balm for every wounded breast —
> 'Tis found above — in heav'n.

There is a soft, a downy bed,
  As fair as breath of ev'n;
A couch for weary mortals spread,
Where they may rest the aching head,
  And find repose in heav'n.

TWENTIETH LECTURE.

THE SANCTUARY AND ITS FURNITURE.

LEV. CHAP. XXIV.

It has been said of the principal part of this chapter, that it gives "what may be called the private duties of the priest." But this is not all that it contains. It embraces provisions which do not refer to the priest at all. It lays commands directly upon the people, as well as upon the priest. It gives what would be much better described by the caption, *Arrangements for the daily service of the Sanctuary.* It speaks of the lamps, and how they were to be kept continually burning; of the oil by which they were to be fed; of the table of shew-bread, and how the loaves were to be made and exchanged; and of the ordering of other things pertaining to the ordinary services of the sanctuary.

Here, then, more than in any preceding portion of this book, are we brought to the consideration of sacred *places*. We have been looking at sacred things, sacred persons, sacred times; but very little at sacred edifices or their furniture. Concerning these, not much is directly said in Leviticus, for the reason that everything pertaining to the Tabernacle was already so fully described in the preceding book. Still, as the regulations for the services which were never to cease in the sanctuary are here brought before us, if we are to speak at all of the sacred places in this connection, this is the proper point for it to be done.

The Tabernacle of Moses, and the Temple of Solomon, (which was only a more substantial and permanent renewal of the same thing,) were as much typical "of good things to come," as the priests who officiated, or the services that were celebrated in them. They were a part of the same grand system, by which God, in those early times, shadowed forth his future dispensations. And we are the more easily led to entertain this belief, from the fact that everything pertaining to the form and furniture of these sacred structures was of divine origin. The model was exhibited to Moses from heaven. God said to him, "Thou shalt rear up the Tabernacle according to the fashion thereof which was showed thee in the mount." Paul says that "Moses was admonished of God when he was about to make the Tabernacle." From all this we would naturally suppose that God meant to express something in the very form and architecture of this sacred building, as well as in the services which it was meant to accommodate. Nay, when we come to an examination of the New Testament, in which the Old receives its explanation and fulfilment, we can have no room for cavil or doubt. The inspired apostle speaks of these "holy places made with hands," and declares them to have been "*the patterns of things in the heavens,*" and "*the figures of the true Tabernacle which the Lord pitched, and not man.*" (Heb. 8 : 2 — 9 : 23, 24.) We do not, therefore, dream when we undertake to read prophecies from the very beams of the temple, and even from the lamps, tables, and curtains of Israel's sacred tent.

To conceive of the shape and appearance of the Tabernacle, you must measure out in your imagination a level ground-plot, about one hundred and fifty feet long, and about seventy-five feet broad; that is, an oblong square, inclosed with linen canvas fastened on stakes, and cords about ten feet in height. Everything relating to the Tabernacle was inside of this inclosed area, which was called *the court of the Tabernacle*. The Tabernacle proper was a smaller inclosure, at the far end of this court, equally distant from the two sides of it. It was formed of boards, overlaid with gold, fifteen feet high, set up alongside of each other in sockets of silver, and held together above by golden bars passing through golden rings fastened to the boards on the outside. The roof of this inner inclosure was formed of heavy curtains of several thicknesses thrown over these rows of upright boards from side to side. This was the Tabernacle proper, which was divided again into two apartments by heavy curtains dropped from the roof. The inmost of these covered chambers, was the *Holy of holies;* and the other, which was the ante-chamber to it, was *the Sanctuary*, otherwise called *the Holy place*.

You thus observe three departments in this sacred structure: first, the inclosed uncovered space outside of the Tabernacle proper; then, the Sanctuary, or first room of the covered part; and third, that peculiarly sacred room in the deepest interior, called the Holy of holies. Nor could any one come to the most holy place, except by passing in through the court, and through the Sanctuary. In all this I see a symbolic history of redemption, and of the sinner's progress from his state of condemnation and guilt to forgiveness and peace in Christ, and to his final glory in the presence of his Lord.

The first apartment was the outside court. It was here that the Jews came to offer their sacrifices. They accordingly appeared there as sinners. There was the altar of burnt-offering, representing Christ crucified as he is held up to a sinful world. By penitently looking to the victim consuming upon that altar, the devout Jew received absolution; and so the sinner by believing on Jesus as his Savior. Approach to that altar was an acknowledgment of sin. A little beyond the altar stood the sea of brass, or the brazen laver. This was between the altar and the door of the Sanctuary, and the priest, in passing into the Tabernacle, had always to wash here before he could proceed; thus acknowledging defilement, and pictorially showing that after justification comes sanctification, and that it is requisite for us to be both forgiven and cleansed before we can come into those higher manifestations found in the Tabernacle proper. The outside court, therefore, represents man in his native condition. It is our place or moral *local* so long as we are only beginning to believe on Christ and to cleanse ourselves from our filthy ways.

The third and most interior apartment, represents the heavenly, post-resurrection, or glorified estate of man. There was the visible presence of the Lord. It was the hidden and guarded place into which vulgar eyes could not look, or unholy ones at all enter. There were the cherubic figures, and there did Jehovah commune with his people. There was the seat of mercy and the throne of glory. It was the grand picture of that celestial invisible world, into which Christ as our forerunner and High-priest has entered, and which he holds in reserve for all his saints in the coming ages.

But, between the outside court and this inmost chamber of the Tabernacle, was *the Sanctuary*, or that department with which the text is directly concerned, and of which I propose more particularly to treat. Its position shows that it refers to a condition of things this side of the heavenly estate, and yet in advance of those rudimental experiences by which we come to be Christians. None but priests were allowed to enter it; but it was properly the priests' apartment. I have heretofore explained who are God's true spiritual priests. Peter says to all real Christians, "*Ye are a royal priesthood.*" He does not say that they shall be priests hereafter only, but that they are priests now, called and ordained "to show forth the praises of him who hath called them out of darkness into his marvellous light." Leaning upon Christ as our sin-offering, and submitting to be washed in the laver of regeneration, we attain to "a holy priesthood," and are advanced to the apartments of the priests. But this process, by which we become priests of God, is the same by which we become members of the Christian Church. The typical reference of the Jewish Sanctuary may therefore be easily reached. It was a picture of the Christian Church estate, that is, of the immunities and relations in which we stand as the accepted followers and servants of Jesus while yet we remain in this world.

With this idea, then, let us take our station in the holy Sanctuary, and simply look around us upon the objects to which the text directs attention.

The chapter before us speaks of *Lamps*. These were the burners upon the famous seven-armed candlestick of gold, which God directed Moses to make for the holy Tabernacle. A full description of it is given in Exodus. To have an idea of this beautiful piece of workmanship, you must figure to yourselves a strong, massive, upright, tall, tapering shaft of gold, with a lamp upon the top. Upon this shaft you must imagine three arms branching out opposite each other on two sides, and curved upward to a level with the centre lamp, each having also a lamp on the top. You thus have a row of seven lamps, on seven different branches, and all supported by one central shaft or stem, to which each branch and lamp is attached as one piece. This fabric is what is called "the seven golden candlesticks." To feed these lamps, the children of Israel were commanded to bring pure oil, beaten from the olive, and the priest was to trim and replenish them night and morning perpetually that they might never cease to burn and shine.

Now, whatever the Jews may have understood from this significant construction, we can be in no great doubt concerning its typical meaning. The Savior himself interpreted it to John, when he said, "The seven stars (or lights) which thou sawest in my right hand, are the seven angels (or ministers) of the seven churches: *and the seven candlesticks are the seven churches.*" The central and all-supporting shaft, represented Christ; or rather, "the right hand" of Christ, on which everything Christian depends. As the seven candlesticks and their lamps were sustained by that massive golden stem, so Christ sustains every member, branch, institution and minister of his universal Church. It is he alone "that is able to keep us from falling." Take him away, and the precious faith and hope, which have been the consolation of millions of poor and sorrowing and dying ones in various ages, at once drops. Take him away, and you take away the foundation upon which humanity has built its last hopes of safety and salvation. Take him away, and you destroy the golden pedestal upon which have been carved and wrought the beautiful flowers and ornaments of grace and goodness in the lives and doings of the saints. Take him away, and the great golden candlestick set up of God for earth's illumination falls with a crash, never to rise again.

You will observe that the number of lamps and branches of this peculiar fabric was *seven*—the complete number—indicating that the whole Church was thereby represented. All rested upon the one central shaft; indicating that there is no true Church, and no branch of the true Church, which does not repose in Christ as its great and only foundation and dependence. The whole fabric was of one piece. The parts were all solidly joined together as one continuous mass of solid gold. And so the holy Catholic Church is *one*. All the branches are compactly joined together in one central support and stay, which is Christ Jesus. And yet, in that unity there was multiplicity and diversity. There were seven branches, and these seven were not all exactly alike. Some were shorter and lighter, and some were longer and heavier; some looked towards the east, and some towards the west; some seemed to diverge very far from the central shaft, others rose immediately by its sides. There was multiplicity and diversity, and yet perfect, unbroken, graceful unity. Beautiful picture of the Church of Jesus! It is not confined to one nation, one dispensation, one **denomination**, but takes in all who are really united to Christ, and built upon him as their only dependence, no matter how diverse or remote from each other they may be in other respects. The Savior never meant his Church to be hemmed in to one form of outward manifestation, worship, government, or details of individual belief. The Gospel itself is *four*, with four separate names, and marked with four distinct individualities; and yet these four are one.

There are people who are greatly offended with Christendom for its many parties, divisions, and denominational distinctions. As well might they revile Creative Power for not making all the planets of one size, form, motion, and distance from the sun — or for making trees of more than one kind, limb and leaf—or for making birds to sing different songs and to wear different plumage—or for making flowers of more than one sort and fragrance—or for not making one man's face just like his neighbor's! Even God himself, in whom unity reaches its deepest intensity, has been let forth to us as Father, Son, and Holy Ghost — three distinctions in adorable and eternal oneness. Why should we have difficulty, then, in finding the one great Church of the Redeemer, embracing many and differing branches and families? It is what we ought to expect. It is accordant with all analogy. There may be distinction without separation, as there are many members in one body, living one and the same life. And so the Church has different outward forms and branches, but one indwelling spirit—variety of provisional organization, but one communion — "diversities of operations," but "one Lord, one faith, one baptism, one God and

Father of all, who is above all, and through all, and in all." And with all the seeming discordances, and the many lines of individual and denominational distinction, which diversify Christendom, all who do inwardly believe and build upon the Lord Jesus Christ as their only hope, though "distinct as the billows," are still "one as the sea."

The object of these candlesticks and lamps was, to furnish light to the sanctuary. The place had no windows, no other modes of illumination. The light which characterizes Christendom as such, is not from nature — not from human reason and philosophy — but from Christ and that pure Spirit which flowed and shone through him and his inspired ministers. Without Christ, and the light which comes from the golden candlesticks of his glory, and the pure olive oil of his Spirit, mankind are in darkness on all sacred things. The night of ignorance, sin and affliction is heavy upon them. Here and there a feeble and uncertain ray may peep into their gloomy habitation to keep up an idea of a better order of things, but not sufficient to dissipate the reigning and distressing obscurity. But in the sanctuary there is light, in which all the priests of God may walk in safety and in peace. The Sun of Righteousness shines for them, if not in unveiled splendor, yet in strength enough to light the soul onward in the holy service of its Maker. "I am the light of the world," says Jesus; and all his people are "the children of light, and the children of day." When God sent his Son into the world, he said, "I the Lord have called thee in righteousness, and will hold thine hand, and will keep thee, and give thee for a covenant of the people, for a light of the Gentiles, to open the blind eyes, to bring out the prisoners from the prison, and them that sit in darkness out of the prison house." With his advent, "the Daystar from on high visited us, to give light to them that sit in darkness and in the shadow of death, to guide our feet in the way of peace." In him and his words, we have the light of wisdom, such as the greatest of earth's sages never knew. In him and the heavy stroke that fell upon him on Calvary, we have the light of forgiveness of sins, purification, and hope, such as all the hecatombs, and prayers, and priestly services of the heathen never could impart. In him and his lifting up in the holy sanctuary, we have the light of joy and peace in the midst of our toils, such as no earthly power could ever give. In him and the lamps he upholds, bright rays of the sunlight of another and better world are made to illumine the steps of mortals, and stars of glory rise even upon the deep darkness of the awful grave.

Yes, "*Light is come into the world!*" From the watch-towers of ancient prophecy, Isaiah saw its rising beams from afar as they first fell on Moriah's golden minarets, and cried, "*Arise; shine; for thy light is come!*" Full-orbed, it rose upon the land of Zabulon and Nepthalim by the way of the sea, and "the people which sat in darkness saw a great light." Jewish priests in their bigotry, and heathen rulers in their bloody tyranny, sought to quench it; but they did but trim its glorious flame and hasten its ascension. And to this day it shines in the ministrations of God's people with a brightness that cannot be extinguished, lighting up the south with a brilliancy superior to its sunny skies, and kindling glory in the north superior to the play of the sunlight on its crystal mountains of unspotted ice. "*Light is come into the world!*" but many see it not, and feel not the mellow bliss that floats exhaustless in its beams. Sin hath blinded their eyes and barred their hearts against its joyous radiance. To behold it, man must come out from the cavernous dens of vice, and throw off the bandages of false philosophy, and lift up his eyes to the heavens. Evil-doers have no willingness for this. Because their deeds are evil, they love darkness rather than light, and come not to where the light shineth, and so abide in the gloom of sin and death. "But he that doeth truth cometh to the light," and thus is made a son of light, whose path shall ever shine more and more unto the perfect day.

But the chapter before us speaks of *Bread* as well as lamps and light. Twelve loaves, baked of fine flour, arranged in piles on a table of gold, ever stood in the holy sanctuary. These loaves were to be renewed every Sabbath, and were to be eaten by the priests in the holy place. This golden table, the same as the supporting shaft of the golden candlesticks, represented Christ, and these unleavened loaves upon it, that pure bread from heaven which he giveth for the sustenance of them that are his.

"*Man liveth not by bread alone.*" There are wants and cravings in our nature which cannot be satisfied with the produce of the fields. There is in us a spiritual man, which must be fed and nourished with spiritual food, or it languishes and dies. "Man's life consisteth not in the abundance of the things which he possesseth." Dives, amid all his earthly plenty and sumptuous fare, became an everlasting starveling. We need higher supplies than this world can furnish, and which can be found only in the holy sanctuary. Jesus furnishes those supplies. "I am the bread of life," says he; "he that cometh to me shall never hunger; and he that believeth on me shall never thirst. This is the bread which cometh down from heaven, that a man may eat thereof and not die. I am the living bread which came down from heaven; if any man eat of this bread, he shall live for ever." It has been touchingly remarked, that "every sigh of Jesus was a crumb of imperishable bread to us." The breaking of his body on the cross has furnished the sublimest feast of time. There "they that hunger and thirst after righteousness" are forever filled. There wisdom hath furnished her table, saying, "Come, eat of my bread, and drink of the wine which I have mingled." Here love hath poured out all her lavish fulness for the famishing children of men. Here the great King throws open his banquet halls, and says, "Come, for all things are now ready." And whosoever will but consent to be made a priest of God, shall find the sacred loaves laid up for him in the holy place, upon which he may be satisfied for ever.

There were to be twelve loaves ever on the golden table — a loaf for every name upon the jewelled breastplate of the priest. And they were ample loaves. *One* omer of manna was enough to serve a man for a day; but each of these loaves contained *two* omers. The bounties provided for our souls in Christ Jesus are superabundant — far more than enough for all that will ever come to partake. Yes, poor, perishing prodigal, in your Father's house there is "enough and to spare"— plenty to satisfy you, and welcome besides, if you will but cast away the husks of sensuality and sin, and come home from your wicked wanderings.

Neither did these loaves ever wax old or become stale. Every Sabbath they were carefully renewed, and thus kept always fresh and sweet. The bread which Jesus gives never moulds, never spoils, and never loses its relish on the tongues of his priests. It is just as fresh and delightful to the aged saint on his dying day, as when first he tasted of it in the days of his youth. It is just as pure and good to us now, as it was to the apostles when they believed on him and were satisfied. Every Sabbath day, rightly spent, brightens it up again with ever renewed beauty and preciousness. It is not that "meat that perisheth;" but "meat which endureth unto everlasting life."

And blessed is he that knoweth of this bread, and cometh to partake of it! His mouth shall be satisfied with good things, so that his youth is renewed like the eagle's. And at the end of days, like Daniel in the school of Melzar, his countenance shall be fairer and fatter in flesh than all the children which eat of Nebuchadnezzar's meat.

— LORD, EVERMORE GIVE US THIS BREAD." —

Having thus looked at the beautiful provisions for light and sustenance which characterized the holy sanctuary, there is yet a thought or two respecting its relation to the holy of holies, to which I will direct your attention.

I have said, that the holy of holies was meant to represent heaven, or that invisible and glorious state into which Christ has entered as our priest and forerunner, and into which all his saints shall enter in time to come. Now, the way into this most holy place was *through the Sanctuary.* There was no other way of entering it. May not this be meant to signify that the way to heaven is through the Church? I know that there has been much unrighteous abuse of the doctrine, that, outside of the Church there is no salvation. It has been the weapon of bigotry, the parent of fanaticism, the shield of harsh uncharitableness; and when limited to any one form or outward order of the Church-state, it is a huge falsehood. But still, there is a solemn truth underlying it. What is the Church? It is the community of those who believe in Christ, and submit themselves to follow and obey him according to the best light within their reach. And unless a man has so far advanced in spiritual things as to be rightfully rated as a member and citizen of this spiritual commonwealth, it would be a contradiction of Christ and all his Gospel to hold out to him the hope of Christian salvation. A man must have faith, and submit to serve Christ, and thus attain to the Christian Church state, or he never shall be where Jesus is. Christ says, "I am the door." "He that entereth not by the door into the sheepfold, but climbeth up some other way, the same is a thief and a robber." "He that believeth and is baptized shall be saved; and he that believeth not shall be damned." We need no plainer words than these; and they are the words of him who openeth and no man shutteth, and shutteth and no man openeth. The way to heaven is through the Church; not this or that particular denomination; not the company of those who stickle for these or those outward forms and ceremonies; but that universal brotherhood of such as take Christ as their

Savior and only hope, and honestly act up to their best light and convictions as to what he requires of us. And if there is any way of salvation outside of this holy Catholic Church. I cannot find it revealed in the Scriptures, and fearful is the risk of him who ventures to trust in it.

But, connected with this is another and more sunny thought. If the Sanctuary is the way to heaven, those who are in that way are very near heaven. Every true member of the Church has but a veil between him and the glorious presence of God and angels. I say every *true* member of the Church; for not all are Israel who are of Israel. There was a Nadab and Abihu among the sons of Aaron. There was a Judas Iscariot among the twelve disciples. There was a Simon Magus among the baptized at Samaria. And the man of sin has never failed from the visible temple. There never yet was an assembly of the saints, but "Satan came also among them." There is therefore a church-membership which is only nominal and outward, possessing nothing of that living power which inwardly connects with Christ and avails for salvation. We may receive upon us the waters of Baptism, and the solemn vows of discipleship, and take and eat of the sacred elements of the Savior's broken body and shed blood, and yet be in the gall of bitterness and the bonds of iniquity. "I have seen a branch," says an eloquent preacher, "tied to a bleeding tree for the purpose of being engrafted into its wounded body, that both might be one; yet, no incorporation followed; there was no living union Spring came singing, and with her fingers opened all the buds; and summer came, with her dewy nights and sunny days, and brought out all the flowers, and brown autumn came, to shake the trees, and reap the fields, and with dances and mirth to hold harvest-home; but that unhappy branch bore no fruit, nor flower, nor leaf. Just held on by dead clay and rotting cords, it stuck to the living tree — a withered and unsightly thing. And so, alas, it is with many; having a name to live, they are dead. They have no faith; they want that bond of living union which alone can make the graft a part of that on which it is grafted—the sinner a real member of the Savior." And, of course, so long as this inward life-principle does not circulate in both, let the man be in what visible Church he may, he is not reached by saving power. He must be vitally joined to Christ. He must partake of his life, drink in his Spirit, and put forth in his strength, or be none of his. But, if our Christianity be real, our faith sincere, our exercises those of the honest heart, our endeavors such as our profession implies, then are we already more than half-way to heaven. A single curtain is all that hangs between us and everlasting glory. As the Sanctuary was the ante-chamber to that in which Jehovah dwelt between the cherubim, so is the Church to those mansions of glory where the pure in heart shall see God. The poet has said,

Heaven lies around us in our infancy;

but heaven lies around us in our manhood too, provided that manhood has attained to citizenship in the community of saints. With heart and spirit set on Christ and good, and earnestly obedient to all the known will of our Lord, we walk in the genial light of golden lamps, and eat of sacred bread from golden tables, waiting only for the lifting of the curtain, when we shall be at home with angels and with God, in the sublime and everlasting dwelling-place of **our** enthroned Redeemer.

> O glorious rest! O blest abode!
> We shall be near and like our God!
> And flesh and sense no more control
> The sacred pleasures of the soul!

We come now, in course, to another episode **in** this book—another accident (so to speak) in the progress of the arrangement of these holy laws, akin to that narrated in the tenth chapter. I will not detain you with it, though it might profitably be made the subject of detailed examination. It was a sort of co-operation of providence with direct revelation to confirm the authority of the Giver of these laws, **and** to draw an outward fence, as Bonar says, around the pavilion of the great King. "The son of an Israelitish woman, whose father was an Egyptian, and a man of Israel, strove together in the camp; and the Israelitish woman's son blasphemed the name of the Lord, and cursed." This seems to have occurred whilst Moses was within the tabernacle conversing with God. It reminds us of that description of the heavenly city given in the last of Revelation where the good come into blessed communication with God, and have a right to the tree of life, whilst "without are dogs, and sorcerers, and whoremongers, and murderers, and idolaters, and whosoever loveth and maketh a lie." And sad is the reflection, that, while Almighty God is engaged in merciful dealings with men, some are quarrelling, striving, and blaspheming. But verily, they shall have their reward. "The Lord spake unto Moses, saying, Bring forth him that hath cursed without the camp, and let all that heard him lay their hands upon his head, and let all the congregation stone him." Sin in Nadab and Abihu brought with it a fearful end, and so did also the profaneness of Shelomith's son. God will not allow his name to be abused, any more than his house to be desecrated with unholy fire. "He that blasphemeth the name of the Lord, shall surely be put to death, and all the congregation shall stone him;" was the solemn injunction of Jehovah to Israel. And it is written, "the children of Israel did as the Lord commanded."

And now, standing, as it were, by the bruised and mangled corpse of the fallen blasphemer, let me suggest to your thoughts those solemn words of the apostle — "He that despised Moses' law, died without mercy under two or three witnesses: of how much sorer punishment, suppose ye, shall he be thought worthy, who hath trodden under foot the Son of God, and hath counted the blood of the covenant, wherewith he was sanctified, an unholy thing, and hath done despite unto the Spirit of grace? For we know him that hath said, Vengeance belongeth unto me, I will recompense, saith the Lord.

It is a fearful thing to fall into the hands of the living God!"

TWENTY-FIRST LECTURE.

THE SABBATIC YEAR AND THE JUBILEE.

LEV. CHAP. XXV.

I HAVE had repeated occasion to remark, in the course of these lectures, upon the number *seven*. It is singular how this number is inwrought with nearly everything sacred. The Scriptures throughout rest upon it with peculiar emphasis. It was on the seventh day that God ceased his work of creation and hallowed a rest, which has made the computation of time by septenaries of days the common and universal method from that day until now. Seven days were given to Noah to gather in the tenants of the ark; and with him came over the flood seven persons, and sevens of all the clean animals. On the seventh month the ark rested on the earth again, and on the seventh day the dove was sent out. Seven years of plenty and seven of famine were sent upon Egypt, as the Lord signified through Joseph. Seven priests, with seven trumpets, were to encompass the walls of Jericho seven successive days, and the seventh day it fell into the hands of Israel. Seven days were the Jews to celebrate sundry of their feasts; seven days were their priests to be in course of consecration; seven days were their unclean to be in cleansing; and seven victims were required in many of their sacrifices. Seven days did Job's friends sit with him, and seven bullocks were to be offered for their sins. Seven years was Solomon's temple in building; seven days was the feast of its dedication; and seventy years was Israel captive at Babylon. Seven years was Nebuchadnezzar degraded as a brute, and seventy weeks were determined until Messiah should be cut off. Enoch, whom God translated, and the first man ever exempted from death, was the seventh from Adam; and, according to Luke, Jesus was the seventy-seventh. Seven hours did the Savior hang upon the cross; seven times did he speak while hanging there; seven times did he show himself after his resurrection; and seven days after his ascension was the Holy Ghost poured out. Seventy was the number of disciples whom he first commissioned. Seven petitions are contained in the prayer which he taught his followers. Seven lamps were in the Tabernacle. Seven Churches we read of in the Apocalypse; and seven seals, seven vials, seven angels, seven Spirits of God, and the finishing of the mystery at the sounding of the seventh trumpet. And one of the most prominent and remarkable features of the Levitical code was that Sabbatic system which pervaded it, making the seventh day, the seventh month, the seventh year, and an additional year every seven times seven years, holy periods and seasons, to be observed with peculiar solemnity and special services. It is these year-sabbaths, and God's ordinances concerning them, which we are now to consider. And may the Holy Spirit direct our meditations, and bring us to a proper and profitable understanding of his will and purposes!

The first of these Jewish year-sabbaths, as presented in the chapter before us, was that which occurred every seventh year. From the time Israel became settled in the land of promise, they were to count seven years, and that seventh year was to be a holy year of rest, especially for the land. It was a year during which all agricultural pursuits and processes were to be interrupted, and the grounds to be left lying fallow. The whole country was that year to be turned into a public common, free to all, the proprietor of his estate not only ceasing to cultivate it, but having no more right to its spontaneous products than any one else. But the people were not, therefore, necessarily required to be idle. "They could fish, hunt, take care of their bees and flocks, repair their buildings and furniture, manufacture clothes, and carry on their usual traffic" (Bush *in loc*). There was nothing to hinder free social intercourse. It was only *the land* that was to rest, and man from tilling it. It was to "be *a Sabbath of rest unto the land*," in which there was to be no sowing, no reaping, and no gathering of what the vine might produce without dressing. This was the leading characteristic of the Sabbatic year, although it doubtless embraced other, religious, economical, civil, and political interests and ends.

The second and most famous of these Jewish year-sabbaths was that which came in at the end of the seventh septennial rest, and occurred every fiftieth year. This was called the great year — the year of Jubilee. It was an institution of the same general Sabbatic character with the seventh day, seventh month, and seventh year, except that it occurred more seldom, and was attended with joys, blessings, and concomitants of good beyond all other sacred seasons. It was also a Sabbath of rest for the land, in which the people were neither to sow, nor prune, nor gather. It was a year of redemption through which no bonds could hold, no contracts bind, no prisons remain locked, and no possessions or estates continue out of the hands of the original owners. When that year came, all debtors were released, all slaves set at liberty, all captives discharged, all exiles brought home, all alienated property restored to those to whom God had given it, and all absent ones once more returned to the bosoms of their families and friends. It was one of those gracious provisions scattered over God's ancient economy, showing the hand and presence of Him who is full of goodness and tender mercies. It was an arrangement which served to equalize and balance society in that uncultivated age, and to prevent many of the causes which so often operate disastrously to a State. Long unrighted wrongs, or depressions too numerous and long continued, are the generators of the temper and passions which give birth to revolutions. Society needs balances and counterpoises against monopolies of wealth and the extremities of ill fortune. And in these, as well as in other respects, a very beneficent and gracious end was subserved by this ancient institute of the Jubilee. It not only contributed to rest the land from the exhaustion of incessant tillage, and to restore the unfortunate; but it was a sort of "restitution of all things," by which a fresh and happy impulse was given to the whole current of affairs. It was a grand year of refreshment and recuperation for a new and more contented life. As long as the Jewish people faithfully kept these Sabbatic laws. they continued to be a prosperous people and a peaceful State; but as they came to disregard them, they were torn and spoiled by intestine strifes, social disorders, and all varieties of political trouble.

There is a feature of these year-sabbaths which would, perhaps, particularly arrest the attention of the political economist, and which is of no less interest to the Christian. It was a bold and hazardous undertaking for a legislator to propose laws which would interrupt the supplies upon which the people subsisted. Yet, this is what was done in these Sabbatic regulations. The ordinary Sabbatic year commenced in the harvest month; but there was to be no seeding during that year, and consequently no harvest until the third succeeding year. The year of Jubilee always begun with the conclusion of the ordinary Sabbatic year, thus bringing together two successive years in which there was neither reaping nor sowing. There would thus be three, if not four, years of complete interruption in the ordinary supplies from the fields. Now, it was no small matter, by mere arbitrary legislation, to strike out of existence three successive harvests every fifty years. The mere partial failure of *one* of our crops, sends stagnation and distress into all departments of society. Three successive failures would fill the whole country with famine, wretchedness, and starvation. What was to prevent a like result from these long and total intermissions in the agriculture of the Jews? So important an inquiry was not overlooked by the framer of these Laws. The Lord directed Moses to say to Israel, "And if ye shall say, What shall we eat the seventh year, seeing we shall not sow, nor gather in our increase? Then will I command my blessing upon you *in the sixth year, and it shall bring forth fruit for three years.*" The people were required to rely upon a miracle for subsistence, and the Lawgiver pledged a septennial miracle in their favor. The fruits of two or three years were to be forthcoming from the earth on the year preceding each Sabbatic year.

Now, from this, I join with others in deducing an important evidence of the truth of the Mosaic narrative and the divinity of these laws. No legislator would ever have proposed, and no people ever would have received, a law which thus required a miracle, *i. e.*, the direct interference of the Power which governs the springs of nature and guides the course of providence, in order to subsist in its observance, without a clear conviction that the law itself came from Him who alone is able to perform what it promised. There must therefore have been entire confidence on the part of Moses that it was God who spoke to him, and that what was promised was really a pledge from Deity certain to be fulfilled. And a similar confidence must have governed in those who accepted the law from his hands, while a few septenaries of years were to settle, by actual demonstration, whether their confidence was well-founded or false. It was a test so direct, so palpable, so certain to expose the falsehood in case there was falsehood, so unlimited as to time, so removed beyond the reach of man to affect the result, and repeated on so grand a scale every seven years, that I cannot see how Moses could have ventured it without certain knowledge that he was speaking by authority of God, or how the people could ever afterwards have regarded him as a divine prophet if it had failed or miscarried. And as Moses certainly did give this law and the pledge connected with it; and as the Jewish people did receive it, and for centuries obeyed and tested it, and still continued ever to honor and reverence him as the prince of all God's prophets; I cannot see to what other conclusion we are to come, but that his communications to Israel proved to be authentic, and that he was just that man of God and legate of heaven which he professed, claimed, and was believed to be.

I do not give this as the only, nor yet as one of the principal evidences of the Divine authority of these laws. It is but one line in the great volume of testimony upon that subject. Indeed, this whole series of discourses, to me has been a gradual and continuous development of an argument for the inspiration of Moses, which I know not how any man can logically set aside. Though our examinations have been somewhat cursory, every chapter, to me, has been luminous with what never could have originated with the mere ingenuity and forethought of man. The declaration with which I began these comments, that the contents of this "third book of Moses" entitled it to be called "the Gospel according to Leviticus," seems to me to have been signally sustained. We have found all its peculiar inculcations radiating from one great centre which has no model but in Christ. and his works and offices of mercy for mankind And to this we have found them to fit and conform in a minuteness of detail, in a profuseness and magnificence of illustration, in a perfection of accuracy, and in a logical and historical correctness, which has astonished and amazed me. They seem more like allegories framed after the occurrence of the facts, than like types instituted fifteen hundred years in advance. The question, therefore, arises, How came

Moses thus to anticipate Christ and the redemption that is in him? How came he to know anything about a character so unique, or about those miraculous facts and wonderful results of the Savior's great and singular history, so as to give such luminous pictures of what God was thus to achieve in the far off ages? Where did he get the idea from which he drew those vivid and living illustrations of the great economy of grace in Christ Jesus? Whence could he have had all this accuracy of information concerning what was to be, but from Him who knew the end of all things from the beginning? It does seem to me, that the denial that Moses acted in these matters under the aid and direction of God, makes of him a greater prodigy, and a more wonderful exception to the experience of mankind, than the inspiration which we claim for him. There was miracle on the one side or other; and I submit it to every candid man, whether it was not most likely on that side to which the great majority of thinkers, and the best and most competent judges in the world, have uniformly assigned it. *And if Moses was inspired*, THEN THE GOSPEL IS TRUE, for we find that Gospel set forth in what Moses commanded and wrote.

But, it is of the typical significance of these year-sabbaths, that I desire more particularly to speak. Thus far, everything in this book has been full of interest. A magnificent panorama has been passing before us for the last five months. Our way has been through a long gallery of Divine pictures of Christ and his work of mercy for man. We have been tracing some of the steps and stairways by which the world has come up to the sublime heights of spiritual wisdom and hope eventually laid open in the New

Testament. All the great facts, appliances, and stages of the redeeming process, have passed in review before us. It only remains for us now to take a glance at its ultimate results and final consummation, and the entire scheme, in all its grand magnificence, will have been exhibited. And to this end serves the Sabbatic system which so singularly characterized the Hebrew ritual.

I do not suppose that these sabbatic regulations referred severally to separate and distinct things. The seventh day, the seventh month, the seventh year, and the year of jubilee, as I take them, all express the same great thought, and are related to each other in signification as the different sections of a telescope. They fold into each other. The one is only a repetition of the other on a larger scale. And they all range in the same line to give a focus for gazing the further into the depths and minuter details of one and the same scene. We have sabbaths of days, and sabbaths of months, and sabbaths of years, and septenaries of years, all multiplied in each other with augmenting interest, to indicate the approach of some one great seventh of time when all God's gracious dealings with man shall come to their culmination, and to point the eye of hope to some one grand ultimate Sabbath, in which the weary world shall repose from its long turmoil and all its inhabitants keep Jubilee.

The word "*Jubilee*" is of doubtful origin and signification. Some derive it from a verb which means to *recall, restore, bring back;* which would very appropriately designate an arrangement which recalled the absent, restored the captive, and brought back alienated estates. Some trace it to Jubal, the inventor

of musical instruments, and suppose that this year
was named after him from its being a year of mirth
and joy, of which music is a common attendant and
expression. In Hebrew, *yobel* means the sounding
of a trumpet; hence some take the word *Jubilee*
as derived from the extraordinary sounding of
trumpets with which this particular year was always
introduced, some making it refer to the kind of instruments used, and others, to the particular kind of
note produced. But, after all, it may have been a
name invented for the occasion, and intended to carry
its meaning in its sound, or to get it from the nature
of the period which it was thenceforward to designate.
It is a word which, if not in sound, yet in its associations, connects with the sublimest joys, ushered in
with thrilling and triumphant proclamations. "Like
the striking of the clock from the turret of some
cathedral, announcing that the season of labor for
the day is closed," says Bonar, "so sounded the notes
of the silver trumpet from the sanctuary, announcing
that the great year of redemption and rest had come
— the year of release and restoration throughout all
Israel."

Some interpret this year of Jubilee as a picture of
the present Gospel dispensation, and consider that
we are now living in this remarkable year. And
there is doubtless an accommodational sense in
which this is true. The Gospel is a trump of gladness, proclaiming liberty to the captives, and the
opening of the prison-doors to them that are bound,
and announcing the moral rest of forgiveness and
peace in Christ Jesus. But I cannot find in this the
direct and highest significance of the Jubilee. The
year of Jubilee did not begin till the close of the day

of atonement. It was only after the High-priest had finished all the services of that solemn day that the silver trumpet sounded for the Jubilee. This day of atonement only began with the Savior's sufferings and death. It is still in progress. Our great High-priest is still within the veil sprinkling the atoning blood. Sinners without are still afflicting their souls and waiting for his reappearance to pronounce upon them the life-giving benediction. Bonds, trials, heavy sorrows, and sore privations still cleave to the saints. Even the holiest Christians have not yet come to the fulness of their rest. The very martyrs, who laid down their lives for the testimony of Jesus, are represented as waiting and crying, "*O Lord, how long!*" With all our peace in Christ Jesus, our portion as yet is connected with dust and tears. The proper Jubilee, therefore, is yet to come. Our priest must first gone forth from the Holy of holies, whither he has gone, and close the reconciliation day, and then only will our joyous rest rightly begin. Jesus must first appear the second time, before our final release and salvation shall be complete.

Many a time have we heard the sounding trumpets of Gospel tidings. Long and loud has the summons to repentance and reconciliation been ringing in the ears of a drowsy world. Many have listened, believed, and accepted, and thereby experienced the glad earnest of the appointed Jubilee; but there is another trumpet—"the great trumpet"—"the trump of God"—which yet remains to be sounded. It is a trumpet which shall never be heard but once in all the revolutions of the ages;—a trumpet whose clangor shall thrill worlds, and startle up the very patriarchs from their long-lost graves, and transmute time itself into eternity;—a trumpet which shall be blown throughout all the earth the moment our High-priest shall have appeared again. "*For the Lord himself shall descend from heaven with a shout, with the voice of the archangel,* AND WITH THE TRUMP OF GOD; *and the dead in Christ shall rise.*" "FOR THE TRUMPET SHALL SOUND, *and the dead shall be raised incorruptible, and we shall be changed.*" And that trumpet is the true trumpet of the true Jubilee. When *it* sounds, shall the great Sabbath of the ages begin. Let us, then, survey some of the sublime features of that coming time.

I. First of all, it is to be *a Sabbath*—a consecrated and holy rest. The year of Jubilee was the intensest and sublimest of the Sabbatic periods. The Sabbath is the jewel of days. It is the marked and hallowed seventh, in which God saw creation finished, and the great Maker sat down complacently to view the admirable products of his wisdom, love and power —blessed type of a still more blessed rest, when he shall sit down to view redemption finished, the years brought to their perfect consummation, and the life of the world in its full and peaceful bloom. The Jubilee is therefore to be the crown of dispensations, and the ultimate glory of the ages, when the Son of God shall rest from the long work of the new creation, and sit down with his saints to enjoy it for ever and ever. Wiped off then shall be the sweat of the toiling brow, and quiet and useless the ploughshare which has so long been bruising and tearing the face of the world. The perfection of the Sabbaths shall then throw its dewy mantle over us for ever.

> Rivers of gladness water all the earth,
> And clothe all climes with beauty.

II. In the next place, it is to be *the period of resti tution.* The year of Jubilee was a year when all property which had been sold or alienated came back to its original owners. Farms and houses that the Jew, through misfortune, had to part with, then became his again. If any one had been reduced to servitude, his freedom returned to him. The land itself received release, and rested in the undisturbed repose which it enjoyed before the fall. Everything seemed to go back to the happy condition in which God had originally arranged things.

Man, in this present world, is a dispossessed proprietor. God gave him possessions and prerogatives which have been wrested from him. God made him but a little lower than the angels, crowned him with glory and honor, and set him over the works of His hands. All creatures were given to him for his service, and he was to "have dominion over every living thing that moveth upon the earth." But, where is all that glory and dominion now! How has the gold faded and the power waned! How much are we now at the mercy of what was meant to serve and obey us! Gone, are our once glorious estates. Gone, the high freedom which once encompassed man. Gone, all the sublime dignity which once crowned him. But we shall not always remain in this poverty and disgrace. Those old estates have not gone from us for ever. When the great joyous trump of Jubilee shall sound, the homesteads of our fathers shall return to us again, nor strangers more traverse those patrimonial halls. With blanching cheek shall the vile intruder then shrink back, and let go his avaricious grasp upon what can be no longer his. Hell then shall cease to vex and rifle those who have taken refuge in the Lord. Our long down-trodden excellence shall then rise from the dust, radiant with the splendors in which it came at first from the great Creator's hand. The crown that has fallen shall then again take its proper place upon the brow for which it was made. The mansions which we have had to exchange for these dissolving tabernacles, shall then be once more our own. And there shall be beauty for ashes, and the oil of praise for the spirit of heaviness; for "in that day shall the Lord of hosts be for a crown of glory, and for a diadem of beauty, unto the residue of his people."

III. Again, it shall be *a time of release for all that are oppressed, imprisoned or bound*. The year of Jubilee struck off the bonds of every Jewish captive, and threw open the prison doors to all who had lost their liberty. We are all prisoners now. Though the chains of sin be broken, the chains of flesh and remaining corruption still confine us and abridge our freedom. Even those pious ones who have passed away from earth, are still held in the power of death. Their souls may be at rest, but their bodies are still shut up in the pit of the grave. There still is groaning and "waiting for the adoption, to wit, the redemption of our body." But when the great trump of Jubilee shall sound, these groanings shall cease, and these fetters all dissolve. Rocky vaults and sepulchres, sealed for ages, shall then suddenly burst open, and the doors of death fall down from their rusty hinges, and broad daylight break into the darkest tombs, and all God's buried saints shake off their damp and mouldy prison garbs, to bid farewell for ever to the dingy cells that now clasp their holy forms. The expecting patriarchs from their ancient tombs shall hear the thrilling call and come; and holy martyrs, whose sacred dust the winds and waters scattered o'er the earth; and "slaughtered saints, whese bones lie scattered on the Alpine mountains cold;" and poor-house paupers, sleeping in Christ in potter's fields; and faithful missionaries, whose hearts the savages have eaten or cast unto the dogs; and sea-lost loved ones, whom shipwreck left to perish on the barren rocks or melt in the still depths of the unfathomed sea — all, all, all, shall then find their sorry fate reversed, and the power of the oppressor gone for ever.

And equally blessed shall be the arrival of that day to those bound sufferers in Christ who shall still be found living in the flesh. The poor consumptive, gradually fading with decay; the trembling paralytic, bound to his sick-room chair; the rheumatic cripple, whose pains have lifted his bones out of their sockets; and the old bed-ridden saint, already half-way in his grave; and the bright youth, wild and parched with intolerable fever; and the maimed soldier of the cross, hobbling sorrowfully on his crutches; and the benighted blind one, feeling his sad way through a world of light and beauty in perfect darkness; and the chained maniac of the mad-house, consuming with rage; and the poor driveling idiot, whom not one flash of reason has ever lit; and the sad, broken-backed daughter, pining in obscurity, cut off from all earthly hope; and the aged grandmother, bowed together with a weight of years that have carried away all the friends of her youth; — these, and ten thousand more that suffer in the Lord, each and all, at that high bugle-note, shall feel the sudden thrill of immortal deliverance, and waste, and sigh, and suffer, and feel their sad privations, no more; for the year of Jubilee has come!

IV. Another feature of that happy time is, that it shall be a time of regathering for the scattered household. Jehovah's word to Israel was, "The fiftieth year shall be a jubilee unto you, *ye shall return every man to his family.*"—It is not possible in this world for families to keep together. A thousand necessities are ever pressing upon us to scatter us out from our homes. The common wants of life, to say nothing of aims and enterprizes for good, honor, or distinction, operate to drive asunder the most tenderly attached of households. And if we should even succeed in overcoming dividing forces of this kind, there are others which do their work in a way which we cannot hinder. Death comes, and, one by one, the whole circle is mowed down, and sleep in separate graves, mostly far apart. One lies in the country church-yard, one in the city cemetery—one in the far-off fatherland, and one in some remote corner of the wide new world. One sleeps in the sunny south, another in the dark and frozen north. One has found his bed on the gory field of battle, and another in the deep wide sea. A sister reposes in the sweet family lot in the flowery city of the dead, and a brother in the waste wilderness, no one knoweth where. There is no complete household upon earth—no family among men—that has not some absent one to mourn.

> There is no flock, however watched and tended,
>   But one dead lamb is there;
> There is no fireside, howsoe'er defended,
>   But hath one vacant chair.

But there cometh a day when all the households of
the virtuous and good shall be complete. The year
of Jubilee shall bring back the absent one. For
when the Son of man shall come, "he shall send his
angels with a great sound of a trumpet, and they
shall gather together his elect from the four winds,
from the one end of heaven to the other." Not one
shall be overlooked or forgotten. That faithful son
that fills the unknown stranger's grave; that brother
who sleeps in a foreign land, or mingles his ashes
with the golden sands of the Sacramento; that mother whose lonely pillow is in the deep cold ground;
that cherub child that slumbers in its little grassy
bed in the far-off hamlet; that loved one whose small
gifts and tokens of affection are all that remains of
him in this world; the lost original of that fading
daguerreotype so often washed with your warm tears;
—all these shall hear the trump of Jubilee, and come
back to their happy, happy homes.

> Then shall love freely flow,
>   Pure as life's river;—
> Then shall sweet friendship glow,
>   Changeless for ever;
> And bliss each heart shall fill;
>   And joys celestial thrill;
> And fears of parting chill
>   Never—no, never!

V. But, there is still another feature of this blessed
time to come, to which I will refer. The sounding
of that trump shall be the summons to a sacred feast
upon the stores laid up by the industry of preceding
years. Though no sowing or gathering was to be
done in the year of Jubilee, Israel was to have
plenty. The bountiful hand of Heaven was to supply

them. Years going before were to furnish abundance for all the period of rest. The Sabbath of the land was to be meat for them. Now is our harvest-time. The fields are waving with beautiful golden products which God means that we shall gather and store for our Jubilee. Industry and toil are required. We must thrust in the sickle, and gather the blessed sheaves, and lay up for ourselves treasures in heaven. It will not do to play the sluggard while that ripe vintage is inviting us to gather. We must work while we may, and lay up while it is within reach. When once the trumpet sounds it will be too late to begin to lay up for the year of rest. *Now* is the accepted time; *now* is the day of salvation. Neglecting this bright, rich, plenteous summer period, we must starve when the faithful are feasting on abundance. But if diligent now, we shall have an ample portion. No Christian effort will ever be lost. Every good deed here done, every gift of charity, every prayer for Zion, every self-denial for Jesus, every cup of cold water given to a thirsty disciple, every word of serious admonition whispered in a sinner's ear, shall contribute to swell the accumulations for a coming festival sublime as heaven. Twenty, forty, sixty years have some been toiling in the exhaustless field. Oft have they been faint and weary. Heavy upon them has been the heat and burden of the day. Hunger and nakedness, peril and bitter soul-sickness have often oppressed them. But, the weight of their long service, their hardships and pains, have all the while been laying up for them "a far more exceeding and eternal weight of glory." And, oh, what abundant treasures have some of them garnered in heaven for the everlasting year of their rest. Blessed storages of good! How will the soul leap when the trump shall sound to come and feast upon them for ever. Then shall "the good wine" come which has been so long delayed. Then shall our Samuel bring us into the celestial parlors which his own hand has fitted up for us, and seat us in the chiefest place, and set before us what has been kept for us, and cause us to feast upon "fat things full of marrow," with Abraham, Isaac, Jacob, and all the saints of God, without interruption and without end.

Hail, then, to the blessed year of jubilee! Hail to the bright year of God's redeemed—year of release for them that sigh—year of the exile's return to his home—year of rest to them that toil—year of finished salvation to the lost! We bid thee welcome! Yea, welcome, thou coronal of time! Welcome, thou opener of the prison doors! Welcome, restorer of our beloved dead! Welcome, health of the nations and liberation to the bound! The weary world waits impatient for thy coming! Millions of saints stir in their mossy graves impatient for thy dawn! Break, sacred morning, and lighten to their birth the glories of the new creation! Let time's slow charioteers drive on without delay, and hasten to the blessed consummation! Behold! "He that testifieth these things saith, Surely I come quickly: Amen. Even so, come, Lord Jesus!"

Friends and brethren, I have done with this "third book of Moses, called Leviticus." For three times seven successive Sabbath evenings we have been traversing the Tabernacle courts together, inquiring into its "meats, and drinks, and divers washings, and carnal ordinances." With the New Testament in our hands, we have endeavored to get a glimpse of what was meant by these services of the ancient fathers. Not in vain, I hope, has been our expenditure of time and study. Luminously have we seen redemption shining through them all. Step by step have we beheld the scheme of grace unfolded in the living pictures of the ancient ritual, until to-night we stand upon the radiant summit of this mount of love and light. And now, as I take leave of the subject, I would fain wish that all the happy things, shadowed in this book, may be possessed by all who have listened to these comments upon them. But what can avail my wishing or your hearing, if these glad tidings be not embraced, believed, pondered, acted upon, and made the light and guide of life? In this solemn hour, then, with your eyes upon the sublimites of the everlasting jubilee, and your hearts moved and softened with the glad visions of what is then to be realized, permit me, in one last closing sentence, to ask and entreat each one of you, now, before leaving this house, to let your honest heart felt vows go up to God, from this forward, to live for Jesus and for heaven. God seal the sacred covenant and make it firm unto everlasting life! Amen, and Amen

THE END.